Leicester Nottingham Studies in Ancient Society 10

TRAVEL, GEOGRAPHY AND CULTURE IN ANCIENT GREECE, EGYPT AND THE NEAR EAST

Edited by

Colin Adams and Jim Roy

Oxbow Books

First published in the United Kingdom in 2007. Reprinted in 2016 by
OXBOW BOOKS
The Old Music Hall, 106–108 Cowley Road, Oxford OX4 1JE

and in the United States by
OXBOW BOOKS
1950 Lawrence Road, Havertown, PA 19083

Paperback Edition: ISBN 978-1-78570-550-2
Digital Edition: ISBN 978-1-78570-551-9

A CIP record for this book is available from the British Library

For a complete list of Oxbow titles, please contact:

UNITED KINGDOM
Oxbow Books
Telephone (01865) 241249, Fax (01865) 794449
Email: oxbow@oxbowbooks.com
www.oxbowbooks.com

UNITED STATES OF AMERICA
Oxbow Books
Telephone (800) 791-9354, Fax (610) 853-9146
Email: queries@casemateacademic.com
www.casemateacademic.com/oxbow

Oxbow Books is part of the Casemate Group

Front cover: The Colossus of Memnon, by Colin Adams

Contents

List of Contributors

COLIN ADAMS is Senior Lecturer in Ancient History at the University of Liverpool.

JOHN BAINES is Professor of Egyptology at the University of Oxford and Fellow of The Queen's College.

THOMAS HARRISON is Rathbone Professor of Ancient History and Classical Archaeology at the University of Liverpool.

MADELEINE JOST is Professor of Classics at the University of Paris X Nanterre.

ELENI KOURINOU is a curator in the National Archaeological Museum, Athens.

ALAN LLOYD is Professor of Classics and Egyptology at the University of Swansea.

JOHN MORGAN is Professor of Classics at the University of Swansea.

ZAHRA NEWBY is Senior Lecturer in Ancient History at the University of Warwick.

YANIS PIKOULAS is Associate Professor, University of Thessaly, Volos.

MARIA PRETZLER is Lecturer in Ancient History at the University of Swansea.

JIM ROY was Reader in Ancient History at the University of Nottingham and is now an Honorary Research Fellow.

List of Figures

Acknowledgements

The papers presented in this book were given at a residential seminar entitled 'Realities and Representations of Travel in Ancient Greece and the Near East' held at the University of Nottingham in April 2002 as part of the Leicester Nottingham Seminar in Ancient Society series. We are keenly aware as editors that the publication of this volume has taken a long time, and we thank our contributors for their patience. We owe our thanks to Chandima Wickramasinghe and Pasi Loman for their assistance. We would also like to thank our colleagues in Nottingham and Leicester for their support and our respective universities for financial assistance. Finally, we would like to thank Clare Litt at Oxbow Books for her interest in the project and help with publication. Figures 30–38 appear courtesy of the Antioch Expedition Archives, Research Photographs, Department of Art and Archaeology, Princeton University.

Introduction

Colin Adams

In recent years there has been a considerable amount of research into travel, travel writing and geography in the ancient world. The foundation is Casson's fundamental work on travel and means of travel (recent editions: Casson 1991, 1994 and 1995), which covers the ancient world from Pharaonic Egypt through to late antiquity. A number of other works have covered particular historical periods or features of travel (e.g. Partridge 1996; Chevallier 1976 and 1988; Adams 2007), but there are still many gaps in the literature. For example, although techniques of transport in Pharaonic Egypt have received some attention, there has been no consideration of travel as a social phenomenon. The same can be said for ancient Greece and the Near East (with the notable exception of the work of Littauer and Crouwel 1979). For the Roman world, no recent general treatment of travel and transport is available and the basic work is now dated (Friedländer 1908–13). There are many directions in which the study of travel and related subjects can go, and this volume presents papers ranging over aspects of travel in Egypt, Greece and the Near East. It can only offer to scratch the surface of a vast topic, and cannot offer the coverage that a full study would provide, but we hope that it will stimulate more research into the various themes raised. For travel and reasons for travel offer a window onto many features of ancient societies – sense of place, perceptions of space, administration, relations with foreign powers, engagement with other cultures, and representation of homelands. Importantly, the collection also shows that the theme of travel in different historical periods and regions can be addressed using a variety approaches (literary texts, inscriptions, archaeology and representation in art). But all seek to explain ways in which travel was embedded in the various cultures of Greece and the ancient Near East.

Some aspects of the broader subject have received considerable attention. Ancient geography has been a particularly rich field of study, heavily influenced by the production of the seminal Barrington Atlas of the Greek and Roman World. Maps and knowledge of space are a central aspect of travel. Ancient cartography has been the focus of much debate (most recently by Kai Brodersen (2001, 2003), Richard Talbert (2004, 2006), and Benet Salway (2001, 2004)), and although it is difficult to provide definitive answers to the questions we would like to ask, it is clear at least that Roman maps had some utility even if they were not to scale, and that their cartography was rather more sophisticated that we might imagine. Collections of edited papers (Adams and Laurence 2001; Ellis and Kidner 2004;

Talbert and Brodersen 2004) have offered new contributions to the field, and have provided a basis for further work. A number of international conferences and seminars are evidence of continuing interest in these fields and offer more in the way of publications (Galsterer and Rathmann 2007; see also the interesting work of the Travel and Religion in Antiquity seminar organised through the Canadian Society of Biblical Studies (http://www.philipharland.com/travelandreligion.htm). Ancient geographical knowledge has also been the focus of important work – especially Strabo, for long curiously neglected (Clarke 1999; Dueck, Lindsay and Pothecary 2005; see also Romm 1992 generally and Batty 2000 on Pomponius Mela). The geographical basis of other authors has also been explored (Clarke 2001 on Tacitus).

Travel writing in the ancient world has been the focus of important work – principally the work of Pausanias, the second century AD writer, and further contributions in the present volume add to this (Habicht 1985; Alcock, Cherry and Elsner 2001; Knoepfler and Piérart 2001; Ellinger 2005 and Hutton 2005), and there has also been an attempt to understand travel writing in much broader cultural terms and historical periods (see esp. Gikandi 1996; Elsner and Rubiés 1999). But a modern discourse is reflected by a similar ancient discourse about travel, and that ancient writers thought about travel in an intellectual manner is evident (see, for example, Pliny the Younger, *Ep.* 8.20; Seneca, *Ep.* 104.15). So why people travelled and how they engaged with other cultures was of interest to intellectuals in the ancient world as today. Travel writing today is a popular genre, and themes and issues in travel are widely disseminated. How true is this of the ancient world? One of the important themes that papers in this book address is just that. Was travel the preserve of the élite? It was certainly important to controlling a region or state and to international relations, as Baines and Lloyd in particular discuss in this volume, but it is certain that it was much more ubiquitous than we might assume. Ordinary individuals travelled, and often for the same intellectual reasons, rather than mere economic necessity. The graffiti of Graeco-Roman Egypt, discussed by Adams, are testament to that. Pretzler also shows that travel was an important aspect of élite intellectual culture and education, and there is certainly a connection between her élites and cultural tourists in Egypt.

Travel also provided a medium for engagement with other cultures and to explore one's own. In Pharaonic Egypt, Baines shows that travel was very closely connected to perceptions of place and space. It also provided a way of exploring the world and its people, demonstrated by Harrison in his discussion of how Herodotus understood geography and what its relationship was with history. Herodotus in some ways constructed his view of the world by people and their spatial relationship – next to the Ionians are the Lydians and so on. So some picture of the world could be envisaged through reading Herodotus. The same is true of Xenophon, discussed by Roy. Xenophon's account of the Persian expedition reads like a travelogue, indeed even like an embellished itinerary. But both also provide a means for understanding other cultures, or perhaps more accurately, of comparing other cultures to their own Greek culture, held to be the standard. Such ideas were not the privilege of the intellectual élite, as Adams argues, for Egyptian graffiti show that Greeks and Romans travelling in Egypt engaged in a dialogue about the Egyptian past, but placing it within a Hellenic context. These traditions and appropriations are evident also in Greek novels, as Morgan demonstrates in his discussion of travel as a literary motif.

Rather like Xenophon's *Anabasis*, Pausanias, the Greek traveller and writer of the second century AD, gives detailed accounts of topography in his catalogue of Greece. Greek identity is again a main theme, but Jost argues that there is also a great regional diversity evident in the writing of Pausanias. He was a cultural tourist, and as Pretzler shows, he was not alone.

All of the papers show that travel was much more common in the ancient world that often assumed. Pikoulas, indeed, provides an import archaeological survey of road systems in the Peloponnese, and shows that roads and communication in Greece were far more developed than assumed, and that the Greeks were important road-builders. It is interesting that Greeks, well known for their seafaring, also developed a land transport infrastructure, and therefore we should not readily assume that proximity for the sea or to navigable rivers necessarily reduced the importance of transport by land (demonstrated for Egypt by Adams 2007).

The representation of travel in art is explored by Kourinou and Newby. Kourinou discusses the depictions of means of transport in reliefs, which not only provides important information about technical aspects of travel, but also its metaphorical importance. Any journey involves coming home, and Newby examines attitudes to homelands shown in the mosaics of Antioch and Zeugma, and this links with the cultural themes discussed in other contributions, for although there is certainly a strong regional identity evident in the mosaics, they also access Greek myth and culture and form an interesting counterbalance to literature and graffiti.

What all of the contributions reveal is that travel is very tightly bound up with culture, and that culture is profoundly influenced by perceptions of the world. Through travel, people could come to understand their environment and culture better through experiencing others.

Bibliography

Adams, C. E. P. (2007) *Land Transport in Roman Egypt: A Study of Economics and Administration in a Roman Province* (Oxford).

Adams, C. E. P. and R. Laurence (eds) (2001) *Travel and Geography in the Roman Empire* (London and New York).

Alcock, S. E., J. F. Cherry, and J. Elsner (eds) *Pausanias: Travel and memory in Roman Greece* (Oxford).

Batty, R. (2000) 'Mela's Phoenician Geography', *JRS* 90, 70–94.

Brodersen, K. (1995) *Terra Cognita: Studien zur römischen Raumerfassung* (Zurich and New York).

Brodersen, K. (2001) 'The presentation of geographical knowledge for travel and transport in the Roman world: *itineraria non tantum adnotata sed etiam picta*', in Adams and Laurence, *Travel and Geography in the Roman Empire*, 7–21.

Casson, L. (1991) *The Ancient Mariners: Seafarers and Sea Fighters of the Mediterranean in Ancient Times* (Princeton, 2nd edition).

Casson, L. (1994) *Travel in the Ancient World* (Baltimore).

Casson, L. (1995) *Ships and Seamanship in the Ancient World* (Baltimore, 2nd edition).

Chevallier, R. (1976) *Roman Roads* (London).

Clarke, K. (1999) *Between Geography and History* (Oxford).

Clarke, K. (2001) 'An Island Nation: Re-reading Tacitus' *Agricola*', *JRS* 91, 94–112.

Dueck, D., H. Lindsay and S. Pothecary (eds) (2005) *Strabo's Cultural Geography: the Making of a Kolossourgia* (Cambridge).

Ellinger, P. (2005) *La fin des maux: d'un Pausanias à l'autre: essai de mythologie et d'histoire* (Paris).

Ellis, L. and F. L. Kidner (eds) (2004) *Travel, Communication and Geography in Late Antiquity: Sacred and Profane* (Aldershot).

Elsner, J. and J. Rubiés (eds) *Voyages and Visions: Towards a Cultural History of Travel* (London).

Friedländer, L. (1908–1913) *Roman Life and Manners under the Early Empire* 4 vols (London).

Galsterer, H. and M. Rathmann (eds) (2007) *Raumwahrnehmung und Raumerfassung in der Antike* (Bonn).

Gikandi, S. (1996) *Maps of Englishness: Writing Identity in the Culture of Colonialism* (New York).

Habicht, C. (1985) *Pausanias' Guide to Ancient Greece* (Berkeley-Los Angeles-London).

Hutton, W. (2005) *Describing Greece: Landscape and Literature in the Periegesis of Pausanias* (Cambridge).

Knoepfler, D. and M. Piérat (eds) (2001) *Éditer, traduire, commenter Pausanias en l'an 2000: actes de culloque de Neuchâtel et de Fribourg (18–22 septembre 1998) autour des deux editions en cours de la Périégèse* (Geneva).

Littauer, M. L. and J. H. Crouwel (1979) *Wheeled Vehicles and Ridden Animals in the Ancient Near East* (Leiden).

Partridge, R. B. (1996) *Transport in Ancient Egypt* (London).

Romm, J. S. (1992) *The Edges of the Earth in Ancient Thought* (Princeton).

Salway, B. (2001) 'Travel, *itineraria* and *tabellaria*', in Adams and Laurence, *Travel and Geography in the Roman Empire*, 22–66.

Salway, B. (2004) 'Sea and River Travel in the Roman Itinerary Literature', in Talbert and Brodersen, *Space in the Roman World*, 43–96.

Talbert, R. (2004) 'Cartography and Taste in Peutinger's Roman Map', in Talbert and Brodersen, *Space in the Roman World*, 113–41.

Talbert, R. and Brodersen, K. (eds) (2004) *Space in the Roman World: Its Perception and Presentation* (Münster).

Travel in Third and Second Millennium Egypt

John Baines

Background

Travel sets sedentary societies apart from nomadic ones, because sedentary people move around less than nomadic ones. It takes a 'home' – a fixed residence – for travel to be distinct in any way; if one has no fixed residence, 'home' is where one is. Nomads can travel, in the sense of going beyond the range of locations they normally traverse. Such movements are common among nomads coming together for significant events, for example where different ethnic or other groups meet (whether or not they form part of the same society), but these practices are not directly relevant to travel in Mediterranean antiquity because they are not characteristic of the complex, sedentary societies of the region.

Travel is at the heart of civilizations, all of which require specialized goods to be conveyed long distances and, more importantly, require people – or rather elites – to acquire experience and culture through interchange and through assimilation of values that are available from, and associated with, particular places. Categories of such places are capital cities and religious centres. Here, civilizations, with their hierarchies of often specialized settlement types – whether in city-state or territorial state configurations – favour travel more than do other types of sedentary society.

Ancient texts do not offer close equivalents for the word 'travel', so that scholars use a concept with a modern definition to investigate the values and practices of ancient societies. This is a legitimate procedure, but requires caution, and the term 'travel' needs to be circumscribed. A minimal definition might be journeying for some distance away from where one lives, that is, from 'home'. Elites may have more than one 'home', for example one in a city and another on their estates or in their region of origin. Movement between homes is more like 'migrating' or 'commuting' than 'travel'. In premodern times elites spent much time in such movements, which were typically seasonal, but because they were oscillations and did not have a special character or constitute moves beyond previous experience, they were part of the creation of a large space for living, rather than travel as I study it here. They are, however, essential to senses of place, provided that economic and climatic factors are included in the analytical notion of a place's meaning; for the actors these meanings are primary motivations for such migratory patterns.

Travel is value-laden. I focus on values, which can be studied through the meaning of particular places or through literary texts. My concern is less with literary or religious aspects of travel (for the latter, see Yoyotte 1960; Volokhine 1998) than with its general significance and with assumptions about it that underlie the exploitation of travel motifs in various genres. Two recent works treat literary aspects of senses of place and thematizations of travel abroad, which developed increasingly autonomous forms from the Middle Kindgom on (Moers 2001; Loprieno 2001, 51–88; see also Loprieno 1988). I attempt to complement these studies, focusing on sources other than imaginative literature. Literature exists in relation to underlying cultural assumptions, often contrasting with and problematizing them; part of my intention is to suggest a background of 'normality' for its more highly coloured formulations.

Literature is not a separate domain. Almost all Egyptian materials that thematize travel – as opposed, for example, to documenting it from artifacts that were transported long distances (e.g. Bourriau 1991) – are complex, elaborately wrought high-cultural products. The impetus to shape and bracket topics is present in them almost as much as in pure narrative fictions, and can take both pictorial and textual form. Less strongly marked thematizations of travel, which may lack some of the detachment and use of conceptual space of belles lettres, offer one perspective among several. Belles lettres emerged relatively late in Egypt and developed in part on the basis of existing written conventions and phraseology. Older inscriptions are therefore crucial, as well as being culturally salient.

In Egyptian literature as in many others, the world beyond the frontier and beyond civilization was an imaginative space where what could not be contemplated within might happen. Travel outside Egypt is mobilized in narratives that vary in structure, tone, and style from folktale plots to superficially realistic and 'factual' presentations of the difficulties of moving around the non-Egyptian world, negotiating with foreigners, and on occasion learning from them. Related attitudes were realized also in visual form, in the decoration of materials from small objects through palaces and tombs to temples. This fictional presentation of an 'other' no doubt had meaning in relation to generally held conceptions that derived from encounters with foreigners, from travel outside Egypt, and at least as importantly from hearsay, exaggeration, and generally held opinion.

I discuss only the rather specialized modes of expression of the third and second millennia (for dates, see Chronological Table), primarily nonroyal sources and texts rather than archaeological materials. I cover only some relevant topics. Alan B. Lloyd explores the rich data from first millennium Egypt in another chapter in this volume.

The world as context for travel

As in many societies, the Egyptians saw where they lived as the World (for places mentioned, see Fig. 1). What was outside might not be part of that world. In early periods there seems to have been no specific word for Egypt,[1] which was 'the Land'

Egypt: chronological table

Late Predynastic	ca. 3200
Early kings including 'dynasty 0'	
Early Dynastic period	ca. 2950–2575
1st dynasty	ca. 2950–2775
2nd dynasty	ca. 2775–2650
3rd dynasty	ca. 2650–2575
Old Kingdom	ca. 2575–2150
4th dynasty	ca. 2575–2450
5th dynasty	ca. 2450–2325
6th dynasty	ca. 2325–2175
7th/8th dynasties	ca. 2175–2125
1st Intermediate period	ca. 2125–1975
9th dynasty (Herakleopolitan)	ca. 2125–2080
10th dynasty (Herakleopolitan)	ca. 2080–1975
11th dynasty (Theban)	ca. 2080–1975
Middle Kingdom	ca. 1975–1640
11th dynasty (all Egypt)	ca. 1975–1940
12th dynasty	ca. 1938–1756
13th dynasty	ca. 1755–1630
14th dynasty	
2nd Intermediate period	ca. 1630–1520
15th dynasty	ca. 1630–1520
16th dynasty	
17th dynasty	ca. 1630–1540
New Kingdom	ca. 1539–1075
18th dynasty	ca. 1539–1292
19th dynasty	ca. 1292–1190
20th dynasty	ca. 1190–1075

or 'the Two Lands' and was also designated by a range of pairings, typical of the Egyptian view that significant unities are composed from dualities, such as 'the Two Banks' or 'the Black Land and the Red Land' (see further Loprieno 2001, 64–76). Of the last of those pairs, the 'Black Land (*kmt*)' – that is, the floodplain with its fertile silt – later became the normal word for 'Egypt'. It was not the term by which other societies designated the country: the Semitic Musur/Mizraim, Arabic Misr, has no ancient Egyptian counterpart. This near-anonymity of the country or world went together with a focus on the centre, but also a concern with frontiers that is evident in the First Cataract around Aswan, where a fortress was constructed on Elephantine Island at the beginning of the dynastic period (Ziermann 1993). 5th and 6th dynasty rock inscriptions with the names of kings display this focus. Two of the 6th dynasty king Merenre state that in different years (?) the king came and went in person and that rulers of three polities to the south prostrated themselves before him (Sethe 1933, 110–1; Roccati 1982, 76–7, 264–5).

More significant for the Egyptians' sense of the world was that they oriented toward the south. New Year was the day when the star Sothis/Sirius became visible again after seventy days of invisibility, an event probably observed in Elephantine, the 'first' place in Egypt, where there was an ancient small temple of the goddess Satis (Dreyer 1986), which seems to be oriented toward the point where Sothis first appeared (e.g. Krauss 1985, 49). Since the Nile enters Egypt from the south, its annual inundation was observed and experienced first from the same point, and came in the same season as the observation of Sothis (Janssen 1987).[2]

These features imply a unitary cosmology and thus a sense that Egypt was a single entity and country. Comparable focuses are also found in uncentralized civilizations, so that this overarching point of reference is not distinctive. It is more distinctive that when the king of Egypt 'extended his borders', to use a typical phrase, this was first done toward the south. The limits farther south that were conquered at various junctures were strongly marked and were appropriated to an enlarged conception of Egypt (see also below). Such extensions did not last indefinitely, but they provided occasions for political action, as well as probably reinforcing Egyptians' sense of what was their core land, with its distinctive spatial and material conditions.

For those who orient to the south, the west is on the right, and the Egyptians were among the relatively few peoples with a positive view of the west, the principal word for which, *jmnt*, belongs to a common Afroasiatic root for 'right' (Posener 1965). The west was also the realm of the dead and was an indispensable domain for a civilization that viewed the dead as one of the four basic components of society – the others were the gods, the king, and humanity – and for which mortuary display was essential. The living constructed monuments and were expected to perform the mortuary cult for the previous generation and to visit them and their monuments.

Both in the requirement to visit tombs and in conceptions of the next world, a premium was placed on movement. The dead aspired to 'walk upon the sacred ways of the west, on which the revered ones walk' (Sethe 1933, 120, 15 – 121, 1; one instance among many). Those 'ways' may have been initially in the necropolis area itself, so that the nonroyal dead, unlike kings, would exist around the tomb. But no later than the Old Kingdom, their next-worldly destiny seems to have been among

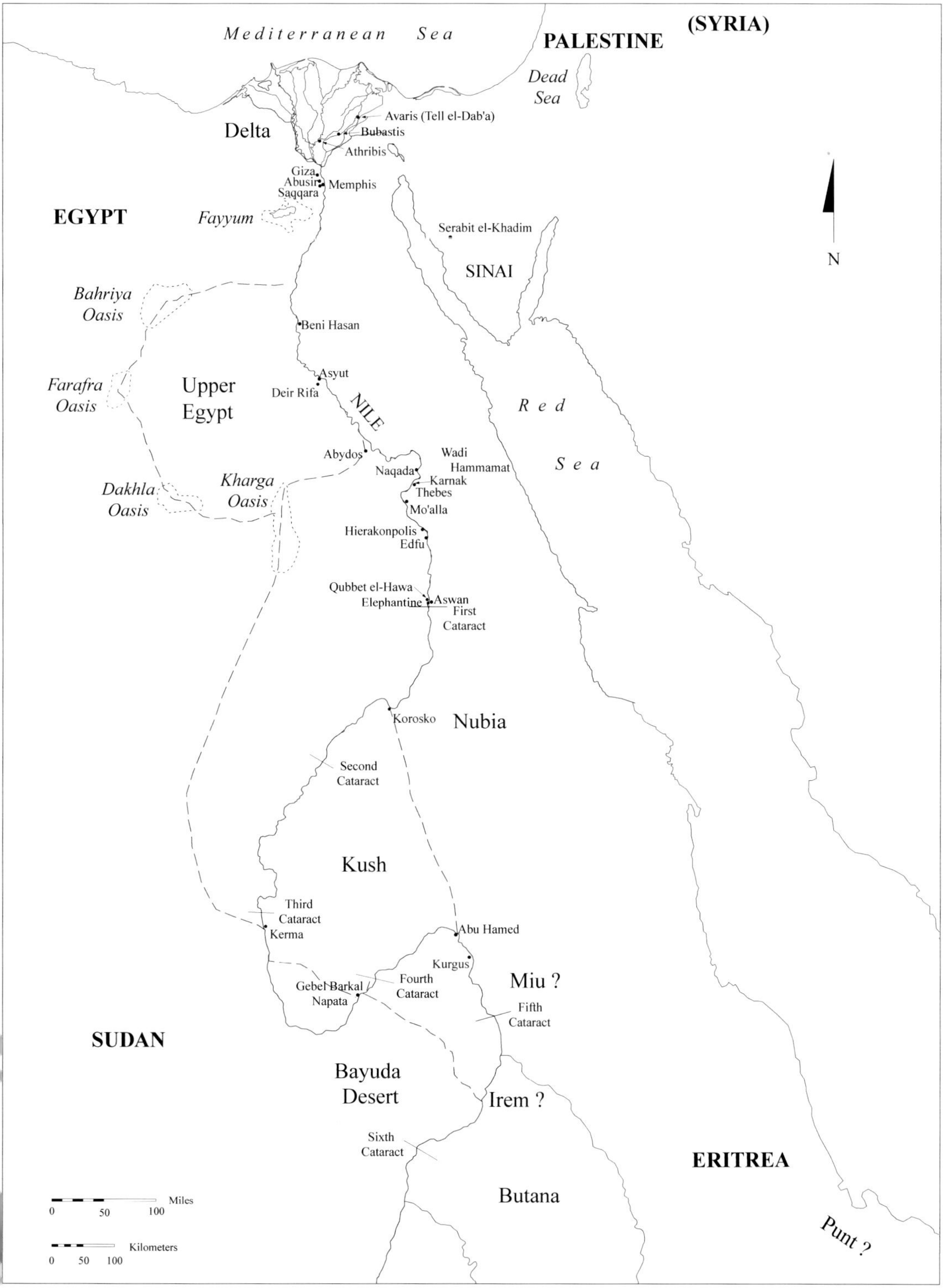

Fig. 1 Map of Egypt.

the stars, participating in a perpetual cosmic cycle realized visually and verbally as the solar barque crossing the sky (Lapp 1986, 51–8). Attaining transfiguration in the next world was contingent on post-mortem travel, in addition to reliance on moral worth and on reciprocity with the living.

As in many languages, values attached to 'ways' were common metaphors (Vittmann 1999). The idea of life as a journey, which seems to be nearly universal, is vital to much in the spatial formulation of worlds and to the values invested in configurations of space and actual or mental movements within them. Metaphorical 'ways' are relevant here because they are goal-directed rather than repetitive and lead into the unknown. They surely underpin a culture's conceptualization of travel.

Rulers and elites

Elites, on whom I focus, complement and contrast with rulers. The patterns of travel of the two are different, even though the ruler almost necessarily travels with a retinue largely drawn from the elite. In Egypt, elites – almost exclusively men – seldom celebrated travel accompanying a ruler unless they could cite a significant exploit of their own. In many cultures, the monarch must move around in order to rule (e.g. Geertz 1983). Some rulers, such as early modern ones of Spain and France, may not have a primary fixed abode (e.g. Elias 1983, 160–3). Others may be required by their role to be constantly on the move – almost to be nomad rulers of sedentary subjects (and superior because nomadism can be seen as nobler) – or to make regular journeys to places that are ideologically significant, for example to ancient sites from which their authority derives or to religious centres in which they must attend or perform important rituals.

In addition to these styles of movement, rulers may need to leave their domains in order to display their power and prowess to subordinate peoples within or outside their areas of rule, to make conquests or, for example in city-state civilizations, to negotiate with political neighbours and participate in events that serve more than one polity.[3] Some of these movements can be termed travel, but the imperatives that govern them should be considered separately from the travel of elites. A problem for the ideological presentation of a ruler is socialization. Elites are in part socialized, or advanced in their social competence and standing, through travel. In earlier periods Egyptian rulers were generally presented as perfect beings and their socialization was not thematized. They were stated to send out missions to foreign lands or to provincial sites where action was needed, but there is hardly any mention of the value of travel to their own selves. While this gap in evidence is probably due in part to the sparseness of sources, it also relates to there being no public presentation of a king's personal development: before the New Kingdom, kings were shown as fully formed, not as people who matured into their superhuman roles.[4]

This does not mean that kings did not travel. The annals of the 1st and 2nd dynasties are largely structured around a biennial 'Following of Horus (*šmsj ḥrw*)', on which the king seems to have moved through the country to raise revenues and give administrative decisions (material: Wilkinson 2000). Small dummy pyramids of the 3rd dynasty imprint royal presence around the country for the next world as well as this one (Seidlmayer 1996). The Following of Horus is not specifically attested from later. It is unlikely that such journeyings ceased, but they may have lost cultural importance as the country became increasingly centralized: almost all significant monuments of the 4th–5th dynasties are near the capital, Memphis. The 6th dynasty biographical inscription of Harkhuf mentions sending a message to the 'Following of Horus', which presumably means to wherever the king happened to be, in accord with earlier usage (Edel 1955, 54; Lichtheim 1973, 25, as 'retinue of [Horus]'). Old and Middle Kingdom material relating to kings focuses around the capital, from which they send out official missions within the country, as well as military, trading, and for example quarrying ventures beyond the Nile Valley and Delta. The king could command and move around by delegation as much as in person: in this respect elite officials were extensions of him. Some 12th dynasty self-presentations ('autobiographies') narrate that their protagonists had accompanied the king on campaigns (see p. 10), while late in the dynasty Senwosret III stated that he had campaigned abroad in person (Lichtheim 1973, 119, ll. 13–5; Eyre 1990). The shift to a more active dissemination of the king's travels and role may have begun during that period.

While in the Old Kingdom the king was the centre to whom others related, economic and political organization required movement around the country. The palace, religious foundations, and members of the elite had scattered estates that were the main sources of their wealth and implied travel between the capital and the various provinces where the estates were (Jacquet-Gordon 1962). Because of this scattering, which probably had the centripetal intent of minimizing local power bases, overseeing them would have had some of the character of 'travel' rather than 'migration'. Moreover, the tension between capital and province, which was played out in different ways when provinces became significant centres from the late Old Kingdom onward, was also an ideological tension between the court at the core, with its focus on ceremony and the exercise of power, and the rural ideal of estates as almost self-supporting and self-contained agricultural entities, some aspects of which may be made visible in tomb decoration (see e.g. Baines 1999a). Very little in the tombs can be taken as depicting specific locations, but they do not represent the court or urban settings. In a royal monument, scenes such as an implied treasury from which rewards are given to the elite point to a central location, while a hunt on a vast scale would be sited in a favoured rural and semi-desert environment, perhaps away from the capital (Borchardt et al. 1913, pls. 52–4 [treasury]; pl. 17 [hunt]; see further Baines 1997, 146–9). Thus, a variety of movement is significant even for the very limited forms in which relations between the third millennium king and his elite were presented.[5]

Early elite movement and travel

Values attached to movement can be seen in the earliest complex societies in Egypt, the polities of the Naqada II period (ca. 3500–3200). The most distinctive product of the period, decorated pottery made from desert clay (known as D-Ware), has as its salient pictorial motif stylized depictions of boats, the essential mode of transport (Midant-Reynes 2000, 189–91). The meaning of these representations cannot be established – it may be otherworldly – but it is significant that boats also occur widely in rock drawings in the Eastern Desert (e.g. Fuchs 1989), where they would have had no function. These drawings express the importance of movement in terms of the dominant Nile Valley mode of boat travel. The pottery both represents and enacts movement, since it was distributed through much of Egypt, probably from just a few production sites – because its style and especially decoration, executed before firing, are rather homogeneous – that are likely to have been near the type site of Naqada. By this date, the Nile provided ease of movement that favoured cultural dissemination among mainly sedentary people over large areas.

The distinction between travel within and beyond borders is important for elites as well as for rulers. In a civilization of city-states, many people, particularly elites, can expect to leave 'home' and go to other states. There is generally no sharp cultural divide between one polity and the next. In a territorial state and civilization like Egypt, the movement of elites around the civilized area may be just as significant, but the country's borders have an absolute and defining quality, and there is a fundamental difference between travel within and beyond them. This difference is mobilized in imaginative literature from the Middle Kingdom to Roman times (Moers 2001), but mentions and depictions of journeys from the Old Kingdom support the assumption that underlying themes went further back. Egypt's extent was defined and its material culture largely uniform by the late fourth millennium; from then on, the distinction between within and outside had essentially the same range of reference as later.

Despite the importance of the division between Egypt and outside, mentions of travel in inscriptions span those two domains without a sharp division. The inscriptions, which are mainly public elite self-presentations that are limited in content and favourable to their protagonists, are a rich source for attitudes to movement and associated values. The genre developed slowly and unevenly over millennia, from the less to the more personal and subjective. Early examples, which tend to state achievements baldly without saying what they signified for their protagonists except in terms of success and rewards, should not be seen as showing that ideas relating to travel were less complex than later. Rather, earlier conventions of personal display were more restrictive and 'objectivizing'. It is therefore worth attempting to identify relevant meanings in earlier texts.

One minimal style of self-presentation or 'ideal biography' states that the protagonist was upright and generous, as well as achieving material success.

He – the genre is male – also 'came back from my town and went out from my estate' (Edel 1944, 47–8). This statement is unspecific, but it exhibits the elite idea of migration and rural focus. Such values require that their holder should not simply remain at the capital, so that they open out into a broader world, if only in limited ways. The values attached to movement were imprinted on the landscape by multiple locations for the mortuary cult and by connections between the cult chapel, the tomb, and the estates that supported the cult. This interlinking can be seen at Elephantine, where at least one mortuary cult chapel in the Old Kingdom town,[6] while the tombs of the elite, but perhaps not of low ranking people, were across the river on the west bank at Qubbet el-Hawa (no convenient publication). These tombs were highly visible and their self-presentations asserted their owners' connection with a wider cosmos, while their titularies, in particular, related them to the capital at Memphis, a thousand kilometres to the north. The river crossing necessary to reach the elite tombs was a powerful metaphor for social difference as well as for passage to the next world. In a widespread usage, death was a 'mooring (*mnj*)' or 'landing (*zmꜣ-tꜣ*)', so that this idea was part of the language. The ideal biography asserts that earlier, during life, the elite member 'ferried the one who had no boat' and 'made a boat for the one who had none' (Edel 1944, 41–2). This relates to local travel, which was unavailable to those without resources. Both the location of the tomb and access to it were hierarchical.

Some elite activities depicted in tombs involved significant movement. While agriculture could take place almost everywhere, hunting in the marshes or on the low desert used favoured locations. Captions to tomb scenes sometimes locate marsh hunting in the Nile Delta, far from the site of a tomb (e.g. Altenmüller 1998, 95–6, pl. 9). It seems to be implied that one would travel for such activities. The distances involved cannot be known, but here again, the separation between elites, for whom movement is significant and pleasurable, and others for whom that is not the case, is vital for display. Movement was also desirable for the next world, both in order to attain a new abode and as part of funeral rituals, in which from early times there were symbolic journeys to sacred places in the Delta (Junker 1940; Altenmüller 1975), and in later, Upper Egyptian tombs to ones in the Nile Valley.

Social landscape and ideal biography provide a context against which should be set narrative presentations of specific exploits; both genres can occur in a single text. Old Kingdom examples include trading and military expeditions to Nubia and to Palestine, as well as a journey to recover the body of a man's father who had been killed by Eastern Desert nomads (Lichtheim 1988, 16). Missions within and outside the country form part of the same texts as the episodes abroad. The distances involved are significant, leading on a conservative estimate to the Dongola Reach in Upper Nubia or, I think more plausibly, to the Butana in central Sudan (O'Connor 1986).

Expeditions to Syria, probably by sea and with partly foreign crews (Bietak 1988), and southward in the Red Sea as far as Punt – perhaps coastal areas of Sudan and Eritrea[7] – are attested in royal sources but not documented in descriptions. In one uncertain case, a dwarf or pygmy 'for god's dancing', comparable with one acquired perhaps a century earlier from Punt, was brought back from a trading expedition to Sudan. This person was from the 'land of the Horizon Dwellers (*tꜣ ꜣḫtjw*)' (Lichtheim 1973, 26; Roccati 1982, 206). This term was later used for the Egyptian Eastern Desert (Couyat and Montet 1912, 98 no. 192, l. 4; Schenkel 1965, 254) and seems to indicate a marvellous and remote land, perhaps to the east – northward or southward – rather than west. A similar term, 'god's land', was used for distant, eastern places from Punt through Sinai to the Lebanese mountains. Despite the Egyptians' stereotyped (not necessarily real) contempt for foreigners and places abroad (see e.g. Baines 1996), remote regions had divine associations, as if they were nearer to the gods, in a conception of a 'world' – that is, Egypt – surrounded by hostile areas, beyond which were inaccessible but idealized places at the edge of the larger cosmos.

The Old Kingdom treatments narrate what protagonists or their heirs selected as the salient and prestigious events of an elite life. These should be set against the experience of others, to the limited extent that it can be modelled. Expeditions involved many people whose presence is often hardly mentioned. When Harkhuf went to Nubia in the 6th dynasty, on one return journey he brought 300 donkeys laden with trade goods, but no figure is given for the human contingent (Lichtheim 1973, 26; Roccati 1982, 205). This pattern fits the premodern – and the modern – world, in which people of consequence have numerous helpers who are of no account for the leader's public persona. The massive Old Kingdom architectural projects involved moving people and goods – specialized materials for construction and agricultural products for subsistence – over long distances. Only when some fact about the personnel on a journey demonstrated that the protagonist had received a privilege were such matters mentioned. The 6th dynasty high official Weni enumerated the categories of overseers and troops he took on a series of military campaigns to somewhere presumably in Palestine; but nothing is said about what then happened to the troops.[8] Two points are emphasized: Weni led a large expedition with numerous supervisors; and he was told the numbers of troops, which was 'classified information', as it would now be termed (Baines 1990b, 17–8), perhaps in part because it was militarily sensitive.

A much later inscription (reign of Ramesses IV, ca. 1150) in Wadi Hammamat recording an expedition to quarry stone, perhaps for elements in his mortuary temple, appends to statistics for the numbers of personnel 'dead, who are omitted from the enumeration: 900' (out of 8638), but does not express regret for the deaths (Christophe 1949, 20–1 with n. r; Kitchen 1983, 14 l. 9).[9] Those who did not return – literary texts present dying away from home as the worst of destinies (e.g. Parkinson 1997, 34, 37) – were presumably not people who mattered. The undertaking was a success; otherwise it would not have been recorded. Counter-examples state that expeditions 'returned without loss' (Erman and Grapow 1926–31, II, 281, 1–4; Cerný, in Gardiner et al. 1952–55, II, 97 l. 15), but one suspects that the precise statistics of the exceptional inscription are more realistic and the realities of these undertakings were often grim.

Two Old Kingdom rock inscriptions in the Eastern Desert imply a little more about the meaning of travel. One of the 6th dynasty, at Bir Mueilha in a mineral-rich southern area, includes several slightly varied conventional statements that the protagonist 'gave water to the thirsty, bread to the hungry' and, more specific to the location, 'I dug these wells(?)' (Rothe et al. 1996, 97–8). The other, in Wadi Hammamat, the principal way through the Eastern Desert and a source of fine stone, may date to the 8th dynasty (Sainte Fare Garnot 1938, 74–6 no. xix, with perceptive comments; Couyat and Montet 1912, pl. xxxv). The text consists of an address to the living to perform an offering prayer: 'Oh living ones who will come to this desert land and who wish to return to Upper Egypt bearing what (you) have acquired for your lord …'. This is a more extensive variation on standard formulas (cited below). Jean Sainte Fare Garnot interpreted its carving in the desert as showing that the protagonist reached out beyond the tomb and his own social milieu in order to enlist as many people as possible to support his destiny in the next world, while giving in return only his aid in returning home – a very significant gift. It is also possible to read the siting of the inscription another way, as implying that someone's personal and moral standing is expressed as much in achievements which are made manifest by travel, especially outside the Nile Valley, as by the monument of the tomb where most known texts of this type are located (later texts also come from temples). The other inscription may fit such a reading still better, since it does not address those who might read it specifically, but rather asserts its protagonist's moral worth in addition to his achievement in reaching the remote place where it was set up.

Late third and early second millennium thematizations of travel

From the 6th dynasty onward, sources become more loquacious, including the evocation of significant stereotypes. The new material does not divide neatly in terms of recognized historical periods. Rather, two roughly contemporaneous developments – a shift of the burials of significant numbers of the elite to the provinces, and more extensive biographical inscriptions – created a context for self-presentations that say more about travel. These changes were not in themselves centrifugal; those who set up their inscriptions in the provinces or beyond the frontiers of Egypt were commissioned from the centre to go there or to reside there. They generally held titles and positions, such as priesthoods in the mortuary cults of kings, that were at least in theory exercised around the capital. The texts are not self-contained, but probably related to oral practices of presentation, for example in funerals, for which the inscribed forms were both more lasting versions and substitutes (see e.g. Baines 1999a; 1999b).

Centripetal idioms of movement appear in the same period in addresses to the living. People visit the tomb 'whether navigating downstream or upstream' (Sainte Fare Garnot 1938, 63, 71–2; the vocabulary derives from movement on the river). Downstream is named first because movement is related to the capital, far to the north in many extant examples. By implication, travel relates to the centre, as is clear also from longer narrative biographies. Visits to the tomb would not necessarily involve long journeys, and if they went from town to necropolis they would move east–west rather than south–north. The evocation of larger distances therefore dignifies the addressees, who are implied to possess an elite range of movement and to focus on the country's ideological centre.

Relatively centrifugal implications of movement are evident in the slightly later inscriptions of Ankhtify, a local potentate of the 9th dynasty, who presented himself as holding the main power from south of Thebes to south of Edfu (Vandier 1950; on his role, see Seidlmayer 2000, 128–33). Ankhtify went to the Abydos area, a couple of hundred kilometres downstream, to meet a representative of the nominal government ruling from near Memphis. His texts accord no prestige to the places he visited, giving the highest status to his own central place of Mo'alla (ancient Hefat), a little way south of Thebes. One passage describes his troops marauding through the Theban area in a vain attempt to provoke a battle. Here, Thebes is not mentioned by name and a couple of place names appear to be substituted by derogatory phrases such as 'the ruin mound they ignored' (Vandier 1950, 198–9 with 201 n. f). In relation to movement, a key difference between Ankhtify's presentation and others is the colouring it gives to evocations of place. The fact that he did not travel to Memphis is exploited to express status. Whereas Old Kingdom elites necessarily related to the capital, he constrained an official to meet him more than half way.

The more numerous Middle Kingdom inscriptions include a fuller range of themes relating to travel both in addresses to the living and in more extensive self-presentations. The religious centre of Abydos has produced thousands of stelae, many with addresses to the living that again invoke passers-by going north or south. The addressees can be in principle everyone, but like those already cited, they largely omit women.

A striking example of the significance of travel is in a benefit that a stela owner holds out as a consequence of pronouncing the offering formula: that 'you should recount your expeditions to your wives' (Sethe 1928, 88 ll. 21–2). Here, the stereotype of many cultures, that men travel and amass experience and women stay at home, is thematized. The casting of the wife in the role of audience is in some ways an elite notion, but it is presented in literary texts as valid also outside the elite (e.g. Parkinson 1997, 58, 62). This evaluation of experience is salient in the literary tale of the *Shipwrecked Sailor*. A central theme of this text is the need for a measured response to adversity (Baines 1990a, 70–72), yet it is cast in the form of a sailor's tale of a journey, on which all his fellows die, that brings him to a paradisiacal island on the edge of the cosmos where aspects of space and time are abrogated.

The snake deity whom the sailor encounters then advises him:

> *If you are brave, master your heart,*
> *and you will fill your embrace with your children,*
> *kiss your wife, and see your house!*
> *This is better than anything.*
> *You will reach home, and remain there,*
> *amongst your kinsmen.*
> (Blackman 1932, 45; translation by Parkinson 1997, 95)

Later, essentially the same passage is repeated, with the addition 'you will be buried', playing on the concern that one should not die abroad while also integrating this-worldly and otherworldly journeys, as is often implicit. An address to the living of the earlier 18th dynasty voices the same concern more strongly, asserting of those who will pronounce the formula:

> *(you who) love life and abhor death,*
> *your local gods will favour you,*
> *you will not taste the fear of another land,*
> *you will be buried in your tombs …*
> (Sethe 1909, 965 l. 15)

Here, travel abroad and associated experience are not straightforwardly positive. Those who can return to recount their experiences value them as contributing to their biography and their standing with their contemporaries of any status, but the dangers are real and are most acute for people of lower standing.

On another level, travel was almost impracticable for many. Peasants appear to have been tied to the land and their movement strongly discouraged (e.g. Posener 1975). Those who absconded were pursued and assigned to compulsory labour institutions (Quirke 1988). A couple of modest stelae of the period celebrate as their protagonists' sole narrated exploits attacks against the 'Oasis dwellers(?)' and the pursuit of 'fugitives' of the 'Western Oasis' (modern Kharga and Dakhla).[10] The owners were among the lowest ranking people who commemorated their travels, and their mission had been to prevent the free movement of their social inferiors. The western oases, from which archaeological evidence of the Middle Kingdom is largely lacking, were later places of forced exile (e.g. Beckerath 1968; in fiction: Caminos 1977); the Middle Kingdom 'fugitives' were presumably in some sense voluntary exiles. Voluntary exile is a denial of the values of a civilization that aspires to be unitary. The difficulty of traversing much of the surrounding territory probably accentuated the sense that departure was treachery. This betrayal of values is exploited to great effect in the *Tale of Sinuhe*, the premier work of Middle Kingdom narrative (Baines 1982, 40–1). Exile is license and degradation, not freedom, which is not an explicitly identifiable value. Nonetheless, freedom of movement is a clear elite aspiration.

As noted earlier, this presentation of restricted movement and associated hierarchical values ignores the many whose travel had no evident prestige, probably in part because they were unable to leave self-presentations and in part because they did not choose whether they travelled. In experiences of travel, Egypt offers no one to compare with the range of early Greek colonists.

Further up the social scale, travel within Egypt is prominent in many Middle and New Kingdom biographies, while travel abroad characterizes those of high rank. A characteristic example is the 12th dynasty high official of Abydos Wepwawetaa, whose two stelae say little about his career but dwell on his ancient family and his ritual roles. The second stela, however, states that he went downstream and upstream visiting the residence and that while he was there he was acclaimed and awarded an office at Abydos. This instance suggests that in order to claim that one had had a significant life, it was desirable to have travelled and to give some specificity to the general notion of navigating down- and upstream (for the residence, see also below).

Wepwawetaa was of limited standing compared to some of those who came to his home town of Abydos to participate, for this life and for the next, in rituals of Osiris (Simpson 1974; O'Connor 1985; Volokhine 1998, 71–6). These included high officials from the residence whom kings commissioned to restore the temple's fabric and cult equipment and to perform rituals as royal deputies.[11] Finds of groups of stelae show that these people travelled with retinues of subordinate officials, presumably also from the capital. Others who deposited stelae were from as far as Athribis in the Delta (Satzinger 1986) or came in large groups from places such as Deir Rifa near Asyut, bringing stelae ready made to be set up in offering chapels (Marée 2002). Marcel Marée argues that clusters among the several thousand Abydos stelae date to spans of no more than a couple of years, so that there would have been some great concentrations of people; these might have been associated with such occasions as the renewal of cult equipment. Thus, Abydos was something like a pilgrimage centre, but the practices are not well understood and pilgrimage may not be the best term for them.[12] Be that as it may, the amount of movement involved was significant and people came from much of the country. It is not known whether only the men who set up self-presentations came or whether the complex extended families and groups of colleagues shown on many stelae came too. The families were to be virtually present at the cult place of Osiris through their depicted figures; whether they came to Abydos cannot now be established.

Other 12th dynasty officials travelled throughout Egypt in the retinue of kings on campaign. Kings were mentioned as making journeys of conquest – which were very highly regarded by the nonroyal and royal alike – more explicitly than they were said to engage in building works or organize trade. The reality of royal movement may have been different, as is suggested by a relatively sober annal inscription in which the king despatches a military expedition to Asia and receives it on its return but does not himself participate (Altenmüller and Moussa 1991, 7 no. 11, 12–14 no. 22, 35–6). The nomarch Amenemhat of Beni Hasan stated that he accompanied the king to Kush – perhaps the second–third cataract region of northern Sudan, further upstream than any territory conquered in the period – and reached the limits of the World (Sethe and Erichsen 1935, 14 l. 15; Lichtheim 1988, 138). The late 12th dynasty official Khusobek, who is attested on two stelae and in a graffito in the second cataract area, campaigned in Nubia and accompanied the king in Palestine, leading his own detachment of troops (Baines 1987b).

These texts mention Nubia first and give more detail about it than about Asia, showing the southward orientation, which is also evident in the large amount of material in the first cataract area, especially Elephantine Island. On the way to and from Nubia or when visiting Elephantine, people made dedications in the shrine of the deified Heqaib, a late Old Kingdom official who had also been a traveller to the south (Habachi 1985). Detlef Franke (1994, 97) notes that a high proportion of the material deposited in the shrine was not set up by locals, that the administrative elite of the period was 'very mobile', and that some of these people made dedications at Abydos as well as Elephantine. From the Old Kingdom on, rocks in the first cataract area were inscribed with 'graffiti' – often formal inscriptions – in addition to memorials placed in temples, tombs, and shrines. Values associated with travel were thus memorialized at places visited.

A still more significant Middle Kingdom feature is the focus on the royal residence, which intensified in the late 12th and early 13th dynasties and counterpointed the despatch of administrators to remote regions and beyond the frontiers. In the early 12th dynasty the residence was moved from Thebes to the Memphite area (Arnold 1991), where it had been in the Old Kingdom. This move had great political and cultural resonance. The word for residence is that for 'interior (*ẖnw*)' and creates a nested vision of the country. From the perspective of abroad, all of Egypt is the 'interior', rather as people living in the British empire commonly referred to Britain as 'Home'. That perspective is exploited notably in literary texts. Within Egypt, the capital and not the country was the 'interior', presumably having been termed thus for the truly enclosed area of the royal residence itself, whose official name was '(Amenemhat I is) he who takes possession of the Two Lands (*jṯ-tꜣwj*)', a designation that related the centre to the entire land and survived in memory into Graeco-Roman times. The extent to which the country focused ideologically on the centre varied, while different cities were seen as central in different periods. These conceptions all related, however, to the fundamental idea of the Egyptian world as an ideological unity, within which the elite valued the symbolic significance of various places. This distributed focus of meaning was a potential stimulus to travel for the sake of experience.

Transition and enlarged horizons

The late Middle Kingdom and Second Intermediate period were times of great change, with a weakening of central rule, loss of control of Lower Nubia, the takeover of the north by an ethnically non-Egyptian dynasty (the 'Hyksos' 15th), and in the far south the expansion of the Kerma state, which overran Lower Nubia.

For a century or more the significance of travel to the centre endured. In the early 17th century a priest from Hierakonpolis in the far south of Egypt narrated as the core of his self-presentation that he had visited the Memphite residence to collect a new cult statue for his god Horus (Hayes 1947), who seems to have selected him for that role through an oracle (Baines 1987a, 89), displaying the cultural and religious importance of extended communication and the need for key artefacts to come from single workshops.

In the following century patterns of communication and travel changed. Immigration from far afield became common, with Sudanese nomads of the Pan-Grave culture settling throughout Egypt and as far south as Kerma, most of them probably as military personnel (Lacovara 2001). Around 1550 the 17th dynasty Theban ruler Kamose proclaimed his intention to reunite Egypt, stating that it was intolerable to be forced to divide it with a Asiatic and a Nubian (Helck 1983, 83–4; Redford 1997, 13). Since from the beginning Kamose probably controlled the land as far south as the first cataract, his claim used an expanded definition of Egypt that seems not to be attested from the Middle Kingdom and that included the former colonial territory of Lower Nubia. His actions seem nearly to have matched his words, at least to the south. There is evidence for his presence in Lower Nubia (but see Krauss 1993), while a stela of a military man states that he spent 'year 3' – the year known for Kamose's campaign north toward Avaris in the Delta – 'beating the drum' and 'I reached Miu, not counting every (other) foreign land, following my lord (= the king) every day, and I reached Avaris' (Baines 1986, 42; interpretation is disputed, see e.g. Störk 1993).

Until recently Miu was generally placed in the second cataract region, which fitted the possible finds of inscriptions of Kamose. It is now established that Miu must be no further north than the fifth cataract region, well over 500 kilometres south-east of Aswan.[13] While it is uncertain how close Kamose came to Avaris in the Delta, within a year he and his army seem to have made raids – not lasting conquests – to south and north that totalled more than 3000 km of travelling.

The same level of mobility and an increased amount of military action characterize the reign of Kamose's successor Ahmose (ca. 1539–1514), the founder of the 18th dynasty and the New Kingdom. Ahmose seems to have conquered at least as far as the second cataract in Nubia and northward into Palestine. His second successor Thutmose I (ca. 1493–1483) carved an inscription on the rock outcrop Hagr el-Merwa near Kurgus, north of the fifth cataract, and asserted that he had reached the Euphrates in Syria (Sethe 1906, 85, ll. 13–4). His grandson Thutmose III (ca. 1479–1425) set up inscriptions next to his grandfather's at these two extremes of Egyptian penetration (Davies 2001, 52), after attaining them more gradually than Thutmose I had done. Nonroyal self-presentations of military personnel from the period cover a comparable range of territory (e.g. Ahmose son of Ebana, Lichtheim 1976, 12–5). In keeping with the more mobile royal role that had emerged, these people did not present an independent role but stated that they accompanied kings.

Kings and nonroyal protagonists of this period seem to have exploited the enlarged southward definition of Egypt ('the Black Land', *kmt*) in the rhetoric of their narratives. Thutmose I, in particular, emphasized having reached the ends of the earth. This idea had a specific realization at Hagr el-Merwa/Kurgus, where heraldic scenes of Thutmose I and III, together with figures of deities and of royal lions, were accompanied by inscriptions commemorating a range of people (the texts also name the region of Miu). Among the names so far identified are Ahmose, the queen of Thutmose I, a king's daughter, several 'king's sons' who could be royal princes or officials and 'viceroys' of Nubia, and high officials including priests and members of the royal entourage. Each person's inscription is distinct and individually commissioned, signifying that their owners came to Kurgus in person.

Kurgus was not the limit of the world the Egyptians knew. Further south-east lay Irem and Nemayu (O'Connor 1987), while Punt was known to be connected geographically with Irem but was normally reached southward along the Red Sea. Kurgus seems to have been ceremonially visited as a marker, probably both to affirm Egyptian territorial claims – bolstered by the unique formulas cursing potential vandals that form part of the inscriptions – and to approach numinous regions, as is suggested by the use of phrases about 'reaching the limits of the World' in relation to expeditions to the far south, as well as the 'land of the Horizon Dwellers' and 'god's land' mentioned above. Kurgus was also the southward, and hence 'forward', limit of annexation of territory, so that in some sense it was part of the country and comparable with the earlier focus on the first cataract area.

This 'cosmological' aspect of travel is not so clearly attested for other directions, although some comparable meaning may have attached to Serabit el-Khadim in Sinai, where there was a temple to the goddess Hathor on a desert ridge (Pinch 1993, 49–58; Valbelle and Bonnet 1996), and to Punt, which was significant in sacred geography as well as being the destination of real journeys. In keeping with the extension of Egyptian possessions and contacts in the New Kingdom, but perhaps also with a more explicit expression of sacral values in reliefs and inscriptions, these features are more clearly attested from then than earlier. By contrast, self-presentations relating to the significance of travel within Egypt – as against transport – are less prominent.

Modes of travel; informal evidence

The example of Kurgus, where a high-ranking, partly civilian group journeyed over vast inhospitable distances, raises questions of modes of travel. Such journeys were difficult into modern times (see e.g. Villamont et al. 1971; Giamberardini 1963); it was not easy even to sail up the Nile into Lower Nubia. Before the advent of the camel in the last centuries BC, desert travel was still more arduous. This difficulty of movement, except on the Nile north of the cataracts in Egypt, fits with the vast majority of evidence relating to travel outside the country, which points to large groups and organized expeditions, mainly under central control. Material describing such undertakings is favoured by patterns of survival, but the picture may not be completely misleading. Sparse populations of nomads inhabited the surrounding regions, notably the Eastern Desert, but numerous Egyptian characterizations make it into a place of terror, where wells might not be found (Fecht 1965, 74–5, 122–3) and the inhabitants were alien and unpredictable (Parkinson 1997, 223 stanza 34). They were not inviting to the lone traveller.

In a non-monetary economy, the food and other essentials required for travel that could not be taken with the traveller could be difficult to acquire, and would often have had to be provided by official sources or by customs of gift exchange and hospitality. Such customs can function well among elites but can hardly apply to large numbers of people and may scarcely operate for the poor. A royal document appended in summary to the 6th dynasty self-presentation of Harkhuf states:

> *(Royal) commands were brought to each Administrator of a New Town and Companion and Overseer of Priests to order that supplies be requisitioned through him from all estates of the granary administration and all temples. No exception was made in the matter.*
>
> (Sethe 1933, 131 ll. 4–7)

This demonstrates that regional storehouses could be expected to provide supplies to groups passing on government business. Since the document would have been delivered throughout the Nile Valley, it shows that there were methods of communication that could alert for the arrival of people on whom significant resources were expended. The citation of the document makes it probable that receipt of such largesse was exceptional and a mark of privilege.

An early 19th dynasty letter shows that such arrangements did not always work by telling the addressee that he should treat a visitor well and assign him a full living allowance, as he had not done for the sender when he visited:

> *… you should look after Merimose when he is there with you. Do not treat him as you did me when I was there in Memphis and half of my provisions (remained) with you for their price in silver.*
>
> (Barns 1948, 36 ll. 8–10; Wente 1990, no. 132)

Nothing is known of provisions for large numbers of people converging on a place, as may have happened at Abydos. While markets existed for trade in small-scale and perishable goods (see e.g. Eyre 1998), they might not have been equal to peak demands like these. Armies inevitably lived off the land and the local community. The 6th dynasty self-presentation of Weni acknowledges this reality by stating that he prevented his troops from stealing from local populations, perhaps in Sinai or southern Palestine (Lichtheim 1973, 20). This detail is probably a 'universalizing' variant of ethical provision for the deprived; the items enumerated in the text parallel the gifts people stated that they gave in their own communities.

The evidence I have cited is largely from formal and public sources, but information about the realities of travel may come better from material that is less highly wrought or less focused on travel as a topic. Such material becomes more frequent in the New Kingdom and includes, for example, a little more information about women in relation to travel than can be found earlier. A mid 18th dynasty letter from a high official about preparations by his own staff a few days ahead of his arrival may have been taken over the desert shortcut between Thebes and the Nag' Hammadi region (Caminos 1964; Wente 1990, no. 118) – a route on which a traveller who paused and carved a graffito in the Middle Kingdom was learned enough to inscribe a passage from a literary text[14] – or perhaps just sent with someone who had to journey at very high speed. But we still know nothing of the background that a late 20th dynasty correspondent took for granted in writing back to Thebes to say that he had arrived in Edfu, where he met someone, and then went on to Elephantine (Wente 1990, no. 308). No detail is given and one cannot tell what sort of contacts or introductions were needed for a traveller to be accepted, where people would meet, what sources there were for provisions or lodging, and so forth.

From the late Old Kingdom on, letters attest to avoidance of travel for specialist supplies or complain of unnecessary travel (e.g. Wente 1990, nos. 40, 132). They also document anxieties of travel and are full of questions about whether the other party has been praying to and consulting local gods to ensure that the absent party will return (Baines 2001). Deities could be invoked to pronounce oracles that would guarantee a child against a vast range of dangers, including those encountered on religious journeys and when travelling by ship or any other means (Edwards 1960, xx, 7, 8, 16).

These anxieties are balanced by travel's prestige in a letter that a widower wrote to his wife in the next world, saying that he had not neglected her and had shown her every care and consideration, even though his successful career had brought him into higher social strata and he had travelled throughout the country accompanying the king (Wente 1990, no. 352).

Conclusion

The widower's assertion to his deceased wife reads almost like the exculpation of a modern executive, but such parallels should not tempt us to underestimate differences between ancient and modern conditions, between means and frequency of travel, as well as perhaps a greater salience of travel in the ancient record, notably in elite self-presentations. Such salience relates in part to the arduous conduct of ancient travel, which meant that voluntary movement over long distances was a major privilege. The New Kingdom journeys to Kurgus show that difficulty was not in itself a severe obstacle. By contrast, the relatively common inscriptions and depictions of the transport of large objects, such as sarcophagi, statues, and obelisks (Helck 1986; Partridge 1996), illustrate that the salience of the activity, in a culture that placed a high value on monuments and on fine stones, could focus on means of movement, which was otherwise kept in the background, and on who accomplished the feat.

Egyptian thematizations of travel set the universals of elite male experience in complex societies in the context of a unitary state and civilization. The culture had a variable attitude to the relation of centre and province and was cautious about the world around, the closest areas of which were environmentally inhospitable, quite apart from their potentially hostile populations. Changes in evidence from different periods relate, among other factors, to changes in the extent of the state and its contacts abroad. Patterns such as the southward orientation of expansion and the association of the east with 'god's land' manifest cultural concerns that may have influenced modes of action profoundly.

Relatively hard evidence for travel – such as rock inscriptions set up abroad or finds of artifacts deriving from remote regions – is quite widespread, but in this chapter I have discussed mainly material in Egypt that is more informative about attitudes than facts. Differences between sources of different periods may be revealing in relation to genre rather than to anything else. The more subjective attitudes to travel that can be identified in Middle and especially New Kingdom sources are unlikely to have been absent earlier and may have been significant in the oral domain. Travel was probably 'good to think with' and good to discriminate with, in patterns characteristic of complex sedentary societies, from as early as there were elites in Egypt.

Acknowledgments

This chapter is a revision of the paper I presented to the conference in Nottingham. I should like to thank Colin Adams for the invitation which stimulated me to work on this topic, which I had long seen as a gap in the literature. Martina Minas and Richard Parkinson most kindly commented on drafts and David Wengrow and Elizabeth Frood were very helpful with references. The final text was completed at the Institute for the Humanities of the University of Michigan, to which I am very grateful for wonderful research facilities.

I presented a second version of the research, partly complementary to this one, in Leipzig in May 2002. This has been published as a booklet of the Ägyptisches Museum der Universität Leipzig, *Die Bedeutung des Reisens im alten Ägypten* (2004); unlike the present chapter, it includes illustrations.

For economy of space, I mostly cite translations of Egyptian texts that give references to primary publications. Translations are my own unless otherwise noted.

Notes

1 The word 'Egypt' derives through Greek from *ḥwt-kꜣ-ptḥ*, an official New Kingdom term for the domain of Ptah in the administrative capital of Memphis. It is thus comparable with Misr, the word for the modern capital city which is also the word for Egypt ('Cairo' is a specialized usage).

2 Contrary to older studies, the visibility of Sothis did not simply mark the first day of the

inundation. The latter could vary by some weeks, while over the millennia the former very slowly shifted later in the natural year, becoming gradually closer to the beginning of the inundation. See Krauss (1985).

3 An Egyptian example is the meeting of Amenhotep II with the rulers of Mitanni, the Hittites, and Babylon in his year 9, in an unspecified location presumably in Syria (Helck 1955, 1309, ll. 13–20; 1961, 40; J. A. Wilson, in Pritchard 1969, 247); the text treats this as submission by the others, but this may be doubted.

4 The 12th dynasty Tale of Sinuhe offers a counterpoint, where the heir to the throne is narrated as being on campaign while the old king remains in the palace (Parkinson 1997, 27–8, 30). This statement in a fictional context contrasts with a historical inscription in which the same heir, in his role as king Senwosret I, asserts his own perfection from birth (Piccato 1997; the inscription, preserved in a later manuscript, may be pseudo-epigraphic).

5 The siting of the king in the country and principles of movement relating to him have a wider resonance among the gods, who both gathered to the centre and were distributed over the entire land (see Hornung 1982, 66–74, for the Early Dynastic period; Begelsbacher-Fischer 1981, 249–70 for the 4th–5th dynasties). This material would repay separate study.

6 F. Junge, in Kaiser et al. (1976, 98–107); Junge (1987, 11). Because town sites are poorly known, it is uncertain how common such cult chapels were. A Middle Kingdom example is attested only from the inscription accompanying a relief in its owner's desert tomb (Sethe 1928, 78 ll. 1–2). On Elephantine Island, a local cemetery next to the town is contemporaneous with the elite tombs at Qubbet el-Hawa, demonstrating a social–spatial separation in death that relates closely to the availability of movement for the elite (Seidlmayer in preparation).

7 See Kitchen (2001); Fattovich (1996). I was not able to take account of S. P. Harvey, in O'Connor and Quirke (2003).

8 Lichtheim (1973, 19–20); Roccati (1982, 193–4). For a Middle Kingdom example where numbers are specified, see Sethe (1935, 15); Lichtheim (1988, 138).

9 Perdriaud (200) reads the text as not stating that these people died, but his interpretation is not convincing.

10 Anthes (1930, perhaps late 11th dynasty); Schäfer (1905, early 12th dynasty). A fragmentary example shows the protagonist with his dogs, like the Anthes example cited, and includes the word 'on his journeys to...', a turn of phrase that can refer to going on royal campaigns or to following a lower-ranking lord: Bisson de la Roque (1937, 134 fig. 821, inv. 2106).

11 Examples include the early 12th dynasty vizier Mentuhotep (Simpson 1991), and Ikhernofret under Senwosret III (Anthes 1974; Lichtheim 1973, 123–5; 1988, 80–2).

12 See notably Yoyotte (1960); Malaise (1987). Compare Lichtheim (1988, 101–34), who remarks: 'Several thousand stelae erected at Abydos in the course of three centuries do not add up to a mass movement' (p. 134).

13 For much of what follows, see Davies (2001). I am very grateful to Vivian Davies for explaining the significance of this material to me.

14 Darnell (1997); Darnell (2002, 97–101). Some of these desert graffiti relate to performance of rituals (Darnell and Darnell 2002, Wadi el-Hôl no. 5), evidently away from home, and to celebrating a 'holiday (*hrw-nfr*)', presumably in the shade of the rock face where they were inscribed (Wadi el-Hôl nos. 17–20). One wonders whether the latter group is partly ironic, but in any case they provide evidence for quite arduous travel for non-pragmatic purposes.

Bibliography

Altenmüller, H. (1975) 'Zur Frage der *mww*', *Studien zur Altägyptischen Kultur* 2, 1–37.

Altenmüller, H. (1998) *Die Wanddarstellungen im Grab des Mehu in Saqqara* (Deutsches Archäologisches Institut, Abteilung Kairo, Archäologische Veröffentlichungen 42, Mainz).

Altenmüller, H. and A. M. Moussa (1991) 'Die Inschrift Amenemhets II. aus dem Ptah-Tempel von Memphis: Ein Vorbericht', *Studien zur Altägyptischen Kultur* 18, 1–48.

Anthes, R. (1930) 'Eine Polizeistreife des Mittleren Reiches in die westliche Oase', *Zeitschrift für Ägyptische Sprache und Altertumskunde* 65, 108–14.

Anthes, R. (1974) 'Die Berichte des Ichernofret und des Neferhotep über das Osirisfest in Abydos', in *Festschrift zum 150jährigen Bestehen des Berliner Ägyptischen Museums*, 15–49 (Staatliche Museen zu Berlin, Mitteilungen aus der Ägyptischen Sammlung 8, Berlin).

Arnold, D. (1991) 'Amenemhat I and the early twelfth dynasty at Thebes', *Metropolitan Museum Journal* 26, 5–48.

Baines, J. (1982) 'Interpreting Sinuhe', *Journal of Egyptian Archaeology* 68, 31–44.

Baines, J. (1986) 'The stela of Emhab: innovation, tradition, hierarchy', *Journal of Egyptian Archaeology* 72, 41–53.

Baines, J. (1987a) 'Practical religion and piety', *Journal of Egyptian Archaeology* 73, 79–98.

Baines, J. (1987b) 'The stela of Khusobek: private and royal military narrative and values', in J. Osing and G. Dreyer (eds) *Form und Mass: Beiträge zur Literatur, Sprache und Kunst des alten Ägypten. Festschrift fur Gerhard Fecht*, 43–61 (Ägypten und Altes Testament 12, Wiesbaden).

Baines, J. (1990a) 'Interpreting the Story of the Shipwrecked Sailor', *Journal of Egyptian Archaeology* 76, 55–72.

Baines, J. (1990b) 'Restricted knowledge, hierarchy, and decorum: modern perceptions and ancient institutions', *Journal of the American Research Center in Egypt* 27, 1–23.

Baines, J. (1996) 'Contextualizing Egyptian representations of society and ethnicity', in J. S. Cooper and G. Schwartz (eds) *The Study of the Ancient Near East in the 21st century: Proceedings of the William Foxwell Albright Memorial Conference*, 339–84, (Winona Lake IN).

Baines, J. (1997) 'Kingship before literature: the world of the king in the Old Kingdom', in R. Gundlach and C. Raedler (eds) *Selbstverständnis und Realität: Akten des Symposiums zur ägyptischen Königsideologie Mainz 15–17.6.1995*, 125–86 (Ägypten und Altes Testament 36, Beiträge zur Ägyptischen Königsideologie 1, Wiesbaden).

Baines, J. (1999a) 'Forerunners of narrative biographies', in A. Leahy and J. Tait (eds) *Studies on Ancient Egypt in Honour of H. S. Smith*, 23–37 (Egypt Exploration Society Occasional Publications 13, London).

Baines, J. (1999b) 'Prehistories of literature: performance, fiction, myth', in G. Moers (ed.) *Definitely: Egyptian literature. Proceedings of the Symposium "Ancient Egyptian Literature: History and Forms", Los Angeles, March 24–26, 1995*, 17–41 (Lingua Aegyptia, Studia Monographica 2, Göttingen).

Baines, J. (2001) 'Egyptian letters of the New Kingdom as evidence for religious practice', *Journal of Ancient Near Eastern Religions* 1, 1–31.

Baines, J. (2004) *Die Bedeutung des Reisens im alten Ägypten* (13. Siegfried-Morenz-Gedächtnis-Vorlesung, Leipzig).

Barns, J. W. B. (1948), 'Three hieratic papyri in the Duke of Northumberland's collection', *Journal of Egyptian Archaeology* 34, 35–46.

Beckerath, J. v. (1968) 'Die "Stele der Verbannten" im Museum des Louvre', *Revue d'Egyptologie* 20, 7–36.

Begelsbacher-Fischer, B. (1981) *Untersuchungen zur Götterwelt des Alten Reiches im Spiegel der Privatgräber der IV. und V. Dynastie* (Orbis Biblicus et Orientalis 37, Fribourg and Göttingen).

Bietak, M. (1988) 'Zur Marine des Alten Reichs', in J. Baines, T. G. H. James, A. Leahy and A. F. Shore (eds) *Pyramid Studies and Other Essays Presented to I. E. S. Edwards*, 35–40 (Egypt Exploration Society Occasional Publications 7, London).

Bisson de la Roque, F. (1937) *Tôd (1934 à 1936)* (Fouilles de l'Institut Français d'Archéologie Orientale 17, Cairo).

Blackman, A. M. (1932), *Middle-Egyptian Stories* (Bibliotheca Aegyptiaca 2, Brussels).

Borchardt, L., E. Assmann, A. Bollacher, O. Heinroth, M. Hilzheimer and K. Sethe (1913) *Das*

Grabdenkmal des Königs Śa3ḥu-Re' II, Die Wandbilder (Ausgrabungen der Deutschen Orient-Gesellschaft in Abusir 1902–1908, Leipzig).
Bourriau, J. (1991) 'Relations between Egypt and Kerma during the Middle and New Kingdoms', in V. Davies (ed.) *Egypt and Africa: Nubia from Prehistory to Islam*, 129–44 (London).
Caminos, R. A. (1964) 'Papyrus Berlin 10463', *Journal of Egyptian Archaeology* 49, 29–37.
Caminos, R. A. (1977), *A Tale of Woe: from a Hieratic Papyrus in the A. S. Pushkin Museum of Fine Arts in Moscow* (Oxford).
Christophe, L. (1949) 'La stèle de l'an III de Ramsès IV au Ouâdi Hammâmât (No 12)', *Bulletin de l'Institut Français d'Archéologie Orientale* 48, 1–38.
Couyat, J. and P. Montet (1912) *Les inscriptions hiéroglyphiques et hiératiques du Ouâdi Hammâmât* (Mémoires publiés par les membres de l'Institut Français d'Archéologie Orientale du Caire 34, Cairo).
Darnell, J. C. (1997) 'A new Middle Egyptian literary text from the Wadi el-Hôl', *Journal of the American Research Center in Egypt* 34, 85–100.
Darnell, J. C. and D. Darnell (2002) *Theban Desert Road Survey in the Egyptian Western Desert* I: *Gebel Tjauti Rock Inscriptions 1–45 and Wadi el-Hôl Rock Inscriptions 1–45* (Oriental Institute Publications 119, Chicago).
Davies, V. (2001) 'Kurgus 2000: the Egyptian inscriptions', *Sudan and Nubia* 5, 46–58.
Dreyer, G. (1986) *Elephantine VIII: Der Tempel der Satet, die Funde der Frühzeit und des Alten Reiches* (Deutsches Archäologisches Institut, Abteilung Kairo, Archäologische Veröffentlichungen 39, Mainz).
Edel, E. (1944) 'Untersuchungen zu der Phraseologie der Inschriften des Alten Reichs', *Mitteilungen des Deutschen Instituts für Ägyptische Altertumskunde in Kairo* 13, 1–90.
Edel, E. (1955) 'Inschriften des Alten Reiches V: Die Reiseberichte des *Ḥrw-ḫwjf* (Herchuf)', in O. Firchow (ed.) *Ägyptologische Studien*, 51–75 (Deutsche Akademie der Wissenschaften zu Berlin, Institut für Orientforschung, Veröffentlichung 29, Berlin).
Edwards, I. E. S. (1960) *Oracular Amuletic Decrees of the Late New Kingdom* (Hieratic papyri in the British Museum, 4th series; 2 vols, London).
Elias, N. (1983) *The Court Society* (trans.) E. Jephcott (Oxford).
Erman, A. and H. Grapow (1926–31) *Wörterbuch der ägyptischen Sprache*. 5 vols (Leipzig).
Eyre, C. (1998) 'The market women of pharaonic Egypt', in B. Menu and N.-C. Grimal (eds) *Le commerce en Égypte ancienne*, 173–91 (Bibliothèque d'Etude 121, Cairo).
Eyre, C. J. (1990) 'The Semna stelae: quotation, genre and functions of literature', in S. Israelit-Groll (ed.) *Studies in Egyptology Presented to Miriam Lichtheim*, 134–65 (Jerusalem).
Fattovich, R. (1996) 'Punt: the archaeological perspective', *Beiträge zur Sudanforschung* 6, 15–29.
Fecht, G. (1965) *Literarische Zeugnisse zur "persönlichen Frömmigkeit" in Ägypten: Analyse der Beispiele in den ramessidischen Schulpapyri* (Abhandlungen der Heidelberger Akademie der Wissenschaften, philosophisch-historische Klasse, 1965, 1, Heidelberg).
Franke, D. (1994) *Das Heiligtum des Heqaib auf Elephantine: Geschichte eines Provinzheiligtums im Mittleren Reich* (Studien zur Archäologie und Geschichte Altägyptens 9, Heidelberg).
Fuchs, G. (1989) 'Rock engravings in the Wadi el-Barramiya, Eastern Desert of Egypt', *African Archaeological Review* 7, 127–53.
Gardiner, A. H., T. E. Peet and J. Černý (1952–55) *The inscriptions of Sinai*. 2, vol. II by Jaroslav Černý. 2 vols, 2nd ed (London).
Geertz, C. (1983) 'Centers, kings and charisma: reflections on the symbolics of power', in C. Geertz, *Local Knowledge: Further Essays in Interpretive Anthropology*, 121–46 (New York).
Giamberardini, G. (1963) *I viaggiatori francescani attraverso la Nubia dal 1698 al 1710* (Studia Orientalia Christiana Aegyptiaca, originally published in *Collectanea* 8, 361–438, Cairo).
Habachi, L. (1985) *Elephantine* IV: *The Sanctuary of Heqaib* (Archäologische Veröffentlichungen des Deutschen Archäologischen Instituts, Abteilung Kairo 33. 2 vols., Mainz).

Hayes, W. C. (1947) 'Ḥoremkha'uef of Nekhen and his trip to Iṯ-towe', *Journal of Egyptian Archaeology* 33, 3–11.
Helck, W. (1955) *Urkunden der 18. Dynastie, Heft 17* (Urkunden des Ägyptischen Altertums 4:17, Berlin).
Helck, W. (1961) *Urkunden der 18. Dynastie: Übersetzung zu den Heften 17–22* (Urkunden des Ägyptischen Altertums: Deutsch, Berlin).
Helck, W. (1983) *Historisch-biographische Texte der 2. Zwischenzeit und neue Texte der 18. Dynastie* (Kleine Ägyptische Texte. 2nd ed., Wiesbaden).
Helck, W. (1986) 'Transportwesen', in W. Helck and W. Westendorf (eds), *Lexikon der Ägyptologie* VI, 743–4 (Wiesbaden).
Hornung, E. (1982) *Conceptions of God in Ancient Egypt: the One and the Many* (trans.) J. Baines (German *Der Eine und die Vielen*, 1971, Ithaca NY).
Jacquet-Gordon, H. (1962) *Les noms des domaines funéraires sous l'Ancien Empire égyptien* (Bibliothèque d'Étude 34, Cairo).
Janssen, J. J. (1987) 'The day the inundation began', *Journal of Near Eastern Studies* 46, 129–36.
Junge, F. (1987) *Elephantine* XI: *Funde und Bauteile, 1.–7. Kampagne, 1969–1976* (Archäologische Veröffentlichungen des Deutschen Archäologischen Instituts, Abteilung Kairo 49, Mainz).
Junker, H. (1940) 'Der Tanz der *Mww* und das Butische Begräbnis im Alten Reich', *Mitteilungen des Deutschen Instituts für Ägyptische Altertumskunde in Kairo* 9, 1–39.
Kaiser, W., G. Dreyer, R. Gempeler, P. Grossmann, G. Haeny, H. Jaritz, et al. (1976) 'Stadt und Tempel von Elephantine: Sechster Grabungsbericht', *Mitteilungen des Deutschen Archäologischen Instituts, Abteilung Kairo* 32, 67–112.
Kitchen, K. A. (1983) *Ramesside Inscriptions, Historical and Biographical* V (Oxford).
Kitchen, K. A. (2001), 'Punt', in D. B. Redford (ed.) *The Oxford Encyclopedia of Ancient Egypt* III, 85–6 (New York).
Krauss, R. (1985) *Sothis- und Monddaten: Studien zur astronomischen und technischen Chronologie Altägyptens* (Hildesheimer Ägyptologische Beiträge 20, Hildesheim).
Krauss, R. (1993) 'Zur Problematik der Nubienpolitik Kamoses sowie der Hyksosherrschaft in Oberägypten', *Orientalia* 62, 17–29.
Lacovara, P. (2001) 'Pan-Grave people', in D. B. Redford (ed.) *The Oxford Encyclopedia of Ancient Egypt*, III, 20–2 (New York).
Lapp, G. (1986) *Die Opferformel des Alten Reiches, unter Berücksichtigung einiger späterer Formen* (Deutsches Archäologisches Institut, Abteilung Kairo, Sonderschrift 21, Mainz).
Lichtheim, M. (1973) *Ancient Egyptian Literature: A Book of Readings* I, *The Old and Middle Kingdoms* (Berkeley).
Lapp, G. (1976) *Ancient Egyptian Literature: a Book of Readings* II, *The New Kingdom* (Berkeley).
Lapp, G. (1988) *Ancient Egyptian Autobiographies Chiefly of the Middle Kingdom: a Study and an Anthology* (Orbis Biblicus et Orientalis 84, Fribourg and Göttingen).
Loprieno, A. (1988) *Topos und Mimesis: zum Bild des Ausländers in der ägyptischen Literatur* (Ägyptologische Abhandlungen 48, Wiesbaden).
Loprieno, A. (2001) *La pensée et l'écriture: pour une analyse sémiotique de la culture égyptienne; quatre séminaires à l'Ecole Pratique des Hautes Etudes, Section des Sciences Religieuses, 15–27 mai 2000* (Paris).
Malaise, M. (1987) 'Pèlerinages et pèlerins dans l'Egypte ancienne', in J. Chélini and H. Branthomme (eds) *Histoire des pèlerinages non chrétiens: entre magique et sacré, le chemin des dieux*, 55–82 (Paris).
Marée, M. 2002. Seminar presentation on Middle Kingdom Abydos stelae. University of Oxford.
Midant-Reynes, B. (2000) *The Prehistory of Egypt, from the First Egyptians to the First Pharaohs* (trans.) I. Shaw (Oxford and Malden MA).

Moers, G. (2001) *Fingierte Welten in der ägyptischen Literatur des 2. Jahrtausends v. Chr.: Grenzüberschreitung, Reisemotiv und Fiktionalität* (Probleme der Ägyptologie 19, Leiden and Boston).

O'Connor, D. (1985) 'The "cenotaphs" of the Middle Kingdom at Abydos', in P. Posener-Kriéger (ed.) *Mélanges Gamal Eddin Mokhtar*, II: 161–77 (Bibliothèque d'Etude 97, Cairo).

O'Connor, D. (1986) 'The locations of Yam and Kush and their historical implications', *Journal of the American Research Center in Egypt* 23, 27–50.

O'Connor, D. (1987) 'The location of Irem', *Journal of Egyptian Archaeology* 73, 99–136.

O'Connor, D. and S. Quirke (eds.) (2003) *Mysterious Lands* (Encounters with Ancient Egypt, London).

Parkinson, R. B. (1997) *The Tale of Sinuhe and Other Ancient Egyptian Poems, 1940–1640 BC* (Oxford).

Partridge, R. B. (1996) *Transport in Ancient Egypt* (London).

Perdriaud, H. (2002) 'Les cas des neuf cents "disparus" de la stèle de l'An 3 de Ramsès IV au Ouâdi Hammâmât', *Göttinger Miszellen* 196, 89–97.

Piccato, A. (1997) 'The Berlin Leather Roll and the Egyptian sense of history', *Lingua Aegyptia* 5, 137–59.

Pinch, G. (1993) *Votive Offerings to Hathor* (Oxford).

Posener, G. (1965) 'Sur l'orientation et l'ordre des points cardinaux chez les Egyptiens', in S. Schott (ed.) *Göttinger Vorträge vom Ägyptologischen Kolloquium der Akademie am 25. und 26. August 1964*, 69–78 (Göttingen).

Posener, G. (1978) 'L'[anachoresis] dans l'Egypte pharaonique', in J. Bingen, C. Préaux, G. Cambier and G. Nachtergael (eds.) *Le monde grec, pensée, littérature, histoire, documents: Hommages à Claire Préaux*, 663–9 (Brussels).

Pritchard, J. B. (ed.) 1969) *Ancient Near Eastern Texts Relating to the Old Testament.* 3rd ed. with supplement (Princeton).

Quirke, S. (1988) 'State and labour in the Middle Kingdom: a reconsideration of the term *ḫnrt*', *Revue d'Egyptologie* 38, 83–106.

Redford, D. B. (1997) 'Textual sources for the Hyksos period', in E. D. Oren (ed.) *The Hyksos: New Historical and Archaeological Perspectives*, 1–44 (University Museum Monograph 96, Philadelphia).

Roccati, A. (1982) *La littérature historique sous l'Ancien Empire égyptien* (Littératures Anciennes du Proche-Orient, Paris).

Rothe, R. D., G. Rapp Jr. and W. K. Miller (1996) 'New hieroglyphic evidence for pharaonic activity in the Eastern Desert of Egypt', *Journal of the American Research Center in Egypt* 33, 77–104.

Sainte Fare Garnot, J. (1938) *L'appel aux vivants dans les textes funéraires, des origines à la fin de l'Ancien Empire* (Recherches d'Archéologie, de Philologie et d'Histoire 9, Cairo).

Satzinger, H. (1986) 'Eine Familie aus dem Athribis des späten Mittleren Reiches', *Studien zur Altägyptischen Kultur* 13, 171–80.

Schäfer, H. (1905) 'Ein Zug nach der Großen Oase unter Sesostris I', *Zeitschrift für Ägyptische Sprache und Altertumskunde* 42, 124–28.

Schenkel, W. (1965) *Memphis. Herakleopolis. Theben. Die epigraphischen Zeugnisse der 7.–11. Dynastie Ägyptens* (Ägyptologische Abhandlungen 12, Wiesbaden).

Seidlmayer, S. J. (1996) 'Town and state in the early Old Kingdom: a view from Elephantine', in J. Spencer (ed.) *Aspects of Early Egypt*, 108–27 (London).

Seidlmayer, S. J. (2000) 'The First Intermediate Period (*c*. 2160–2055 BC)', in I. Shaw (ed.), *The Oxford History of Ancient Egypt*, 118–47 (Oxford).

Seidlmayer, S. J. (in preparation) *Elephantine* XII: *Ausgrabungen in der Nordweststadt von Elephantine 1979–1982, Ein Gräberfeld des Alten und Mittleren Reiches und andere Befunde* (Deutsches Archäologisches Institut, Abteilung Kairo, Archäologische Veröffentlichungen, Mainz).

Sethe, K. (1906) *Urkunden der 18. Dynastie* (Urkunden des Ägyptischen Altertums IV, 1, Leipzig).
Sethe, K. (1909) *Urkunden der 18. Dynastie* (Urkunden des Ägyptischen Altertums IV, 4, Leipzig).
Sethe, K. (1928) *Ägyptische Lesestücke zum Gebrauch im akademischen Unterricht: Texte des Mittleren Reiches* (2nd ed, Leipzig).
Sethe, K. (1933) *Urkunden des alten Reiches* (Urkunden des Ägyptischen Altertums I, 1; 2nd ed., Leipzig).
Sethe, K. and W. Erichsen (1935) *Historisch-biographische Urkunden des Mittleren Reiches* (Urkunden des Ägyptischen Altertums VII, 1, Leipzig).
Simpson, W. K. (1974) *The Terrace of the Great God at Abydos: the Offering Chapels of Dynasties 12 and 13* (Publications of the Pennsylvania–Yale Expedition to Egypt 5, New Haven and Philadelphia).
Simpson, W. K. (1991) 'Mentuhotep, vizier of Sesostris I, patron of art and architecture', *Mitteilungen des Deutschen Archäologischen Instituts, Abteilung Kairo* 47, 331–40.
Störk, L. (1993) 'Der Trommler des Königs', *Göttinger Miszellen* 133, 101–9.
Valbelle, D. and C. Bonnet (1996) *Le sanctuaire d'Hathor, maîtresse de la turquoise: Sérabit el-Khadim au Moyen Empire* (Paris and Aosta).
Vandier, J. (1950) *Mo'alla: la tombe d'Ankhtifi et la tombe de Sébekhotep* (Bibliothèque d'Etude 18, Cairo).
Villamont, J. de, J. Somer, C. Burri, and S. Sauneron (eds) (1971) *Voyages en Egypte des années 1589, 1590 & 1591* (Collection des Voyageurs Occidentaux en Egypte 3, Cairo).
Vittmann, G. (1999) *Altägyptische Wegmetaphorik* (Beiträge zur Ägyptologie 15, Vienna).
Volokhine, Y. (1998) 'Les déplacements pieux en Egypte pharaonique: sites et pratiques cultuelles', in D. Frankfurter (ed.) *Pilgrimage and Holy Space in Late Antique Egypt*, 51–97 (Religions in the Graeco-Roman World 134, Leiden).
Wente, E. F. (1990) *Letters from Ancient Egypt* (Writings from the Ancient World 1, Atlanta).
Wilkinson, T. A. H. (2000) *Royal Annals of Ancient Egypt: the Palermo Stone and Its Associated Fragments* (Studies in Egyptology, London).
Yoyotte, J. (1960) 'Les pèlerinages dans l'Egypte ancienne', in *Les pèlerinages*, 19–74 (Sources Orientales 3, Paris).
Ziermann, M. (1993) *Befestigungsanlagen und Stadtentwicklung in der Frühzeit und im frühen Alten Reich: Elephantine 16* (Deutsches Archäologisches Institut, Abteilung Kairo, Archäologische Veröffentlichungen 87; Mainz).

Egyptians Abroad in the Late Period

Alan Lloyd

The timespan of this paper is the Late Period, a term of dubious precision. For present purposes I propose to define it as the period initiated by the beginning of the Twenty-first Dynasty c. 1069 BC.

The term 'abroad' in my title might seem to need no explanation. When we use it in normal discourse, it means 'not in our own country but in some other place on the surface of the globe'. The Ancient Egyptian world-view, however, offers more options than that. This point emerges clearly from one of the most valuable and interesting of all literary survivals from the Late Period, the cycle of Setne Khaemwese preserved in Demotic papyri of the Ptolemaic and Roman periods (Griffith 1900; Lichtheim 1980, 125–51; Ritner in Simpson 2003, 453–89).

In the first tale of the cycle we encounter a passage which describes a contemporary perception of the world very clearly:

> *When you [recite the first spell you will] charm the sky, the earth, the netherworld, the mountains, and the waters. You will discover what all the birds of the sky and all the reptiles are saying. You will see the fish of the deep [though there are twenty-one divine cubits of water] over [them]. When you recite the second spell, it will happen that, whether you are in the netherworld or in your own form on earth, you will see Pre appearing in the sky with his Ennead, and the Moon in its form of rising.*

The outcome is subsequently described as follows:

> *He (i.e. Neneferkaptah) recited a spell from it; [he charmed the sky, the earth, the netherworld, the] mountains, the waters. He discovered what all the birds of the sky and the fish of the deep and beasts of the desert were saying. He recited another spell; he saw [Pre appearing in the sky with his Ennead], and the Moon rising, and the stars in their forms. He saw the fish of the deep, though there were twenty-one divine cubits of water over them. He recited a spell to the [water; he made it resume its form].*

In these extracts we are confronted with a perception of the world which is operating with a number of different levels: in the first place, and most obviously, the text speaks of physical elements as physical elements — the sky, the earth, the mountains, and the waters (the distinction between earth and mountains reflecting the typically Egyptian distinction between flat land and mountain). Amongst

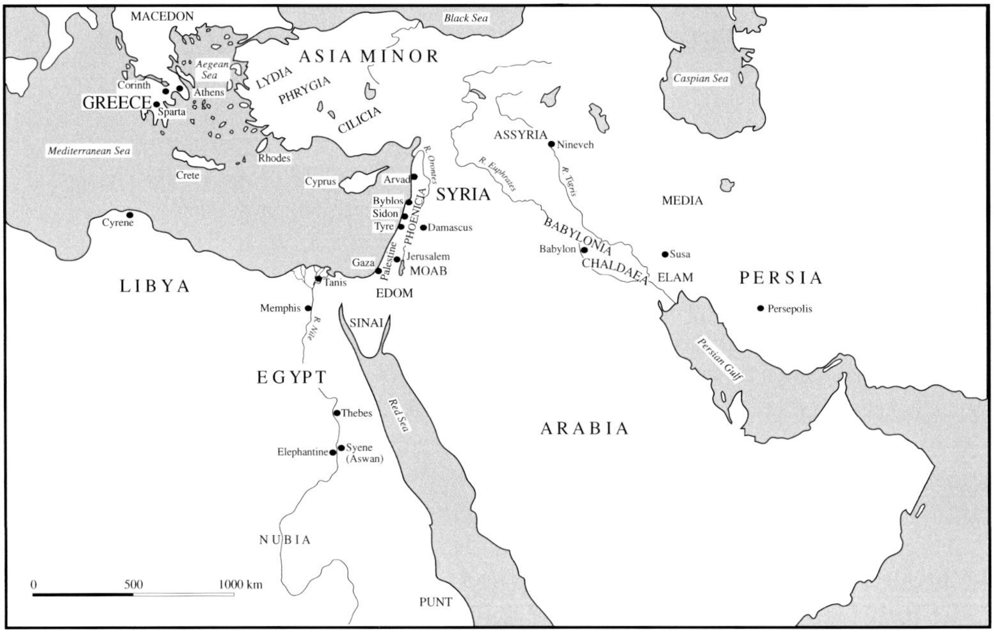

Fig. 2 Map of Egypt and the Near East.

living beings birds, fish, and reptiles are singled out, presumably since gaining communication with them was considered to be particularly problematic because of their habitat and, therefore, required the mobilization of arcane knowledge. All of these elements are parts of the phenomenal world with which we ourselves are completely familiar. There are, however, features which lie well outside that: the netherworld is treated as having the same existential status as sky, earth, mountains, and waters; one of the heavenly bodies, and probably all, are regarded as divine beings; and, most important of all, it is clear from this and later passages in the Setne texts that, provided one possesses the requisite arcane knowledge, it is possible not only to move into and out of the underworld, but even to hear the conversations of birds, fish, and reptiles, and fly through the air. There are, therefore, two axes to this world, a horizontal and a vertical, and it is possible for some people, at least, to travel both in a horizontal and a vertical plane. I propose to take my lead from Setne Khaemwese and deal with travel on both these axes. Let us begin with travelling by land.

Overwhelmingly, the available evidence of Egyptians abroad in the Late Period relates to activity in Asia which normally presents itself in military form (Fig. 2). Throughout most of the first four centuries of the period under discussion the major military force in the Near East was Assyria, the ambitions of such kings as Tiglath Pileser I (1114–1076BC) bringing the Assyrians and their armies to the Mediterranean Sea to receive tribute from such ancient associates of Egypt as Tyre, Sidon, and Arvad (Pritchard 1955, 274–301; Kitchen 1973, Index, s.v. Assyrians; Grayson 1991, 71–161; Onasch 1994). This factor quite clearly dominated Egyptian activity in Syria-Palestine, and the Assyrians evidently presented themselves as a recurrent threat to Egypt's interests and, above all, security until the end of the seventh century. The Egyptian response to this threat was frequently indirect, taking the form of guaranteeing a buffer zone to the north-east of Egypt, either by military or diplomatic means, but direct military action against Assyria was common, as was direct diplomatic activity. The diplomatic option may well be reflected by the fact that a collar on the mummy of Psusennes I (d. 991 BC) bore a bead with the name of a daughter of an Assyrian grand-vizier upon it (Kitchen 1973, 267). Strategic moves to counter the advance of the Assyrian juggernaut will certainly lie behind Egyptian involvement in the struggle between King David (c. 1010–970 BC) and Edom (1 Kings 2.14–22), though there is no detail on the extent of an Egyptian presence in the Edomite kingdom (Kitchen 1973, 273). Similarly, there is evidence suggesting that the Pharaoh Siamun (c. 978–59 BC) attacked the Philistines, and the strategic implications of that action are so obvious that they need no exegesis from me (Kitchen, 1973, 279–83). The marriage of an Egyptian princess to King Solomon (1 Kings 9: 16: cf 1 Kings 3.1; 7.8; 9.16, 24; 11.1) looks like a piece of diplomacy with a distinctly strategic dimension. Indeed, this action is a particularly striking indication of the seriousness with which the Egyptians took the situation when we recall the firm refusal of Amenhotep III in the late XVIIIth Dynasty to give an Egyptian princess to Kadashman Enlil I of Babylon, despite the fact he had received one of his daughters into his own harim. The comment preserved in an Amarna letter speaks volumes: 'From of old, no daughter of an Egyptian king is given to anyone' (Avruch 2000, 163; Meier 2000, 169). In the reign of Shoshenk I (c. 945–24 BC) the picture of relations with Syria-Palestine is altogether more variegated. We know that he maintained good relations with Abibaal, king of Byblos, and this must have brought Egyptians to the city. Osorkon I and Osorkon II followed suit. Whilst the strategic dimension will certainly be there, a powerful additional motive in these activities must have been the maintenance of the age-old commercial ties with the city, which were particularly designed to guarantee access to the high-quality timber resources of the Lebanon. In this they were in direct rivalry with the Assyrians who were also keenly aware of this resource, as emerges from the records of Tiglath-Pileser I:

> *I went to the Lebanon. I cut (there) timber of cedars for the temple of Anu and Adad, the great gods, my lords, and carried (them to Ashur)*
>
> (Pritchard 1955, 275).

It should also be remembered that the major Egyptian north-east Delta city of Tanis, a major dynastic centre at this period, was ideally suited to function as a focus for trade with the Near East and had certainly not failed to avail itself of that opportunity (Kitchen 1973, 257).

Less benign was Shoshenk I's reaction to the kingdom of Israel. On the death of Solomon (c. 931/30 BC) a great assault was mounted against Israel (1 Kings 14.25–26; 2 Chronicles 12.3–4) which was brilliantly successful. In his fragmentary victory stela it is claimed that this was the result of an Asiatic attack, a claim which does at least concede that a military motivation was at issue, and the text reiterates the old claim that the military action was supported by the god Amun (text, Breasted IV, 1906–7, §724A; Kitchen 1973, 294). The assertion that much destruction was wrought would suggest the implementation of a deliberate policy of neutralizing a perceived threat to Egypt's position in that area. There were, however, other benefits which would not have been accidental: the economic return on these actions is much to the fore in the surviving documentation in the claim that much booty accrued. Unsurprisingly, much of this wealth was immediately devoted to a sizeable building programme.

Possibly we should locate at about this time the career of Pediese, son of Apy, who has left us an inscribed statuette clearly intended for funerary purposes. The date is problematic. The statue itself appears to be of Middle Kingdom date, i.e. is about 1000 years earlier than Pediese, but it has been usurped with inscriptional material which was dated by Steindorff no earlier than the XXIInd Dynasty. Pediese is stated on this monument to have been 'commissioner for Canaan and Philistia', and Steindorff is inclined to regard him as an agent of Shoshenk I suggesting that ' … through permanent messengers or commissioners amicable relations were set up, which facilitated in particular the exchange of goods'. He also points out that the name of Pediese's father has a very Semitic look to it (Steindorff 1939, 30–3). If that is true, we may speculate that we are dealing with an agent of mixed ethnic origins acting as an official link between the Egyptians and their eastern neighbours. Sadly, since neither Pediese's date nor ethnicity can be established beyond doubt, these suggestions can amount to no more than attractive possibilities.

The success of Shoshenk, sadly for the Egyptians, did not set a precedent. Probably in the reign of Osorkon I (c. 924–889 BC) an Egyptian force under a Nubian called Zerah was defeated by the Assyrians and put to flight in Syria-Palestine. Osorkon II (c. 874–850 BC) did rather better when he joined a Syro-Palestinian anti-Assyrian alliance, and we hear of 1000 Egyptian soldiers participating in the Battle of Qarqar in 853 BC which halted the southward advance of Assyrian forces, but in 720 the Egyptian expedition under Raia sent to assist the king of Gaza against the Assyrians was a total failure (Pritchard 1955, 285). The overall picture is that Egyptian involvement in military operations in the area was regarded as a recurrent possibility by all concerned, but heroism was not always the order of the day: there is Assyrian evidence of Egyptian tribute being sent, i.e. they were buying off the Assyrians, e.g. in 716 we find Osorkon IV sending a present to pacify Sargon II:

> *Shilkanni, king of Musri (i.e. Osorkon), a remote {region}, the fear of the effulgence of Assur my lord [overwhelmed him], and he (had) brought to me as his present*

twelve large horses of Egypt without their equals in the land (of Assyria)
(Pritchard 1955, 286; Kitchen 1973, 376).

In 712 Shabako shows himself equally pragmatic in handing over the rebel Iamani of Ashdod to Sargon II, and his name even features on a seal-impression from Nineveh, a fact which is more likely to reflect cordial relations than hostility (Kitchen 1973, 380).

Shebitku embarked on a confrontation with Sennacherib c. 702 alongside rulers of Syria-Palestine, and a force was sent to their assistance under his brother Taharqa. They saw action at the Battle at Eltekeh, north of Ashdod, where they were defeated by the Assyrians, and the Egyptians were eventually forced to retreat (Pritchard 1955, 287–8).

Not very surprisingly the Assyrians eventually lost patience and embarked on the ultimate solution to the Egyptian problem. On his accession to the throne Taharqa (c. 690–664 BC) continued to meddle in Syria-Palestine, and this led to the invasion of Egypt by the Assyrians under Esarhaddon which resulted in the expulsion of Taharqa and his flight to Nubia. This was followed by an attempt to consolidate Assyrian power in Egypt by installing Egyptian quislings in key cities. This had only a short-lived success (Kitchen 1973, 391–3; James 1991, 699–700).

In the reign of Assurbanipal an Egyptian rebellion headed by these vassals created another context in which the Egyptians could find themselves on foreign soil. The Egyptian vassals of the Assyrians conspired with Taharqa to re-establish Nubian control, but, when the plot came to light, many of the guilty were transported to Nineveh. The Assyrian record is graphic:

And they (the officers) put to the sword the inhabitants, young and old, of the towns of Sais, Pindidi, Tanis and of all the other towns which had associated with them to plot, they did not spare anybody among (them). They hung their corpses from stakes, flayed their skins and covered (with them) the wall of the town(s). Those kings who had repeatedly schemed, they brought alive to me to Nineveh. From all of them, I had only mercy upon Necho and granted him life. I made (a treaty) with him (protected by) oaths which greatly surpassed (those of the former treaty). I clad him in a garment with multicolored trimmings, placed a golden chain on him (as the) insigne of his kingship, put golden rings on his hands; I wrote my name upon an iron dagger (to be worn in) the girdle, the mounting of which was golden, and gave it to him. I presented him (furthermore) with chariots, horses and mules as means of transportation (befitting) his position as ruler. I sent with him (and) for his assistance, officers of mine as governors. I returned to him Sais as residence (the place) where my father had appointed him king. Nabushezibanni, his son, I appointed for Athribis (thus) treating him with more friendliness and favor than my own father did
(trans. Pritchard 1955, 295).

Psammetichus' programme of liberation of Egypt from the Assyrians led at the beginning of his reign to an alliance with Gyges of Lydia (Lloyd 1975–88, I, 14–16). It is more than likely that this saw Egyptian soldiers or diplomats appearing in Sardis, but we do not, as yet, have any evidence of that. Whatever the detail, the Egyptians established their independence of Assyria, but, very quickly, we find a complete realignment of the great powers of the Near East. The Nabopolassar Chronicle for 616 speaks of Egyptian troops fighting in Mesopotamia beside the Assyrians against the Chaldaeans, and they appear again in this capacity in cuneiform records in the reign of Necho II (Lloyd 1975–88, I, 14–23). I do not want to discuss in detail the long duel of the Egyptians and the Chaldaeans. Suffice it to say that the same factors and methods operated as with the Assyrians and that ultimately, despite major disasters, the Egyptians prevented the Chaldaean occupation of the country. Whilst military activity dominates our sources, it is evident that there was also diplomatic activity in the Greek world intended to strengthen ties with useful, or potentially useful, allies, e.g. we have evidence of Necho's dedications at Branchidae and in the temple of Athena Polias at Ialysus. This must have entailed visits by Egyptian ambassadors, but there is no explicit statement to that effect.

The next major threat was the rise of Persia (Olmstead 1959; Ray 1988, 254–86; Frye 1962; Lloyd 1994, 337–60). As usual this led to a speedy realignment of forces, old enemies becoming new friends in the time-honoured way, but now we find new actors appearing on the stage. Clearly the rise of Persia was an immediate threat to the Chaldaeans, less immediate, though real, to Lydia and the Greek states of Asia Minor. Not surprisingly, therefore, we find a flurry of diplomatic activity, intended to put together an anti-Persian alliance which included Cyrene, Lindus, Polycrates of Samos, and Sparta. Here again the diplomatic activity must have brought Egyptians to the states in question, but here again the Egyptian sources are inexplicit.

The sea played an important role in all these activities. According to the Thalassocracy List of Castor of Rhodes the Phoenician thalassocracy was followed by that of the Egyptians who were succeeded, in turn, by the Milesians. The chronology of this list is notoriously eccentric, but, as I have argued in a recent paper, the sequence strongly suggests a date in the early seventh century, i.e. there was a tradition accessible to Castor which knew of serious Egyptian naval involvement in the Eastern Mediterranean at that time, and nothing in our data contradicts that view, quite the contrary (Lloyd 2000b, 82–3). Necho II continued this tradition in the Mediterranean but also took the further dramatic step of establishing a fleet in the Red Sea. The latter measure is particularly intriguing. It probably reflects an interest in reopening or, at least developing, commercial relations on the Red Sea coast, the warships being designed to preserve merchant vessels from interference by Edomite or Sabaean attack (Lloyd 1977, 145–8). Apries continued the commitment to naval power, clearly as part of his overall strategy for dealing with the Chaldaean threat, and we hear of successful operations against Cyprus and Phoenicia (Herodotus 2.161).

Whilst Asiatic operations dominate the surviving evidence, other quarters of the globe were also foci of attention. Through much of the period under discussion Nubia was an independent power and a force to be reckoned with. Karnak texts from the reign of Shoshenk I speak of tribute being brought from Nubia in a context which leaves no reasonable doubt that this activity took place as the result of military action there. We also have inscriptional evidence of a naval expedition into Nubia by Necho II (610–595BC) (Kaiser 1975, 83–4; Lloyd 2000b, 84); we know that Psammetichus II (595–589BC) dispatched a great expedition into the area at least as far as the Fourth Cataract, allegedly to forestall a Nubian attack on Egypt (Sauneron and Yoyotte 1952; Der Manuelian 1994, 337–71); we have archaeological evidence that the Egyptians were occupying a fort on the island of Dorginarti at the northern end of the Second Cataract from at least the middle of the sixth century, a fact which must surely indicate the presence of further military installations linking this outpost with the Egyptian frontier installations at Elephantine (Heidorn 1991, 206–9); finally, there is a reference in a Demotic papyrus of regnal year 41 of Amasis (530/29 BC) to an expedition into Nubia which, as far as we can tell, consisted of scribes, rowers, soldiers, Nubians, Palestinians, and Syrians — probably one of many such enterprises conducted there at this period under the aegis of Egyptian military control (Erichsen 1942, 56–61).

Another area of interest which drew Egyptians out of Egypt was Cyrene, a prosperous and powerful Greek colony on the North African coast which had the potential to constitute a serious threat to Egypt's western frontier. Apries dispatched a disastrous expedition against this state for motives which are not entirely clear in Herodotus who is our major source. In all probability it was inspired in part by a request for assistance from the Libyans who were being put under pressure by Cyrene, but this motive may well have been strengthened by pressure from the *Machimoi* class in Egypt, who were themselves of Libyan origin and also by the rich economic pickings which control of Cyrene would guarantee. Amasis is presented as taking an altogether more benign view of his Greek neighbour to the west. He concluded an alliance at least as early as 567 and married a Cyrenean woman who was beyond any reasonable doubt the daughter of Battus II (c.590–560BC) (Lloyd 1975–88, III, 233–5).

After the Persian conquest in 525 Egypt lay firmly in the Persian Empire, apart from the odd rebellious episode, for over a century, and Egyptian perceptions of their own security needs were no longer a significant factor in taking Egyptians abroad. Nevertheless, they could easily find themselves on foreign soil in a different capacity, i.e. in the service of the Great King. Herodotus informs us at 6.6, that Egyptian ships formed part of the naval resources deployed by the Persians against Miletus during the rebellion of Histiaeus in 499, though he does concede that the Phoenicians were the most enthusiastic contingent in the fleet. Almost twenty years later they provided 200 ships for Xerxes' great expedition against Greece together with contingents of heavily armed marines under the command of Xerxes' brother Achaemenes. Egyptians were also responsible, with the Phoenicians, for the production of ropes of papyrus and linen for Xerxes' bridging equipment (7. 25.1; 34). The Egyptian fleet particularly distinguished itself at the Battle of Artemisium where it captured five Greek ships with their crews. It is very much of a piece with this that at the end of the fifth century we find an Egyptian called Tamos functioning as governor of Ionia, a role which he may well have inherited from another commander of Egyptian origin.

The period of Egyptian independence marked by the XXVIII–XXXth Dynasties sees a recurrence of the Syro-Palestinian merry-go-round which characterised the period before the Persian conquest of 525, this time designed to guarantee that the Persians were not able to reassert control over Egypt (Lloyd 1994, 337–49; Lloyd 2000a, 385–90). In this endeavour the Egyptians were successful until the reconquest of Egypt by Artaxerxes III in 343. This event inaugurated a short-lived Second Persian Period which provided further opportunities for Egyptians to show their capacity for collaboration, and this opportunity was evidently taken up by Somtutefnakhte, a priest of Herakleopolis, who was involved in some capacity in the great battles in Asia between Alexander the Great and the Persians leading to the Macedonian occupation of Egypt in 332. His statements of gratitude to his local god include the comment: 'You protected me in the combat of the Greeks, when you repulsed those of Asia. They slew a million at my side, and no-one raised his arm against me'. Indeed, he appears to have lost contact with whatever force he was initially involved with. 'I crossed the countries all alone, I sailed the sea unfearing, knowing I had not neglected your word' (see Tresson 1931, 369–91 for text and commentary, Lichtheim 1980, 41–4 for a translation).

It lies in the nature of our historical sources that war and related activities dominate ancient descriptions of Egyptians abroad, but civilian activity certainly features, clearly because Egyptian expertise in certain areas led to their being invited or compelled to travel to foreign parts. One example is Udjahorresnet who speaks as follows in his great biographical inscription (see Lloyd 1982, 166–80):

> *The Majesty of the King of Upper and Lower Egypt, Darius, ever-living, commanded me to return to Egypt — when his Majesty was in Elam and was Great Chief of all foreign lands and Great Ruler of Egypt — in order to restore the establishment of the House of Life ... after it had decayed. The foreigners carried me from country to country. They delivered me to Egypt as commanded by the Lord of the Two Lands.*

In Herodotus we find Egyptian doctors appearing at the court of Darius (3.129) where a group of them had been gathered as the best Egyptian doctors he could find. They tried unsuccessfully to heal a dislocation in the ankle of the king who had to have recourse to the renowned Greek physician Democedes of Croton to solve the problem. Whether the tale is true or false, it reveals that the reputation of Egyptian doctors was sufficiently high for the Greeks to think that they could be invited to display their skills at the highest level outside Egypt itself. This high repute of Egyptian medicine is, of course, as old as Homer, and finds a most intriguing fictional reflex in the pseudo-epigraphic Bentresh Stele which dates either to the Persian or the Ptolemaic period (see Lichtheim 1980, 90–4; Kitchen 1996, 113–6). Here the daughter of the prince of Bakhtan, a name possibly based on Bactria, is taken ill, and a messenger is sent to Egypt for assistance where he petitions the Pharaoh Ramesses II:

> *I have come to you, O King, my lord, on account of Bentresh, the younger sister of Queen Nefrure. A malady has seized her body. May your majesty send a learned man to see her.*

The learned scribe Djehutyemheb was accordingly dispatched to Bakhtan. He discovered that the source of the trouble was an evil spirit whom it was possible to defeat, and he sent a message to Egypt to dispatch a god, i.e. the statue of a god, to do the job. The god Khons-the Provider-in-Thebes was allocated transport consisting of boats and a chariot and horses to go to Bakhtan to bring about a cure which he did, indeed, achieve.

To date we have been talking of movement by land and sea in historical space and time and literary reflections of that, but to the Egyptians these were not the only options even if the other options were only open to very few. I pointed out at the very beginning of this paper that the underworld was placed on the same existential plane as the earth, sky, and the waters, and the corollary of that is that this can also be visited on a temporary basis by living Egyptians. In the second tale of Setne-Khaemwese, which survives in a papyrus of the Roman period, Si-Osiri takes his father Setne Khaemwese down to the Underworld to instruct him in the workings of the judgement of the dead. The message is: 'He who is beneficent on earth, to him one is beneficent in the netherworld. And he who is evil, to him one is evil. It is so decreed [and will remain so] for ever. The things that you have seen in the netherworld at Memphis, they happen in the forty-two nomes [in which are the judges] of Osiris, the great god …'. Whilst, however, this journey is possible for some, it is out of the question for most. The key to this capacity is arcane knowledge. It is said of Si-Osiri: ' … he was put to school. [After a short time he surpassed] the scribe who had been given him for instruction. The boy Si-Osiri began to recite writings with the scribes of the House of Life in [the temple of Ptah. All who heard him thought him] the wonder of the land … [When the] boy Si-Osiri [reached] twelve years of age, it came to pass that there was no [scribe and learned man] in Memphis [who could compare] with him in reciting spells and performing magic'. It is mastery of *heka*, 'words and rituals of power', and that alone which opens up this area to the select few (Ritner 1993; Pinch 1994; Koenig 1994).

Even the sky can be opened up to some. In the second tale of Setne Khaemwese we hear of the existence of Egyptian boats which are capable of flying through the air. At one point 'Horus-the-son-of-the-Wolf recited a spell: he created a (flying) boat of papyrus and made it carry away a vault of stone. It halted with it at 'Great

Lake', the big water of Egypt.' A little later a character pleads: 'If you will give us a sky-boat, we will not return to Egypt ever again'. Eventually, 'Horus-the-son-of-the-Wolf … gave a (flying) boat to Horus-son-of-the-Nubian-woman and the Nubian woman, his mother, and they flew to the land of Nubia, their home'.

What exactly is the conceptual background to these narratives of movement on what I have chosen to call 'the vertical axis'? The immediate reaction might be to argue that we are dealing with fiction and that this is simply fantasy, but 'fantasy' seems to me to be a highly culturally loaded term. There is a wealth of evidence from all periods of Egyptian history that the Egyptians took the view that, if one possessed *heka*, it was possible to use it to bring about alterations in one's world. To the Egyptians the world was a continuum of possibilities. There was the normal, which is the stuff of everyone's experience, and there are things in the world which are, in varying degrees, abnormal, though not miraculous. The learned man is capable, through his arcane knowledge, of opening a much greater range of the spectrum of possibilities than ordinary mortals, and for such men voyaging in the vertical axis would be perfectly feasible.

There is one motivation for foreign travel which certainly operated in the world of Greece and Rome but not in Egypt. At Herodotus 1.29–30, we are informed that Solon travelled abroad after passing his legislation for the purpose of *theoria*, 'sightseeing', and there are many accounts, reliable or otherwise, of distinguished Greek and Roman visitors to Egypt who are engaged in what we might call cultural tourism. We never, as far as I know, encounter anything similar in an Egyptian context. Egyptians were perfectly prepared to pay visits to their own ancient monuments, and they not infrequently left rather amusing messages of the 'Kilroy was here' variety to record their passage, but I know of nothing similar outside Egypt. The reason for this situation must lie in a highly egocentric view of Egyptian culture. In a previous study I commented:

> *The Egyptians often used the word rmṯ, 'man', in the sense of 'Egyptian', thereby indicating that all non-Egyptians were non-human. They evidently saw themselves as the possessors of cultural attributes which not only distinguished them from, but made them superior to, all foreigners and were capable of describing their foreign acquaintances in the most contemptuous terms. Their world-view expressed this attitude as an always latent and sometimes actual state of war between Pharaoh and outsiders who are often regarded as the agents of chaos, the confederates of Seth*
> (Lloyd 1975–88, II, 157).

This attitude led to an almost complete lack of interest in what other cultures did. The Egyptians might assimilate certain features of religion or take over elements of technology which they perceived to be of value to themselves, but we find nothing remotely like Solon's desire for study, enquiry, or visiting other countries out of curiosity. It is, therefore, not surprising to find that, when in earlier periods the Egyptians engage in imperialist adventures, their approach is either to establish themselves as a parallel culture alongside the native peoples with little cross-fertilization or they engage in a radical assimilation of the local population to Egyptian norms (Smith 1995).

Despite the foregoing observation, it is possible to detect in the Late Period a process which begins slowly but gathers a gradual momentum until eventually it sweeps Egyptian civilization away almost completely. This process involves another kind of journey, a migration of perceptions and a move into a foreign intellectual world which led to a situation as far as it is possible to go from that which I have described. Let us consider briefly just one example of what I mean – here I could again have used the tale of Setne Khaemwese, but I have chosen to go elsewhere.

The frequent forays into Asia which form so conspicuous a part of Egyptian activity abroad during the Late Period could not fail to find their parallels in literature. One of the most fascinating of these is the *Tale of Prince Pedikhons and Queen Serpot* (Volten 1962; Lichtheim 1980, 151–6). This story survives in a much damaged text of the Graeco-Roman period and presents us with the spectacle of Prince Pedikhons embarking on a great campaign into Syria with an army made up of Egyptians and Assyrians. Here his great enemy is Queen Serpot, the 'Pharaohess' (so the Egyptian!) of the Land of Women, i.e. she is Queen of the Amazons. Here we do not only have a fictional reflex of a recurrent phenomenon in Egyptian history, but a journey into another cultural tradition which has led to the importation and assimilation into Egyptian literature of a distinctively Greek legend, but the cultural balance eventually changes from a situation where the Egyptian dimension is in the ascendant to a situation where the Egyptian is swamped. The Egyptians spent too long in this foreign cultural landscape, and it eventually became theirs too with little more than a residue of their ancient culture remaining. This pervasive process of cultural interaction ended by producing the remarkable Graeco-Egyptian culture of late Antique Egypt whose most striking manifestation is the artistic tradition which we are accustomed to call Coptic Art (see, generally, Thomas 2000).

It is time to summarize. The underlying determinant governing Egyptian travel is a deeply Egyptocentric attitude to what lies outside Egypt and this determines everything which is done on our horizontal axis when Egypt is an independent power. The prime consideration, whether we are dealing with Asia, Libya, or Nubia is the defence of Egypt, and this is followed by a requirement to guarantee access to foreign resources of which Egypt had need. In the Late Period the Egyptians adopted a highly pragmatic approach to achieving these ends. If they could get away with force, that was applied both by land and sea, sometimes by a strategy of indirect approach, sometimes direct, but diplomacy, including buying off the enemy, was also employed as and when it was in Egypt's interest to do so. When Egypt was under foreign control, other issues could take Egyptians abroad: they might be used as soldiers or sailors in the foreign military; they might rise to high office abroad; or they might be used as technical experts, in particular, as doctors. The Egyptians also inhabited a conceptual world where it was possible to move on a vertical axis, either to the Underworld or to the sky, but the capacity to do this was believed to reside solely with learned man with access to arcane knowledge. Unlike Greeks or Romans, there is no evidence of the Egyptians engaging in cultural tourism, no doubt again a reflection of their cultural egocentricism. There is, however, an intellectual and even spiritual journey on which the Egyptians were imperceptibly engaged in the Late Period, and this journey took them for ever out of their old Pharaonic world into the world of Late Antique Egypt which was, in all matters of any significance, the world of late Graeco-Roman culture.

Bibliography

Avruch, K. (2000) 'Reciprocity, Equality, and Status-Anxiety in the Amarna Letters', in R. Cohen and R. Westbrook (eds.), *Amarna Diplomacy: The Beginnings of International Relations*,154–64 (Baltimore and London).

Breasted, J. H. (1906–7) *Ancient Records of Egypt. Historical Documents from the Earliest Times to the Persian Conquest*. 5 vols. (Chicago).

Der Manuelian, P. (1994) *Living in the Past: Studies in Archaism of the Egyptian Twenty-Sixth Dynasty* (London and New York).

Erichsen, W. (1942) 'Erwähnung eines Zuges nach Nubien unter Amasis in einem demotischen Text', *Klio* 34, 56–61.

Frye, R. (1962) *The Heritage of Persia* (London).

Grayson, A. K. (1991) 'Assyria', in *The Cambridge Ancient History* III, 2, 71–161. (Cambridge, 2nd edtion).

Griffith, F. Ll. (1900) *Stories of the High Priests of Memphis* 2 vols (Oxford).

Heidorn, L. A. (1991) 'The Saite and Persian Period Forts at Dorginarti', in W. V. Davies (ed.) *Egypt and Africa. Nubia from Prehistory to Islam*, 205–19 (London).

James, T. G. H. (1991) 'Egypt: The Twenty-Fifth and Twenty-Sixth Dynasties', in *The Cambridge Ancient History* III, 2, 677–747 (Cambridge).

Kaiser, W. *et al.* (1975) 'Stadt und Tempel von Elephantine: Fünfter Grabungsbericht', *Mitteilungen der deutschen archäologischen Instituts (Abteilung Kairo)* 31, 39–84.

Kitchen, K. A. (1973) *The Third Intermediate Period (1100–650 BC)* (London).

Kitchen, K. A. (1996) *Ramesside Inscriptions. Translated Annotated. Translations Volume II. Ramesses, Royal Inscriptions* (Oxford and Cambridge Mass.).

Lichtheim, M. (1980) *Ancient Egyptian Literature III: The Late Period* (Berkeley, Cal. and London).

Lloyd, A. B. (1975–88) *Herodotus Book II. Introduction and Commentary* 3 vols (Leiden).

Lloyd, A. B. (1977) 'Necho and the Red Sea: Some Considerations', *Journal of Egyptian Archaeology* 63,142–55.

Lloyd, A. B. (1982) 'The Inscription of Udjahorresnet: A Collaborator's Testament', *Journal of Egyptian Archaeology* 68, 166–80.

Lloyd, A. B. (1994) 'Egypt, 404–332 BC', in *The Cambridge Ancient History VI: The Fourth Century B.C.*, 337–60 (Cambridge, 2nd edition).

Lloyd, A. B. (2000a) 'The Late Period (664–332 BC)', in I. Shaw (ed.) *The Oxford History of Ancient Egypt*, 369–94 (Oxford).

Lloyd, A. B. (2000b) 'Saite Navy', in R. Brock, G. J. Oliver, T. J. Cornell and S. Hodkinson (eds.) *The Sea in Antiquity* 899, 81–91 (Oxford).

Meier, S. A. (2000) 'Reciprocity, Equality, and Status-Anxiety in the Amarna Letters', in R. Cohen and R. Westbrook (eds.) *Amarna Diplomacy: The Beginnings of International Relations*,165–73 (Baltimore and London).

Olmstead, A. T. (1959) *History of the Persian Empire* (Chicago and London).

Onasch, H-U. (1994) *Die Assyrischen Eroberungen Ägyptens*, Ägypten und Altes Testament 27/1–2 (Wiesbaden).
Pinch, G. (1994) *Magic in Ancient Egypt* (London).
Pritchard, J. B. (1955, 2nd edition) *Ancient near Eastern Texts Relating to the Old Testament* (Princeton).
Ray, J. D. (1988) 'Egypt 525–404 BC', in *The Cambridge Ancient History IV. Persia, Greece and the Western Mediterranean C. 525–479 B.C.*, 254–86 (Cambridge).
Ritner, R. K. (1993) *The Mechanics of Ancient Egyptian Magical Practice*, Studies in Ancient Oriental Civilization 54 (Chicago).
Sauneron, S and J. Yoyotte (1952) 'La campagne nubienne de Psammétique II et sa signification historique', *Bulletin de l'institut français d'archéologie orientale* 50, 157–207.
Simpson, W. K (ed.) *The Literature of Ancient Egypt* (New Haven and London).
Smith, S T. (1995) *Askut in Nubia. The Economics and Ideology of Egyptian Imperialism in the Second Millennium BC* (London and New York).
Steindorff, G. (1939) 'The Statuette of an Egyptian Commissioner in Syria', *Journal of Egyptian Archaeology* 25, 30–3.
Thomas, T. K. (2000) *Egyptian Funerary Sculpture: Images for This World and the Next* (Princeton).
Tresson, P. (1931) 'La stèle de Naples', *Bulletin de l'institut français d'archéologie orientale* 30, 369–91.
Volten, A. (1962) *Ägypter und Amazonen*, Mitteilungen aus der Papyrussammlung der Österreichischen Nationalbibliothek (Papyrus Erzherzog Rainer) n. s. 6 (Vienna).
Wiseman, D. J. (1961) *Chronicles of Chaldaean Kings (626–556 B.C.) in the British Museum* (London).

The Place of Geography in Herodotus' *Histories*

Thomas Harrison

Herodotus has fathered any number of academic disciplines: history, anthropology, ethnography, the history of religions – and there can be little doubt that someone somewhere at some time has claimed him as the father of geography, the father of travel writing, and much else.[1] Before we rest on Herodotus' laurels, however, we should question what such claims to paternity mean. What history? What geography? A recent survey of modern geographical work by an ancient historian, Katherine Clarke in her *Between Geography and History*, confirms what an outsider might suppose, that geography can mean a range of very different things: from what my parents' generation were taught at school (learning the rivers of France by heart), through what I was taught at school (how to find the best site for a power station), to, at the other extreme of the 'new cultural geography' something nearly indistinguishable from cultural studies (Clarke 1999, ch. 1; for human geography as indistinguishable from cultural studies, see e.g. McDowell 1997). Though one view of the order of composition of Herodotus' *Histories* has it that Herodotus began with a geographical monograph on Egypt, and only later discovered history, whether Herodotus had a conception of geography, let alone one approximate to any modern definition, is also questionable. This chapter then is necessarily *in search of* geography and its place in the *Histories.*

* * * * *

By one definition at least, geography is to do with maps. Herodotus has a map. This is, of course, the map which Aristagoras of Miletus, in his attempt to secure support for the Ionian revolt against Persian rule, showed to the Spartan king Cleomenes (5.49.1): 'he went to confer with him, the Lacedaimonians say, having a brazen tablet, on which was engraved the circumference of the whole earth (*periodos gês*)[2] and the whole sea and all rivers.' This passage has been used recently as a kind of trump card to demonstrate that Herodotus and the Greeks (and consequently the Romans) could conceive of abstract space.[3] Leaving aside that larger question for now, this is not perhaps the perfect passage with which to prove the point. Aristagoras' accompanying blurb – which of course *may* embellish a much more cartographically subtle map – takes us from people to people along an imaginary journey to the city of Susa. '"They live adjoining one another as I will show you.

stance: 'that they [the Egyptians] always were, as long as men have been, and that as the soil gradually increased many of them remained in their former habitations and many came lower down'; if the Delta were not a part of Asia and Libya, then the Ionians should rightly create a fourth continent, that of the Delta. Herodotus, on the other hand, considers – a bluff, common-sensical view – 'the whole country inhabited by Egyptians to be Egypt, just as that inhabited by Cilicians is Cilicia, and by Assyrians Assyria'; the only boundary between Asia and Libya is the frontier of Egypt. In support of this, he cites finally an oracle given to the peoples of Apis and Marea, on the borders of Egypt and Libya. These people were convinced that they were not Egyptian but Libyan; 'they had no relation to the Egyptians', they had said, 'because they lived out of the Delta, and did not speak the same language as them'; they desired in particular to be able to eat beef. But the god, Zeus Ammon, forbade them and countered with another definition of what it was to be Egyptian: that all the country which the Nile irrigates is Egypt, and that all those were Egyptians who dwelled below the city of Elephantine, and drank of that river' (see Thomas 2000, 177–8). Herodotus adds that the Nile floods reach as far as two days' journey to either side of the river.

Here again we see the problematisation of conventional geographical distinctions, the attempt to find boundaries between continents and countries that make sense – an issue to which we will return. He is notably more explicit in his discussion of the bounds of Egypt than in the case of Greece – a unit which sometimes seems to encompass all Greeks (7.157), including those in Sicily, and on other occasions has precise geographical boundaries (7.175–6), with a clear point of entry at Thermopylae. What is striking here is also, however, the link posited between land and people. The people of Apis and Marea will be Egyptians willy-nilly; 'self-determination' has nothing to do with it. Distinguishing customs – language or the desire to eat beef – are also irrelevant, as the people of Apis and Marea are forced to conform to the customs of the land to which they belong; the possibility that they might get up and leave is not considered.

This model, of men and women rooted to the land, is not quite a universal pattern. There is, in particular, one celebrity case of a group 'upping' and leaving, the Egyptian 'deserters' (2.31). Members of the Egyptian warrior caste, disenchanted with continually manning garrisons in remote locations (amongst them, Marea), they resisted king Psammetichus' entreaties not to desert their gods or abandon their wives and children, one of their number dangling his genitals in the king's face and declaring that so long as he had these he could find himself more wives and children. But the colourful character of this anecdote, together with Herodotus' perhaps exaggerated interest in the possibility of peoples or individuals being transplanted across the Persian empire,[7] suggest the very exceptional status of such a scenario. A similar turn of argument should be employed in the case of another exception: the Scythians, the archetypal nomads with their only connection to the land the tombs of their ancestors (see Hartog, 1988). The example of the Scythians might suggest an appreciation on Herodotus' part (albeit in a rather schematic form) of another theme common in recent geographical studies, the subjectivity of experience of the physical environment, place as 'lived in space', structured by human experience (cf. Clarke, 1999, 17). It is not, however, accidental that such an appreciation emerges in an ethnographic context. Similarly, it is not an accident that it is characteristically in an ethnographic context that we find an emphasis on man-made barriers to, or devices for, communication. Egypt was once easily covered by land, but has since become impassable through the construction of canals (2.108; cf. 1.185).[8] (Egypt, as a result, is a distinctly monarchical landscape). Conversely, Persia can be crossed regardless of natural circumstances, due to the royal messenger service (8.98) – though politically subversive messages can still be smuggled through in the bellies of hares, on the wooden base of wax tablets or on the tattooed heads of favourite slaves (1.123, 3.126–8.5.35, 7.239).

Foreign lands then provide an opportunity for a kind of geographical experimentation, for Herodotus to explore, in the abstract, the relations of lands and people, and the range and limits of the human manipulation of the landscape. Clearly, however, we could become too carried away by the detection of aspects of Herodotus' work dimly reminiscent of the insights of modern or post-modern geographers. Just as in other areas of his thought and preconceptions, so in his geographical mentality Herodotus is significantly not a colleague.

To begin, a relatively uncontroversial example. In the majority of instances, Herodotus sees geographical distances, whether they are in the Greek world or in foreign lands, as comparable; that is to say, he assesses them on the same scale. So, for example, the distance from Heliopolis to the sea is the same as that from Athens to Pisa (2.7); the Taurian coast resembles the coast of Attica or (for those who are unfamiliar with this stretch of coast, with an equivalent stretch of Italian coastline, 4.99); when Egypt floods, its cities take on the appearance of Aegean islands (2.97); the Nile delta is compared with the alluvial plain of the Maeander or of the Achelous in Acarnania (2.10). But as that final example demonstrates, comparison can break down: 'if', Herodotus qualifies, 'I may be allowed to compare small things with great, for of the rivers that have thrown up the soil that forms these countries, not one can justly be brought into comparison, as to size, with any one of the five mouths of the Nile.' Different countries indeed may require different scales, as Herodotus' calculation of the length of the coast of Egypt shows up (2.6; cf. 3.89.):

> *The length of Egypt along the sea coast is sixty schoeni, according as we reckon it to extend from the Plinthinetic bay to the Lake Serbonis, near which Mount Cassius stretches: from this point then the length is sixty schoeni. Now, all men who are short of land measure their territory by fathoms* (orguiêsi)*; but those who are less short of land by stades; and those who have much by parasangs; and such as have a very great extent by schoeni. Now a parasang is equal to 30 stades, and each schoenus, which is an Egyptian measure, is equal to 60 stades. So the whole coast of Egypt is 3600 stades in length.*

We are dealing here, it seems, not only with another instance of Herodotus' putting the Greeks in their proper place (parallel, for example, to his observation on how the Greeks are children in their knowledge of the gods, 2.53.1). Rather we are looking through a lens which magnifies the far-off. This is reflected also in some slightly pyschodelic visions of foreign landscapes: the river Araxes is reported to have 'many islands in it, some nearly equal in size to Lesbos' (1.202.1); the Caucasus is the largest and tallest of mountains, and contains within itself 'many and varied peoples of men' (1.203.1).

I move on to a more controversial theme, that of the symmetry of Herodotus' world. (We are treading here on very well-worn ground). Herodotus, as a number of scholars have observed (see esp. Hartog 1988, Redfield 1985, Romm 1989, Cartledge 1993), envisages the world in a number of ways in symmetrical or schematic terms. The Scythian climate is the reverse of all other countries, with rain and thunder in summer but rarely in winter (when thunder occurs in winter it is counted as a *teras*, a prodigy or omen, 4.28). Inferring from what is known to what is unknown, he assumes, without excluding the possibility of comparison, that the Nile and the Danube mirror each other (2.33–4; cf. Thomas, 2000, 66), and he then goes on implicitly to associate this natural reversal with the reversal in Egypt of human customs: 'the Egyptians, besides having a climate peculiar to themselves, and a river different in its nature from all other rivers, have adopted customs and usages in almost all respects different from the rest of mankind' (2.36); women go to market, men stay at home and weave, women urinate standing up and men sitting down, and so on.

Another form of Herodotean schematism – how it relates to these mirror-images or polarities is an issue to which we will return – is a geographical ethnocentrism, a conception of the world in which the Greeks (or some Greeks, the Ionians) are central. This emerges most clearly in Herodotus' observations on the ideal nature of the Ionian climate (1.142.1–2):

> *These Ionians, to whom the Panionion belongs, have built their cities under the finest sky and climate of all men that we know; for neither the regions that are above it, nor those that are below, nor the parts to the east or west,*[9] *are at all equal to Ionia; for some of them are oppressed by cold and rain, others by heat and drought.*

We find a similar schematism, though, in his discussion of the extremes of the inhabited world in Book III (3.106–16), for example in his observation that the inhabited world is flanked by regions which give forth the rarest produces (little economic sense here, 3.106–16). Strikingly also he ascribes a linguistic ethnocentrism to the Egyptians, observing that they call all those who are not of the same language barbarians (2.158.5),[10] and to the Persians he ascribes a world view by which they measure the virtue of peoples according to their proximity (1.134.2–3).

Finally, Herodotus appears to give a strong emphasis in his *Histories* to a distinction between Asia and Europe. It is this distinction that appears both at the beginning and the end of Herodotus' work, and so confirms that the end of the *Histories* are indeed the end (see esp. Boedeker 1988, Dewald 1997): through the stories of reciprocal abductions between the continents, and of the Persian Artayctes' execution overlooking the Hellespont, and in the repeated statement that the Persians believed that all of Asia belonged to them (1.4.4, 9.116.3). But the Asia-Europe distinction is not a merely ornamental feature; it also provides an explanatory framework for much of the *Histories*. The rule of Asia is seen repeatedly as a single, distinct prize (cf. 3.88.1, 4.1, 4.4, 7.1.2). Cyrus, as his grandfather Astyages' dreams (of urine or vines spreading from his daughter's genitals) had foreboded, had been destined to rule all of Asia (1.107–8; cf. 1.209); through his defeat of Astyages, and the finishing touch of his conquest of Assyria (1.177–8.1), the dream was fulfilled. The Persian lust for world conquest is represented as the desire to combine Asia and Europe, not just in Themistocles' famous speech after Salamis (8.109), but also in a number of other contexts: as early as book I, Cyrus dreams that the son of Hystaspes, Cyrus' own successor Darius, sprouted wings which overshadowed Asia and Europe (1.209.1); this theme is continued, for example, by an olive wreath of Xerxes' which grows over the whole earth (7.19; cf. 7.53, 209), or in Xerxes' own statement that, should the Greeks not be defeated, they would inevitably capture Asia (7.11).

There are some difficulties of interpretation here, however. To begin with the distinction between Asia and Europe, the first question that we face is how to square this emphasis with Herodotus' (to modern eyes, arguably more admirable) observations on the continents. Rosalind Thomas has suggested that we have here essentially the meeting of two world-views (Thomas, 2000, 99–100):

> *Perhaps we can suggest that Herodotus' narrative of the Persian wars is bound by widespread perceptions of the importance of the Europe-Asia crossing, carried along by its emotional and symbolic importance ... while at the same time Herodotus is aware of the intellectual problems with the conventional divisions of the continents, and any over-determined sense of their eternal significance... This is one of the most striking examples of the combination of the traditional and the new in Herodotus, in which the narrative has a symbolic logic which Herodotus elsewhere distances himself from.*

To talk of the 'widespread perception' of the importance of these conventional units – insinuating apparently a distinction between Herodotus on the one hand, and a popular milieu on the other – underestimates, however, the weight that these themes are given elsewhere in the *Histories*. Similarly, the 'symbolic logic' of a narrative is perhaps too easily seen as something residual or secondary, by comparison with the contemporary intellectual currents to which we may prefer to give prominence. At other points, for example, Thomas suggests that the analogy of Nile and Danube is a loose one, or anomalous (Thomas 2000, 112), or that it 'seems safely reminiscent of an earlier world of crude and schematic map-making of the early Ionians' (Thomas 2000, 200); this, however, is balanced by the fact that 'the manner in which he introduces, explains and defends his use of such analogy, belongs to this mode of discourse.' Our priority, however, should not be to award points to Herodotus or any other author for being abreast with the latest fashions, but rather to do justice to the *interpenetration* of what appear (in our terms, but not necessarily Herodotus') progressive and traditional attitudes.

So, in the case of the continents, it is possible that we are in search of a solution to an imaginary problem. The central question here is the status that we should attach to Herodotus' problematisation of the continents, or of other conventional geographical units. 'Herodotus sees as meaningless', in Thomas' words again, 'the conventional geographical divisions into continents' (Thomas 2000, 79). But does he? In Book II, his criticisms of the Ionians are for the boundary that they choose between Asia and Libya; in its place, however, he suggests equally conventional and arbitrary boundaries for Egypt, that Egypt is the area flooded by the Nile, two days' journey on either side. Herodotus' discussion of the continents in Book IV ends significantly with his choosing to use the conventional names: 'Let no more be said on this subject; we will use the customary names.' Clearly he is uncomfortable with the conventional names; at the same time, however, 'there is a lingering idea … that the distinctions of language *should* reflect real rather than merely arbitrary distinctions; he wants the names to make sense and is disappointed that they do not' (Harrison 2000a, 257).

Herodotus' closing formula could, of course, be seen as elegantly dismissive (Thomas 2000, 245; cf. e.g. Lateiner 1989, 64–7, 196–205). This, however, misses the significance of a possible parallel between the names of the continents and the names of the gods. Herodotus' speculations on the names of the gods are accompanied by very similar statements of caution. The names of the gods are likewise conventional – and seen quite clearly to be so (e.g. 2.53) – but this does not imply disbelief in the conventional gods of myth or ritual. Rather the conventional terms are protected by the catch-all defence of the unknowability of the divine: because the divine is unknowable, in other words, you might as well continue to use the conventional classifications (see further Harrison 2000a, 191–2). It is in the same light that Herodotus' return to the conventional names for the continents should be viewed. This should be connected, in turn, to a large body of ideas in the *Histories* that suggests that the natural world is divinely sanctioned, his emphasis on the impiety of crossing natural boundaries, or of creating man-made boundaries (Harrison 2000a, 92–100, 238–9, Harrison 2004). In the repeated emphasis on Persian Kings' attempts to master nature – taming the Hellespont, dividing the river Gyndes into 360 streams so shallow that women could cross without wetting their knees (1.189–90), and so on – we see have what one might, very tentatively, term an environmental theology.[11] In other words, it is not so much that Herodotus' belief in the timeless significance of Asia and Europe is a literary left-over, but rather that Herodotus' spirit of independent scientific enquiry is framed, and constrained, by his sense of the significance of conventional boundaries.

More broadly, there is a danger here of setting too high a threshold for Herodotean schematism or polarity.[12] (In this, Thomas is representative of a broader backlash (e.g. Miller 1997, 1; Davidson 2002)). 'It has been claimed influentially', Thomas continues, 'that [Herodotus] virtually created his observations of foreign peoples via a 'rhetoric of inversion', that is, creating an inverted image of "the other" from Greek customs. Certainly he looked on with the eyes of a Greek observer, intrigued by those elements which ran counter to Greek experience – and it is hard to see how he could do anything else. So certain Greek ideas of normality may have coloured his account. But what *kind* of ideas or preoccupations may have guided these interpretations?' (Thomas 2000, 44–5). The answer is that Herodotus was following similar lines of enquiry to contemporary medical writers or 'inquirers into nature'; he was concerned with general human nature and sameness rather than ethnic difference for its own sake. 'This seems very different', Thomas concludes, 'from the clichés about barbarians which we find, for instance, in much Athenian literature'.

This choice, however – a repeated choice between, on the one hand, scientific curiosity, and, on the other, a crude ethnocentrism – is a significantly false one. Of course, we will not find evidence of a 'simple bipolar scheme', because the polarities which we find in the *Histories* constitute part of a broader mentality, one reflected already by Pindar, for example (Pindar fr. 105ab; cf. fr. 215a). Hence their lack of consistency: if one were to try to map one strand of Herodotean geographical schematism onto another – the model by which the Nile mirrors the Danube with that in which Ionia marks the centre of a climatic circle – we would end up with a confusing muddle. (To observe this lack of consistency is not intended to detract from the force of such polarities; nor should it be understood as a criticism of Herodotus.) Another possibility that is excluded, finally, is that that scientific discourse itself may have been informed by a similar 'rhetoric of inversion'. Thomas, it should be said, finds place for a number of grids and opposites: Herodotus sees 'Libya and Scythia – as opposed to other pairs – as climatic opposites; they are part of a climatic grid' (Thomas 2000, 54). Polarities, it seems, are fine so long as they are not harnessed to crude ethnocentric ends. If the purpose of Herodotean ethnography were 'simplistically to reaffirm Greek character and Greek identity', we are told elsewhere, it would surely be odd for Herodotus (in the passage referred to above on the Ionian climate) to choose the grid of hot and cold, wet and dry along which to do so (Thomas 2000, 71). But do all polarities have to be equally pronounced in their chauvinism for us to claim any chauvinism or ethnocentrism in ancient texts?[13] Are there not significant *affinities* between this scientific ethnocentrism and other forms which employ different criteria? And perhaps most importantly, can you have a scientific curiosity that is pure and disinterested, divorced from issues of power?[14]

* * * * *

This brings us back to the text. In understanding the place of geography in the *Histories*, there is another context that has been so far overlooked: the context of Herodotus' own work. How do Herodotus' geographical and ethnographic 'digressions' relate to the text of the *Histories* as a whole?

One answer would be that they are simply a reflection of the heterogeneity of the contents of the *Histories*, of the breadth of Herodotus' interests. Libya, Egypt and Scythia are given such emphasis, at least in part, because of their central role in contemporary enquiries into nature (Thomas 2000, 53–4, 77). But, no matter the importance of that intellectual background, scientific and medical questions take up only a relatively small portion of Herodotus' ethnographic sections. Though we may enjoin ourselves repeatedly to read the whole of the *Histories* in the light of those flashes of scientific curiosity,[15] inherent in the important recent work on Herodotean ethnography is a centrifugal tendency, a temptation to see the *Histories'* contents as essentially disparate, to settle for a model of the Histories in which different portions are inspired by different motives (Clarke 1999, 64–5).

Even were we to settle for a model of outright heterogeneity, moreover, this would itself require further explanation. First, we must interrogate the very idea of the 'digression'. Digression from what? The term suggests a main thread of narrative from which we step aside. Though Herodotus asserts his intention to digress, or rather that his *logos* has sought out 'additions' (*prosthekas*) from its outset (4.30.1), his very defence of digression, his assertion of its central role, detracts from any conclusion of a clear (narrative or other) thread. Moreover, it is easy to underestimate the complex relationship of any logos to the surrounding narrative, to suppose that a digression is straightforwardly subordinated to the text that frames it. As Richmond Lattimore observed, 'This passage has been called the Arabian Logos; and if there is any such thing as an Arabian Logos, this must be it. But it is not an organised free-standing anthropology of Arabia or the Arabians, rather a sequence of notices which grows organically out of its place of occurrence in the Persian progress' (Lattimore 1958, 14; Griffiths 2001 on 'kissing cousins').

A parallel question, alluded to earlier, is whether Herodotus has any distinct conception of geography, how geography (in our sense) is framed and presented within the *Histories.* Even in the narrowest sense of charting rivers and mountains and seas, geography for Herodotus is not apparently a discrete topic.[16] Aristagoras' map – or rather Herodotus' commentary on Aristagoras' map – includes geological resources and the character of peoples alongside the itinerary of the royal road to Susa. In conclusion to his description of the Scythian rivers Herodotus notes that, because of them, the greatest commodities were easily available to the Scythians (4.59); then he turns to their other customs (*ta de loipa nomaia*), in particular their religious customs. Natural wonders are included side by side with others. Scythia has nothing which is the object of wonder except the rivers and a footprint of Heracles two cubits long (4.82). Similarly, the two prime wonders of Lydia are the gold dust of the river brought down from Mt. Tmolus and the monument to Alyattes (1.93).

How then are the 'digressions' connected to the narrative? In one sense, clearly, as Richmond Lattimore observed, the narrative hook on which Herodotus hangs the descriptions of the *nomoi* of foreign peoples, which fill much of the early books, is the Persians' gradual expansion.[17] The relationship of 'digression' and narrative is not simply one of narrative convenience, however. First, in a relatively straightforward way. Knowledge of the landscape and customs of Scythia, for example, is clearly vital for understanding Darius' flawed attempt at conquest. Herodotus' narrative of the Greek landscape encountered by Xerxes has similar practical applications: the land and the sea will prove to be the Persians' greatest enemies, Artabanus foresees (7.49); his prophecy was fulfilled when the landscape of Artemisium, Thermopylae and Salamis proved to the Greeks' advantage. The landscape is an even more active participant in other episodes (cf. Clarke 1999, 31): when cliffs form themselves by an optical illusion into ships to frighten off the Persians (8.107.2), or in a number of natural miracles. Herodotus' narrative of Persian conquest also implies other, subtler, morals. Herodotus repeatedly attaches cults and aetiological myths to the localities passed by the Persians: stories such as of how Thetis was stolen away at Cape Sepias (told to the Persians by the Ionians, 7.191) or of Aphetai where Heracles was 'left behind' by Jason and the Argonauts (7.193). This construction of an 'imaginary Greece' – to echo the title of Richard Buxton's excellent book – reinforces a sense of the divine possession of the Greek landscape, of a persistent undercurrent that pulls against the Persians in their attempt to appropriate Greece.[18]

We need also, however, to put the geographical digressions in the context of the *representation of geographical knowledge* in the *Histories*. The opening of the *Histories* presents us with a world of discrete populations. The Phoenician ship that wends its way from the Red Sea through the Mediterranean to Argos (cf. 7.89), where the abduction (or elopement?) of Io triggers a cycle of war between Greeks and barbarians, is represented, it seems, as if it were the first contact between these peoples. The possibility of populations remaining discrete is reflected in a number of subsequent passages: for example, in the advice given to Cambyses by the king of the Ethiopians (to stay at home and be grateful that god had never inspired the Ethiopians to take others' land: 3.21.2–3; cf. 1.27, 71, 206), or in the Babylonian queen Nitocris' construction of bends in the Euphrates as barriers between herself and the 'restless empire of the Medes', to prevent them becoming acquainted with her affairs (1.185–6). Of course, Nitocris' efforts to hide Babylon are in vain, and so implicitly are any such attempts: contact and conflict are inevitable.[19] The early books of the *Histories* see a cumulative growth in the contacts between peoples: through Persian expansion, the thickening of individual contacts (Solon, Syloson, Democedes, Aristagoras, Demaratus) and through other broader means, by the development of trade,[20] or through the diffusion of religious customs or names of gods, again apparently beginning from a blank slate (Rudhardt 1993; Harrison 2000a, ch. 8 and appendix 2).

It is in the context of this historical process, the gathering of all peoples together into a single *oikoumenê*, that Herodotus' ethnographic-geographical digressions need to be seen. I have argued elsewhere for an interpretation of this accumulation of contacts as essentially a fatalistic, amoral, account (Harrison 2002, 556–8, Harrison 2003, 249–51): his remark on the twenty ships sents by the Athenians in support of the Ionian revolt, and in response to Aristagoras' entreaties (5.97.3), far from being a comment on the wisdom of their decision, is an observation of the fateful moment at which first contact was made between Persians and Athenians, at which the lengthy fuse for the Persian wars was lit. Similarly, the coincidence of factors that provokes Aristagoras to make the decision to revolt essentially gives him no choice (5.36.1). This account, however, misses an important ingredient of the historical process according to Herodotus: that is, power.

The relationship of geographical knowledge and power is an important theme in much modern geographical literature (Godlewska and Smith 1994, Godlewska 1995, Harley 1992, Driver 2001, Edney 1990, Kearns 1998); it has also been explored by students of ancient geography, notably by Christian Jacob (albeit in a later context) (Jacob, 1991, 149), by Katherine Clarke and by Claude Nicolet, who noted that the 'first maps in Western history appeared during the Persian Wars as visualizations of the distances that were destined to mark, or mask, the balance of power' (Nicolet 1991, 5). This link between power and geographical knowledge was also one recognised by Herodotus himself.

Much of the geographical material in the *Histories* is framed through the imperial ambitions of the Persians. It is Xerxes' wonder at the mouth of the Peneius gorge, for example, and his thought of diverting the river, which leads to Herodotus' explanation of why it has the form it does (7.128–30). It is Darius' wonder at the Black Sea which leads to Herodotus' 'eye-witness' report of his measurement of it (4.85–6). Similarly Herodotus' reports during Xerxes' invasion of many of the myths and rituals associated with the landscape of Greece are triggered by the King's interest; the questioning figure of Xerxes is apparently ever-present in the narrative (e.g. 7.196–7, 208–9).

There is also a regular association of listing and measuring with kingship and empire, an association that goes beyond the common-sense truth that rulers need to know the extent of their rule. On the verge of crossing the Danube bridge into Scythia, Darius chooses to commemorate the peoples under his command (4.87). Xerxes is always nervously counting and surveying his subjects. And Herodotus, partly to build up the stakes of Greek-Persian conflict, and partly perhaps as a reflection of this association of kingship and geographically organised power, includes perennial reviews of the number of peoples under the King's command, in timely contexts such as after Darius' accession to the throne (3.88 ff.; Harrison 2000b, ch. 7). Only on one occasion does a list of Persian resources originate from an enemy of the Persians, but even in this case the rhetorical force of the list is to compel submission to Persian power: at the outset of the Ionian revolt (5.36),

Hecataeus of Miletus (the probable author of Aristagoras' map) lists all the peoples of Asia in order to persuade the Ionians not to revolt; when this argument fails, he argues (significantly, in the light of later Athenian imperialism) that they should aim for mastery of sea.

To turn to measuring, Artaphernes' settlement of Greeks of Asia Minor in the light of the Ionian revolt involves, first, the surveying of their territory in parasangs (6.42).[21] Is the choice of unit only pragmatic? Or does it imply, in Herodotus' view, a symbolic subordination? Just as the poverty of the Greek landscape embodies in some senses their independence – they have to be virtuous to earn rain from Zeus (cf. 7.102), unlike the Egyptians who merely rake in their agricultural wealth, and who rely (presumptuously?) on the Nile flood (2.10; cf. 1.193) – Persian rule and Persian decadence are mapped, projected onto the landscape itself. All Persia – like all Laconia – unites to mourn the death of a King (6.58; see Arrian, *Anab.* 7.14.19 for the mourning decreed for Hephaistion). 'The whole territory over which the King reigns', Herodotus observes in the context of the wealth of Babylonia, 'is divided into districts for the purpose of furnishing subsistence for him and his army, in addition to the usual tribute' (1.192). He goes on to report that Tritantaechmes son of Artabazus, who held this district from the King, received a whole artaba of silver every day from the region. 'And he had a private stud of horses, in addition to those used in war, of 800 stallions, and 16,000 mares, for each stallion serviced 20 mares. He kept too such a number of Indian dogs that four considerable towns in the plain were exempted from all other taxes and appointed to find food for the dogs.' The Persians' mapping of the land of their empire, like that of modern empires, seeks to objectify its own administrative units. The map becomes, in the words of Thongchai Winichakul, 'a model for, rather than a model of, what it purported to represent… It had become a real instrument to concretize projections on the earth's surface' (cited by Anderson 1991, 173–4). But it is then distorted through the Greeks' gaze, with the Persian system of taxation transformed into a bureaucracy of decadence. This is most clearly demonstrated by a passage of the Platonic *Alcibiades* (Pl., *Alc.* 123b), in which Plato puts this description of the journey up country to the King into one of his characters' mouths (*Alc.* 123b): 'For I myself was told by a trustworthy person, who had been up to their court, that he traversed a very large tract of excellent land, nearly a day's journey, which the inhabitants called the girdle of the King's wife, and another which was similarly called her veil, and many other fine and fertile regions reserved for the adornment of her consort; and each of these regions was named after some part of her apparel.'

Another significant pattern is that of Persian exploration prior to conquest (Martin 1965). The Persians like to know what they are getting: this is why, for example, Cambyses' sends the Fish-eaters to Ethiopia, to discover the customs of the country (3.1–25). This also underlies the importance of individuals such as Syloson of Samos, who led the Persians to 'net' his home island (3.139–49), or of Democedes of Croton who, to ensure his own return home, persuaded the Queen, Atossa, to convince her husband to send him on a fact-finding mission to Greece; the Persians who accompanied him were the first Persians, according to Herodotus, to come from Asia to Greece (3.134–8). It is this pattern of obsessive exploration prior to conquest, coupled with a degree of Hellenocentrism (a conviction on the Greeks' part that they were worthy of such obsession), that lies also behind the traditions that Xerxes knew the contents of Delphi better than those of his own palace (8.35), that Darius kept up with Greek wrestling (so that he was impressed when Democedes married the daughter of the famous Milo, 3.137) or that Darius invaded Greece because of his passion for Attic figs (Dinon *FGrHist* 690 F 2). At the first point of contact between the Greeks of Asia Minor, the Spartans had sent heralds to Cyrus to tell him not to meddle with the Greeks; the King replied by asking 'who are these Spartans?' and threatening them (1.153.1), a form of questioning that forms a significant motif in Greek representations of Persia (Harrison 2000b, ch. 4). As the Persians' geographical horizons expand, it is implied, so conquest will continue.

Ironically, however, in the event, the Persians reveal a striking ignorance of what they are conquering. Mardonius, possibly disingenuously, sells Greece as a land of fertility (7.5.3), a theme that then Xerxes adopts as his own, claiming that they would acquire through the campaign a land no less wealthy than that which they now possess (7.8.a2). The Persians' delusions are cruelly revealed when the landscape of Greece fails to support them. A similar pattern can be traced in the case of Croesus, who attacks the Persians, despite the wise advice of Sandanis – strikingly reminiscent of Aristagoras' to Cleomenes (5.49) – that 'you are preparing to make war against a people who wear leather trousers, and the rest of their garments of leather; who inhabit a barren country and feed not on such things as they choose, but such as they can get' (1.71). (A similar almost resolute ignorance of the realities of geography is shown, of course, by the Athenians in the case of Sicily – one of a number of significant parallelisms between Herodotus' Persian invasion and Thucydides' Sicilian expedition (Rood 1999, Harrison 2000c)).

The same association of gradually expanding geographical knowledge and imperial expansion can be seen in Herodotus' treatment of another burgeoning power, that of Athens. Polycrates was the first man, excepting Minos, to aim at rule of the sea (3.122). It was rule of the sea that Hecataeus recommended to the Ionians as the only possible way of defeating the Persians (6.136). The Athenians then, implicitly, take on the baton. Like Polycrates, who was offered the money with which to realise his ambitions – by Oroites, only to discover that it was a trap and so to be killed – the Athenians' ambitions increase as their horizons widen. Aristagoras' lecture to the Spartan Cleomenes mocked the Greeks for fighting over wretched scraps of land when larger prizes were available (5.49.8). 'But now you must carry on war for a country of small extent, and not very fertile, and of narrow limits, with the Messenians, who are your equals in valour, and with the Arcadians and Argives, who have nothing akin to gold and silver, the desire of which induces men to hazard their lives in battle'. The same lecture, we are told – if not also the same map – was presented also to the Athenians, only with the added reminder of the Athenians' kinship with the Milesians: it was this promise of the wealth of Asia then which induced the Athenians to lend their fateful twenty ships (5.97). The Athenians' part in the Ionian revolt, except in its consequences, was something of a damp squib: after burning the temple of Kybebe in Sardis – accidentally, or so we are told (Parker 1983, 168 n. 133) – they came home and took no further part. But their eyes lift up once more after Marathon. The end of book VI sees a whole string of glimpes of Athenian imperialism: the story of the suitors for the hand of Agariste, with its concluding reference to the birth of Pericles (a lion, as his mother dreamt the night before his birth, 6.131),[22] Miltiades' repossession of Lemnos (following an ancient grievance against the Pelasgians, 6.137–40), and his failed attempt to capture Paros (6.132–6). His alleged motive for attacking Paros was that the Parians had furnished a single ship to the Persian fleet (a familiar fig-leaf for imperialism?); his real motive was a grudge against an individual, Lysagoras son of Tisias, who had slandered him to the Persian Hydarnes. What is particularly significant here, however, is the way in which Miltiades persuades the Athenians to support his venture, with its echo of Aristagoras' words to Cleomenes, or Oroites' promise to Polycrates: 'having asked of the Athenians 70 ships, and troops and money, without telling them what country he purposed to invade, [he said] that he would make them rich if they would follow him, for he would take them to such a country from which they would easily bring away abundance of gold' (6.132).

A similar resurgence in Athenian ambition takes place after Salamis. This can be seen, for example, in the profiteering activities of Themistocles (8.110–12),[23] but also more significantly at the very end of book 8 in the Athenians' explanation to the Spartans of their reasons for rejecting an alliance with the Mede (8.144). They put down the Spartans for supposing that they might even entertain Persian overtures of peace (which they then entertain in book IX in an attempt to galvanise the Spartans: 9.11). The language that they use, however, in its allusions to Aristagoras' promise of untold wealth is strongly suggestive of their incipient imperialism: 'you appear to entertain an unworthy dread; for there is neither so much gold anywhere in the world, nor a country so pre-eminent in beauty and fertility, by receiving which we should be willing to side with the Mede and enslave Greece'. It is in this context also that another slightly earlier passage can be seen. After Salamis Herodotus describes a lengthy stand-off between the Greek and Persian fleets (8.132). The Greek fleet would go no further east than Delos (perhaps a significant location, in the context of the Athenians' later alliance), the Persians no further west than Samos. Herodotus comments on the Greeks' perspective: 'For all beyond that [Delos] was dreaded by the Greeks, who were unacquainted with those countries, and thought all parts were full of troops; Samos, they were convinced in their imaginations, was as far distant as the pillars of Hercules.' It has been suggested that this passage 'reads like a quiet rebuke to mainland Greeks for their ignorance of the Asian side of the Aegean' (Thomas 2000, 11). It is perhaps more convincingly seen in the context of

Herodotus' representation of Athenian power than in a scientific context. How far could the Athenians go if they got the habit – if they were indeed to discover the whereabouts of the Pillars of Hercules?

It is on this pregnant note of impending imperial expansion that Herodotus also ends his *Histories*, with Pericles' father, Xanthippus' barbaric execution of the Persian Artayctes overlooking the Hellespont (Boedeker 1988). Thucydides arguably moves this plot further – if one accepts the hypothesis of a close intertextual relationship between his Athens and Herodotus' Persia – when his Athenians are envisaged as aiming not only for Sicily but for Italy and Carthage (Thuc. 6.15.2; cf. 7.66.2, Plut., *Nic.* 12, *Alc.* 17.3), just as the Persians' real aim was not only to conquer Athens, but all Greece and Europe, to create an empire coterminous with the sky (1.209.1, 7.8.g2–3, 7.19.1, 7.54.2, 8.53.2, 8.109.3). But we can also supplement this picture from other sources. Isocrates' *Philip* (112) contains the passing statement that the Pillars of Hercules were set down as the limits of Greek territory. The Old Oligarch's picture of the openness of Athens to foreign influences can be set against Herodotus' comment on the Persians, that they were the most ready of all peoples to adopt foreign customs (1.135; cf. 4.76.1, 1.79.1, 1.91.1), the famous comic fragment of Hermippus which lists the goods that come to Athens from her empire (parodying perhaps the language of the Persian king, as seen in the Susa Foundation charter, Kent 1953 DSf), or in Pericles' vision of Athens drawing in resources from around the whole world (*ek pasês gês)* (2.38; emphasised by Clarke 1999, 223). Athens – in aspiration, if not in reality – becomes a world empire on the model of Persia before her: there are scarcely bounds to her power.[24]

* * * *

Two final questions remain. The first is where, for Herodotus, this historical pattern is going to end. Can the Ethiopian, brave and upright and resistant to the lures of imperial expansion, remain an Ethiopian, in other words, or will contact with other, more restless powers, lure him also into the competition for power? Is it an immutable matter of national character that dictates that Cleomenes (or, more accurately perhaps, his daughter Gorgo) will resist Aristagoras' rhetorical snares while the Athenians will be sucked in?[25] One story in the *Histories*, a neat parallel to the story of Io that initiates contact between Phoenicians and Greeks, suggests a model of contact between different peoples that might *not* lead inexorably to conflict: a story of the peaceful trade between Carthaginian traders and a Libyan tribe beyond the Pillars of Hercules (4.196), in which each side leaves its goods or its payment and then scuttles away and watches from a distance to see whether its proposed rate of exchange is satisfactory. National character, however, is not immutable in the *Histories* – though it may change in strange and sudden ways (Thomas 2000, e.g. 107–8, 113, 134). The Persians are characterised repeatedly as restless (hence Nitocris' introduction of bends in the river), but they were not always so. It was only when Cyrus – for the most personal reason, inspired by

Harpagus' grudge against Astyages – gained them their freedom that they became so (1.123–6). Similarly, it was when the Athenians gained their freedom from tyrants, and when each man began to work for himself, that their military fortunes rose and they defeated their neighbours the Chalkidians and Boiotians (5.78). There are ominous signs in the *Histories* that other peoples too could rise up. When Herodotus notes that the Thracians could be the most powerful people were they to find a single ruler or a single purpose (5.3), the implication seems to be either that other empires are waiting in the wings, or just that there will be an increasing mêlée of world powers.

The final question is that of the implications of this picture for Herodotus' historical project. If geographical knowledge, in his perspective, is inextricably associated with imperial expansion, and if this position is a deliberately formulated and developed one (as has been suggested here), how then could Herodotus fail to be self-conscious in writing a work which, by implication, is not only a reflection of aggressive expansion but will also facilitate it? To borrow the formula of Simon Gikandi (1996, esp. ch. 3), is Herodotus a critic or a proponent of an 'imperialized knowledge'? This question takes us to the heart of the *Histories*, to the larger conundrum of the extent to which, or limits within which, Herodotus' agents can act to avert their fates. But, of course, we do not have to believe – with a Crimean archaeologist cited by Neal Ascherson in his *Black Sea* (1995, 52) – that Herodotus was an agent of imperial expansion, measuring the Black Sea in the service of Pericles, to suppose that his purpose was, in some less crude and direct form, a Hellenising, a proto-imperial one (cf. Vasunia chs. 2–3).

Despite his occasional put downs of the Greeks vis-à-vis barbarians, there is still reason to believe that the *Histories* are in part a celebration of the Greek victory in the Persian wars, as well as, more broadly, of the possibilities of human achievement. But it is not just a simple question of whether or not Herodotus can be described as a 'barbarian-lover'.[26] In his treatment of the Victorian culture of travel, Simon Gikandi has shown how a number of rhetorical schemas can coexist even in the same narrative (1996, ch. 2): Anthony Trollope, for example, far from lamenting (in the words of another famous account of the West Indies) that 'Dominica is English in name only', lambasts the English abroad for their slavish devotion to English cuisine ('They will give you ox-tail soup when turtle soup would be much cheaper'). His autopsy lends him a special authority to correct the standard myths and ideologies of the time. Trollope's irony, however, is – perhaps predictably – bordered by a set of paradigms, especially concerning race, that predate his travel – and which also find confirmation there. We should expect no less complexity from Herodotus and the Greeks. Herodotus' put-downs of the Greeks vis-à-vis foreign peoples, his ironic identification of incipient Athenian imperialism with that of the Persians (and so on) do not preclude the possibility that the very frame of his *Histories* reflects and reinforces the structure of attitudes that allows for the expansion of Greek power. Nor do we need to choose between curiosity and interest, on the one hand, and contempt for foreign culture on the other.[27] As a number of scholars have recognised, the assimilation of foreign peoples through myth (the Persians descended from Perseus etc.) – a process that appears to run counter to a pattern of polarities – may itself be a form of appropriation, a kind of mythical colonisation (Bickerman 1952, Hall 1989, e.g. 172–81).

We can perhaps see traces of this proto-imperialism also in what was made of Herodotus. Arrian's account of Alexander is rich in allusions to Herodotus' Persians.[28] (The extent to which the history of Alexander is one dictated by his historians' literary predecessors has been underestimated). Some of these parallelisms do not necessarily reflect well on Alexander. Though he turned down the opportunity to have Mt Athos carved into his image, for him, as for Persian kings, mountains no matter how high and precipitous are mounted (4.18.6, 4.21.1, 3, 4.28.1, 4, 5.26.5). He takes a similar, rather personal, approach to rivers; he would feel ashamed, he tells his lieutenant Parmenio, if after crossing the Hellespont, this petty stream, the Granicus, held him back (1.13.6). Alexander prays at Troy just as Xerxes had before him; he also propitiates the Hellespont (1.11.5–8). And the accounts of his 'last plans' – regardless of their historicity (Bosworth 1988, ch. 8) – again cast him very much in the same mould as Herodotean imperialists, with geographical exploration and conquest almost as synonomous. 'From the Persian gulf', Alexander tells his mutinous troops by the river Hyphasis (5.26.2), 'our fleet shall sail round to Libya, as far as the pillars of Heracles; from the Pillars all the interior of Libya then becomes ours, just as Asia is in fact becoming ours in its entirety,[29] and the boundaries of our empire here are becoming those which God set for the whole continent' (cf. Arr., *Anabasis* 7.1.1–4, 7.20.7 ff). Oswyn Murray and now Katherine Clarke have suggested that Herodotus' popularity in the Hellenistic Age derived from his having provided a model for accommodating the peoples of the Successor kingdoms (Murray 1972; Clarke 1999: 68–9). Arguably, that is not a coincidence. As Edward Said and many other writers have stressed, 'the enterprise of empire depends upon the *idea* of having an empire' (Said 1993, 10). Herodotus here did much of the thinking.

Notes

1 There is, at any rate, a journal *Hérodote*, subtitled the *Revue de géographie et de géopolitique.*

2 For the suggestion that Hecataeus of Miletus was the author of Aristagoras' map, see Jacob 1991, 43–4. For a recent account of the development of Greek geography focussing on Hecataeus, see Heilen 2000.

3 Clarke 1999, 9; Clarke's distinction of an ancient and post-enlightenment mentality relies heavily on *Categories of Medieval Culture* by A.J. Gurevich, 1985 (whose own familiarity with the ancient evidence is very limited: e.g. with such generalised statements as that ancient conceptions of space and time were still profoundly marked by mythological conceptions).

4 See also here Jacob 1991, 58–9; for Egypt as shaped like an axe (broader at the Mediterranean end, narrowing around Memphis, and then broadening), see also Pseudo-Scylax, in C.

Muller (ed.) *Geographi Graeci Minores* (Paris, 1855) i.80–1.

5 Cf. Jacob 1983, 53: 'il "geographo" vuole costruire un'immagine coerente del mondo, dominabile dall'occchio e dalla memoria, sopratutto riproducibile e trasmettibile'.

6 2000, ch. 3. For the separate issue of Herodotus' position (esp. in relation to Hecataeus) on the number of the continents, two or three, see now Zimmermann 1997; contrast Alonso-Nuñez 2002, 146.

7 E.g. the case of Metiochus the son of Miltiades, 6.41, with a Persian wife and children – historical parallel to the conceit of *Dissoi Logoi*, DK 90 B 6 (12), that if a small (Greek) child were transported to Persia, he would speak Persian, and *vice versa*. For the threatened transportation of Greeks, cf. 6.4, 20, 119; for lands without people, see also 3.149, 4.18, 4.46, 6.31, 8.61 (for the Athenians' Persian war 'nomadism').

8 Cf. Pind., *Isthm.* 6.22–3 ('Thousands are there of broad roads cut out endlessly for your great deeds, even beyond the sources of the Nile and through the land of the Hyperboreans.') Space and distance for Herodotus are also confounded in different ways by synchronisms such as that between Plataea and Mycale; cf. Gauthier 1966, Clarke 1999, 121–2.

9 This last phrase is bracketed by both Hude and Rosén.

10 As Redfield argues, however, 1985, this Egyptian ethnocentrism serves to justify a Hellenocentric perspective: 'cultural relativism becomes ethnocentric'.

11 For the Persians' attempted appropriation of natural phenomena, cf. 1.188–9, 3.117, 4.91, 7.27.2, 7.35, 54, 128–30, 8.97 (for non-Persians, cf. 1.75, 174, 184–5, 2.168), with Harrison 2000a, 238–9; the Persians, at the same time, however, venerate rivers to an exceptional degree, and refrain from urinating, spitting or washing in them, 1.138.2.

12 The schematism/polarity traced by e.g. Hartog, Hall, Cartledge is characterised repeatedly as a body of mere clichés: 'a mass of fairly standard Greek preoccupations and prejudices' (Thomas 2000, 74); on another occasion ethnography is contrasted with 'the anti-barbarian obsessions of Athens and Athenian literature' (2000, 96).

13 Thomas' presumption against chauvinism is perhaps most marked in her account of the Hippocratic *Airs, Waters, Places*, when the author notes the effects of custom, esp. monarchy, on the Asian *genos* – in contrast to his general thesis of the debilitating effect of climate and environment – Thomas notes that 'it is hardly expressive of Greek triumphalism or Greek cultural chauvinism' (2000, 93; cf. p. 90).

14 Cf. Thomas 2000, 28–9: 'We will also find that ethnographic material and speculation have a role in early Greek science which stands somewhat apart from the preoccupations with Hellenism, Greek identity and Greek conflict against the barbarian that emerge from studies of the barbarian in Greek tragedy and fifth-century Athens.'

15 Cf. Thomas 2000, 272 (cf. p. 19): 'The implications are that Herodotus' narrative history of the Persian Wars in the later books, and his occasional personal comments, are considerably more barbed than sometimes thought, critical, polemical, and well aware of alternative damaging versions.'

16 A cause for regret for Pédech 1976, 48–54, who blames Herodotus for his (influential) subordination of geography to history, and for his inclusion of baroque customs in his geographical sections. Contrast, however, Alonso-Nuñez 2003, 152, heralding him (for similar reasons) as the first universal historian.

17 Cf. Clarke 1999, 16. Contrast e.g. Murray's emphasis, 1988, 261–3, on two distinct 'elements' in the *Histories*: the 'collection of *logoi*' and the history of events.

18 Cf. 7.58.2, 7.176.3, 7.189.3, 7.192.2, 7.198.2, 7.200.2. For the relationship of landscape and myth, see esp. Buxton 1994, ch.6.

19 This qualifies the important insight of Balot 2001, 107 that Herodotus assumes a conception of a just allocation of resources between peoples ('moral "facts" about the global distribution of goods are thus inscribed in the physical boundaries of the world').

20 1.163.1: 'These Phocaeans were the first of all the Greeks to undertake long voyages, and they are the people who discovered the Adriatic and Tyrrhenian seas and Iberia and Tartessus...' (cf. 2.154 for the origins of deep contact between Egypt and the Greek world from the time of the Greeks settlement in Egypt.)

21 Cf. 2.109 for Sesostris' allocation of equal units of land to the Egyptians, and for the Greeks' borrowing of this Egyptian land-surveying; cf. also the Delphic oracle given to the Spartans, 1.66.2.

22 For the significance of this image, see esp. Dyson 1929, more recently Thomas 1989, 270f.

23 On Themistocles' central role in the characterisation of the Athenians in terms of greed, see Balot 2001, 117–21.

24 I do not mean to accept as historical fact the implicit Athenian claim that Persian power concluded with the end of the Persian wars against Greece.

25 Is it, as Jesper Svenbro – cited by Christian Jacob, 1991, 45–7 – suggests, due to the tribal and monarchic nature of the Spartans and the democratic and egalitarian conception of space of the Athenians? Probably not.

26 Cf. Thomas 2000: 273: 'His reputation as *philobarbaros*, and his openness to barbarian habits and influences seem far removed from at least the popular and official attitudes in Athens of the time.'

27 An extreme example of the possible overlap of scientific curiosity and imperial ideology is the expedition of Halford Mackinder to climb Mt Kenya: Mackinder shot eight local servants on his way to the summit and then sawed off the peak. See further Kearns 1998.

28 Vasunia 2001, 256–61, Harrison 2004. Of course, it is necessary for my argument for some of these features to originate with his sources Ptolemy and Aristoboulus.

29 For the 'rule of Asia', see also Arr., *Anabasis* 2.14.9, 3.9.6, 3.18.11, 3.24.3, 6.29.8.

Bibliography

Alonso-Nuñez, J. -M. (2002) 'Herodotus' conception of historical space and the beginnings of universal history', in P. S. Derow and R. Parker (eds.) *Herodotus and his World*, 145–52 (Oxford).

Anderson, B. (1991) *Imagined Communities: Reflections on the Origin and Spread of Nationalism* (London).

Armayor, O. K. (1978) 'Did Herodotus ever go to the Black Sea?' *Harvard Studies in Classical Philology* 82, 45–62.

Ascherson, N. (1995) *Black Sea* (London).

Balot, R. K. (2001) *Greed and Injustice in Classical Athens* (Princeton)

Bickerman, E. J. (1952) 'Origines gentium', *Classical Philology* 47, 65–81

Boedeker, D. (1988) 'Protesilaos and the end of Herodotus' *Histories'*, *Classical Antiquity* 7, 30–48.

Bosworth, A. B. (1988) *From Arrian to Alexander* (Oxford).

Buxton, R. (1994) *Imaginary Greece: The Contexts of Mythology* (Cambridge).

Cartledge, P. (1993) *The Greeks* (Oxford).

Clarke, K. (1999) *Between Geography and History* (Oxford).

Davidson, J. (2002) 'Too much other?', *Times Literary Supplement* 19 April 2002.

Dewald, C. (1997) 'Wanton kings, pickled heroes and gnomic founding fathers: strategies of meaning at the end of Herodotus' *Histories*', in D. H. Roberts, F. M. Dunn and D. Fowler (eds.) *Classical Closure*, 62–82 (Princeton).

Driver, F. (2001) *Geography Militant: Cultures of Exploration and Empire* (Oxford).

Dyson, G. W. (1929) '*Leonta tekein*', *Classical Quarterly* 23, 186–95.
Edney, M. H. (1990) *Mapping an Empire: The Geographic Construction of British India 1765–1843* (Chicago).
Gauthier, P. (1966) 'La parallèle Himère-Salamine au Ve et au IVe siècle av. J.-C.', *Revue des études anciennes* 68, 5–32.
Gikandi, S. (1996) *Maps of Englishness: Writing Identity in the Culture of Colonialism* (New York).
Godlewska, A. (1995) 'Map, text and image. The mentality of enlightened conquerors: a new look at the *Description de l'Égypte*', *Transactions of the Institute of British Geographers* 20, 5–28.
Godlewska, A. and N. Smith (eds.) (1994) *Geography and Empire* (Oxford).
Griffiths, A. (2001) 'Kissing cousins: some curious cases of adjacent material in Herodotus', in N. Luraghi (ed.) *The Historian's Craft in the Age of Herodotus*, 161–78 (Oxford).
Gurevich, A. J. (1985) *Categories of Medieval Culture*, tr. G.L. Campbell (London).
Hall, E. (1989) *Inventing the Barbarian. Greek Self-Definition through Tragedy* (Oxford)
Harley, J. B. (1992) 'Deconstructing the map', in T. J. Barnes and J. S. Duncan (eds.), *Writing Worlds: Discourse, text and metaphor in the representation of landscape*, 231–47 (London).
Harrison, T. (2000a) *Divinity and History: The Religion of Herodotus* (Oxford).
Harrison, T. (2000b) *The Emptiness of Asia: Aeschylus'* Persians *and the History of the Fifth Century* (London).
Harrison, T. (2000c) 'Sicily in the Athenian Imagination: Thucydides on the Persian wars', in C. J. Smith and J. Serrati (eds.) *Ancient Sicily from Aeneas to Cicero*, 84–96 (Edinburgh).
Harrison, T. (2002) 'The Persian invasions', in E. Bakker, I. de Jong and H. van Wees (eds.) *Brill's Companion to Herodotus* (Leiden), 551–78
Harrison, T. (2003) '"Prophecy in reverse"? Herodotus and the origins of history', in P. S. Derow and R. Parker (eds.) *Herodotus and his World* (Oxford), 237–55
Harrison, T. (2004) 'Mastering the landscape', in *Titulus. Studies in Memory of Dr. Stanislaw Kalita. Electrum* vol. 8 (Krakow), 27–34
Hartog, F. (1988) *The Mirror of Herodotus: The Representation of the Other in the Writing of History*, tr. J. Lloyd (Berkeley).
Heilen, S. (2000) 'Die Anfänge der wissenschaftlichen Geographie: Anaximander und Hekataios' in W. Hübner (ed.) *Geographie und verwandte Wissenschaften, Geschichte der Mathematik und der Naturwissenschaften in der Antike* 2, 33–54 (Stuttgart).
Jacob, C. (1983) 'Carte greche', in F. Frontera (ed.) *Geografia e geografi nel mondo antico* (Rome).
Jacob, C. (1991) *Géographie et ethnographie en Grèce ancienne* (Paris).
Kearns, G. (1998) 'The imperial subject: geography and travel in the work of Mary Kingsley and Halford Mackinder', *Transactions of the Institute of British Geographers* 22, 450–72.
Kent, R. G. (1953) *Old Persian. Texts, Grammar, Lexicon* (New Haven)
Lateiner, D. (1989) *The Historical Method of Herodotus* (Toronto).
Lattimore, R. (1958) 'The composition of the *History* of Herodotus', *Classical Philology* 53, 9–21.
Martin, V. (1965) 'La politique des Achéménides. L'exploration prélude de la conquête', *Museum Helveticum* 22, 28–38
McDowell L. (1997) *Undoing place? A Geographical Reader* (London).
Miller, M. C. (1997) *Athens and Persia in the Fifth Century BC: A Study in Cultural Reciprocity* (Cambridge).
Murray, O. (1972) 'Herodotus and Hellenistic culture', *Classical Quarterly* 22, 200–13.
Murray, O. (1988) 'The Ionian Revolt', *The Cambridge Ancient History* IV², 461–90 (Cambridge).
Nicolet, C. (1991) *Space, geography, and politics in the early Roman empire*, tr. H. Leclerc (Ann Arbor).
Parker, R. (1983) *Miasma: Pollution and Purification in Early Greek Religion* (Oxford).
Pédech, P. (1976) *La geographie des Grecs* (Paris).
Redfield, J. (1985) 'Herodotus the tourist', *Classical Philology* 80, 97–118, reprinted in T. Harrison (ed.) (2001) *Greeks and Barbarians*, 24–49 (Edinburgh).

Romm, J. (1989) 'Herodotus and mythic geography: the case of the Hyperboreans', *Transactions of the American Philological Association* 119, 97–113.
Rood, T. (1999) 'Thucydides' Persian wars' in C. S. Kraus (ed.) *The Limits of Historiography*, 141–68 (Leiden).
Rudhardt, J. (1992) 'Les attitudes des Grecs a l'égard des religions étrangères', *Revue de l'Histoire des Religions* 209, 219–38, reprinted as 'The Greek Attitude to Foreign Religions' in T. Harrison (ed.) *Greeks and Barbarians* (Edinburgh), 172–85.
Said, E. W. (1993) *Culture and Imperialism* (London).
Spang, R. (2000) *The Invention of the Restaurant: Paris and modern gastronomic culture* (Cambridge Mass.).
Thomas, R. (1989) *Oral Tradition and Written Record in Classical Athens* (Cambridge).
Thomas, R. (2000) *Herodotus in Context: Ethnography, Science and the Art of Persuasion* (Cambridge).
Vasunia, P. (2001) *The Gift of the Nile: Hellenizing Egypt from Aeschylus to Alexander* (Berkeley).
Zimmermann, K. (1997) 'Hdt. IV, 36, 2 et le développement de l'image du monde d'Hécatée à Hérodote', *Ktema* 22, 285–98.
Zingross, M. (1998) *Herodotus' Views of Nature* (Athens).

Xenophon's *Anabasis* as a Traveller's Memoir

Jim Roy

Xenophon's *Anabasis* is the major surviving autobiographical account of a journey by a classical Greek. It offers some insights into how Xenophon at least viewed the physical effort of travel, but its main interest as a travel memoir is in its presentation of non-Greek territories and cultures, especially some very ungreek areas in eastern Anatolia. The book is of course much more than a traveller's memoir. It is also the story of the Greek mercenaries who marched with the rebel Persian prince Cyrus against his brother King Artaxerxes, and then after Cyrus' defeat and death at Cunaxa made their way out of the Persian Empire back to the political complications of Hellas. When writing Xenophon certainly also had in mind the problems that eventually drove him into exile from Athens, as he briefly acknowledges in the *Anabasis*. And the book is a good read, for Xenophon tells a good story, and his journey left him with several good stories.

A good deal has been written about the *Anabasis*, and is still being written. In 1995, for instance, two commentaries appeared, by Lendle and Stronk. However, many of the issues considered in this paper were reviewed in a 1995 conference at Toulouse, of which the proceedings have been published by Briant 1995, and there is an excellent and penetrating review of these proceedings by Tuplin 1999. There is therefore little reference in this paper to the very large body of earlier work.

Book 1 of the *Anabasis* first sets the scene and explains why Cyrus recruited the Greeks, then describes their march under Cyrus' command to the heart of the Persian Empire, and closes with Cyrus' defeat and death at Cunaxa. Until the battle Cyrus' forces had met no major opposition, and had generally been able to follow readily practicable routes, while Cyrus had ensured that provisions were available. For the Greeks the first of the work's seven books thus depicts their easiest conditions for travel. After Cunaxa however the Greeks had to fend for themselves, finding supplies as best they could and looking for guides to show the way. They frequently had to fight hard, and lost many men. Nobody travelling with them then would have the same leisure for observation that could have been enjoyed before Cunaxa. For that reason it is worth beginning by considering how Xenophon chooses to describe travel in Book 1, when he was much less subject to the constraints experienced after Cunaxa.

Before considering Book 1, however, it is worth noting that for Xenophon routine travel, e.g. across the Aegean, is taken for granted. He passes over in a very brief phrase his journey from Athens to Sardis to join his friend Proxenus who was with Cyrus (3.1.8). He does not even mention Proxenus' own journey across the Aegean with the mercenaries whom he raised for Cyrus (1.1.11). Later a general comment on men who sailed out from Greece to join Cyrus notes only that some had additional expenses, no doubt because they too recruited for Cyrus and had to pay to bring their recruits to Asia Minor (6.4.8). Xenophon, a highly selective writer, does not spend words on travel so conventional.

In Book 1 the march of Cyrus' army is largely recorded in routine, almost mechanical, terms. Though there are notorious difficulties for those who seek to reconstruct in detail the movements described in Book 1 and later – difficulties which there is no time to pursue here (see Tuplin 1997, 404–417 and 1999, 332) – I believe that Xenophon kept a diary or at any rate some form of notes. Progress is recorded in stages (i.e. days of march) and parasangs, as in 1.2.19: 'From there he marched three stages, twenty parasangs, and arrived at Iconium, the last city of Phrygia. There he stayed three days.' We do not know why Xenophon chose to record distances in parasangs, nor who measured the distances he records: these and other problems arising from Xenophon's use of parasangs are analysed by Tuplin (1997, 404–417), who notes the difficulty of finding satisfactory answers. Xenophon names towns, and describes them by some or all of a group of set terms – large (*megale*), prosperous (*eudaimon),* and the puzzling inhabited (*oikoumenê* or some equivalent verb): e.g. at 1.2.20 '... he marched four stages, twentyfive parasangs, across Cappadocia and arrived at Dana, a city *oikoumene,* large and prosperous.' (References to towns in the *Anabasis,* and also to other settlements such as villages, are reviewed by Nielsen 2000). Geysels (1974) argued that *oikoumene* meant 'politically organised', and is followed by Brulé (1995, 12–13), but serious objections have been raised by Tuplin (1999, 334–5). The word may mean 'populous'. Villages are also noted, in areas where no town is recorded, but are not named, though they may be identified in some way, like those given to the queen Parysatis (1.4.9). Palaces are recorded, and hunting parks (*paradeisoi*) attract particular attention, as e.g. at 1.2.7–8 on Celaenae, where Cyrus had a palace and a paradeisos and there was also a palace of the king. Major rivers are named, and their width is given in plethra or, for the largest, stades: at 1.4.1 'From there he marched two stages, ten parasangs, and arrived at the river Psarus, the width of which was three plethra.' The rivers are obstacles to be crossed by travellers proceeding by land, and are not considered even incidentally as waterways (Baslez 1995, 84–85, cf. Tuplin 1999, 333 n. 5). Mountains are of no inherent interest and the effort of marching over them does not deserve mention (Tuplin 1999, 340 suggested that mountains were "ordinary"): they are referred to only rarely when they have some military relevance, and they are never named. Plains are also noted (Tuplin 1999, 340 n. 15), especially a fertile plain in Cilicia (1.2.22). Other features of the landscape are rarely mentioned, but the desert is briefly described (1.5.1, 5–6). Xenophon does note how the Greeks got food. Generally the Greeks buy their own supplies, while Cyrus ensures that supplies are available. Exceptionally he allows them to loot Lycaonia as hostile territory (1.2.19). Occasions when there is some problem with supplies are noted. When there is an opportunity to hunt, it is recounted with enthusiasm, the more so because it is hunting of a kind not available in Greece: at 1.5.2–3 Xenophon describes hunting, and eating, wild asses, bustards, and deer in what he calls the Arabian desert, and also recounts how the Greeks tried and failed to catch ostriches. There is little interest in the local human populations, though those who earn a living in the desert by extracting stone from the riverbanks and making millstones to sell in Babylon attract Xenophon's attention (1.5.5). Brulé argues that Xenophon sees the areas he moves through as a Greek, and filters out what appears normal to him, recording what is novel or otherwise noteworthy. This is certainly correct in general, but it hard to believe that the temperature in the desert was ignored as something that Greeks were used to (Brulé 1995: 6): it is simpler to believe that weather and climate were of no interest to Xenophon, unless they affected the Greeks' progress (as they did later in the march). As Tuplin (1999, 342) has pointed out, Xenophon makes little effort to contextualise his account, and does not refer for instance to what Herodotus had said on the areas the army was crossing. In general throughout the *Anabasis* Xenophon tells his story in isolation (which makes it easier for him to pass over various political complications, such as the degree of Sparta's support for Cyrus). There are rare exceptions, such as his explanation that the river Marsyas at Celaenae (1.2.8) was so called because Apollo overcame Marsyas there and hung his skin in the grotto where the river rises, and his reference to the Spring of Midas near Thymbrion (1.2.13), where Midas was said to have caught the satyr Silenus. Xenophon also mentions that Xerxes was said to have built the royal palace and the acropolis at Celaenae after his defeat in Greece (1.2.9). Such brief allusions to myth or history, all reported in the form "it is said", sound like snippets of information picked up on the spot, but, being so few, suggest that Xenophon was not very interested in gathering such material, or at least declined to include much of it in his narrative.

The battle of Cunaxa changed the Greeks' situation radically. From then on the Greeks had to fend for themselves. Book 2 recounts their uneasy negotiations with Persians, until several of the Greek leaders are seized. In Book 3 the Greeks move north away from the Persian heartland, and in Book 4, still moving broadly north despite detours, they cross mountains to reach the southern shore of the Black Sea. In Books 5 and 6 they make their way along the Black Sea coast towards Byzantium, and in Book 7 they face the complex problems of the Greek world, and notably the power of the Spartan authorities in and around Byzantium. They briefly fight for the Thracian leader Seuthes in European Thrace, and the story ends when they pass from his service to that of the Spartan commander Thibron. Obviously for the mercenaries and in particular for Xenophon, there are more adventures to come, notably under the Spartan king Agesilaus in Asia Minor and then in Greece, but the

Anabasis does not carry the story so far. Thus the whole story from Book 2 onwards is the tale of a return to Hellas – as the text frequently says (e.g. 3.1.2) – though the army's actual arrival in Hellas is confused and – at least as far as the *Anabasis* takes the story – inconclusive.

Obviously the changed circumstances of the Greeks after Cunaxa mean that in Books 2 to 7 concerns are evident that had played little if any part in Book 1. The army has to feed itself, and has to find guides. It frequently has to fight its way through hostile terrain. In Books 5 and 6, because the mercenaries no longer have an employer, and are for the most part not in such extreme danger as they often were in Books 2 to 4, the ordinary soldiers become much more ready to question the authority of their officers and the army's structure of command. There is also a desire to take booty so that they do not return empty-handed to Hellas (e.g. 6.1.17–18). These developments clearly would have affected Xenophon's ability to observe and record the people and places the Greeks were encountering. Yet the later books of the *Anabasis* as a record of travel show marked similarities with Book 1.

Progress is still measured in stages and, till the end of Book 4, in parasangs. Towns are still named and described by the same set terms as in Book 1. The use of *polyanthropos* ('populous', of Sittace 2.4.13), while new, does not mark any real change. There are however two significant changes in the way Xenophon writes of towns. One is more or less automatic, namely the addition of *Hellenis* to Xenophon's set terms for towns once the army comes to Greek towns on the Black Sea coast. That *Hellenis* then disappears again is, however, more telling. From Trapezus to Heracleia Xenophon tells us that cities are Greek, and often specifies that they are in non-Greek territory: e.g. 5.3.2 'Marching for three days they arrived at Cerasus, a Greek city by the sea, a colony of the Sinopeans in Colchian territory.' However, once the Greeks reach Chrysopolis opposite Byzantium Xenophon no longer feels the need to mention that towns are Greek, or indeed to deploy other terms from his set vocabulary to describe towns: 6.6.38 'On the sixth day they arrived at Chrysopolis in Calchedonia ...' and 7.2.11 'When the Greeks arrived at Perinthus ...' Evidently between Heracleia and Chrysopolis the Greeks have returned to Hellas, and in Hellas much more can be taken for granted about towns. The Greeks did not pillage towns. Xenophon reports himself as upbraiding the Greeks when they seemed about to loot Byzantium with the words (7.1.29) '... if we were not willing to seize any barbarian city, though we were conquerors, but will sack this, the first Greek city into which we have come.' There is here more rhetoric than logic, but the narrative of the *Anabasis* suggests that the Greeks preferred to attack villages. From Book 2 onwards, as in Book 1, villages are again recorded in areas where no particular town is mentioned. It is true that (2.4.21) a messenger told the Greeks in general terms that the area between the Tigris and a large canal was vast and included many towns and villages, but specific towns and villages are not recorded in close proximity to each other. Only at the very end of the *Anabasis*, in the account of Xenophon's marauding expedition against the Persian Asidates, do we hear of villages under the walls of the town (*polisma*) Parthenion in the plain of the Caïcus (7.8.21). Villages are above all sources of supplies: they are very rarely mentioned without some report of what provisions they could offer: e.g. 3.5.1 'Those with Cheirisophus went down and camped in a village full of many good things. And there were many other villages full of many good things in that plain along the river Tigris.' They also offered shelter, all the more important because the Greeks had burned their tents to reduce their baggage-train (3.3.1). Palaces (3.4.24, 4.4.2, 4.4.7) and a paradeisos (2.4.13) continue to attract Xenophon's notice, though now rarer. Major rivers are again named, and their width measured in plethra or stades. That the two rivers between the territories of the Macronians and the Scytheni (4.8.1–2) are not named is a rare exception. Mountains become a major problem for the army, particularly in Book 4, and are very often mentioned in accounts of fighting against local forces. Yet they are described in purely military terms, and only Mount Theches, the mountain from which the Greeks again saw the sea, is named (4.7.21). Most often the landscape is mentioned in terms of the obstacles that it presents to the Greeks' progress, or the tactical opportunities it offers to hostile forces to impede the Greeks. Otherwise it appears as a source of produce. A special case is the site at Calpes Limen, which Xenophon thought particularly suitable for founding a new city: he describes at some length both the space which could be used, and the crops which the countryside bore (6.4.1–7). From Book 2 onwards finding the way is a problem, and the Greeks generally get the guides they need by capture. Though the Greeks had burned their wagons (3.3.1), they still had a considerable train of pack-animals (e.g. 4.2.13). Xenophon consistently uses the term *hypozygia*, which means literally "draught animals" but can also mean pack-animals (Pikoulas 1995: 364–365) and after 3.3.1 the word clearly refers to pack-animals, as the synonym *skeuophora* 3.2.26 shows. The Greeks therefore needed to find routes which their baggage-train could use (4.1.24, 4.2.10). The Greeks treated some of their captive guides brutally: they caught two of the Carduchi, and when one refused to show them a route, they cut his throat in front of the other, who then agreed to guide them (4.1.23–24). Occasionally guides were provided by temporary allies, sometimes for their own purpose: the ruler of the city Gymnias gave the Greeks a guide who took them through territory hostile to Gymnias and urged them to burn and pillage, which showed – obviously enough, but Xenophon chooses to note the fact – that the guide was acting out of a desire to harm his enemies and not out of friendship for the Greeks (4.7.19–20). Very rarely the Greeks themselves discovered a route: a march without guides is mentioned explicitly at 4.2.24, and on one occasion two young soldiers found a badly needed river-crossing (4.3.10–12). The Greeks also needed interpreters, and apparently found them without much difficulty: Xenophon seldom records how the Greeks came by an interpreter, save for the serendipitous case of the Macronian ex-slave serving in the army as a peltast who came to Xenophon to say that he recognised his fellow-countrymen and then conducted successful negotiations on behalf of the generals (4.8.4–6). The weather is mentioned several times when it creates major problems for the Greeks, particularly when they have to face deep snow and icy winds in the mountains (e.g. 4.5.3–4, 4.5.15–21). This bitter cold cost lives, and Xenophon even notes that at one point the Greeks abandoned men who were suffering from snow-blindness and frost-bite (4.5.12). In Xenophon's narrative however the severe weather does not last for long, even though the army crossed mountain terrain in winter. This anomaly has given rise to considerable modern debate, raising questions also about Xenophon's chronology of the march: the issues are reviewed by Glombiowski 1994. While different solutions have been proposed, it is at any rate safe to accept the judgment of Tuplin (1998, 287): 'Bluntly, the time X[enophon] assigns to Kurdistan/Armenia seems inadequate to match climatic parameters'. The weather occasionally helped the Greeks: at 4.2.7 a convenient early-morning fog allowed a party of Greeks to approach the enemy unseen. As in the first book Xenophon makes little effort to contextualise his account, and rarely refers to anything outside his immediate narrative. Rare exceptions are the deserted cities Larissa (3.4.6–9) Mespila (3.4.10–12), about both of which Xenophon says that they had formerly been inhabited by Medes and that the Persian king, when taking over power from the Medes, had failed to capture them. He also mentions (6.2.2) that at the promontory Acherousias near Heracleia Heracles had descended to Hades to find the dog Cerberus, and that "they" now show as proof a hollow more than two stades long.

During most of the *Anabasis* the Greeks were moving through non-Greek areas, but the peoples whom they encountered as they moved from the upper Tigris through eastern and northern Anatolia were the most alien. Xenophon's description of these communities thus illustrates in the most extreme form how he chose to represent non-Greek cultures. Cartledge (1993, 44) wrote of Xenophon's 'ethnocentric ethnography', and Brulé develops the idea that Xenophon employs 'le modèle hellénique' (1995, 4) to assess what he sees, recognising some familiar features and noting some that are alien. It is of course true that Xenophon writes from a Greek viewpoint, never more obviously than in saying that (5.4.34) 'Those on the march said that those [the Mossynoeci] were the most barbarian they encountered and the furthest removed from Greek standards'. These words of course imply that, even without saying so explicitly, Xenophon has measured other cultures against Greek standards and found them more or less alien, even if not so strikingly non-Greek as the Mossynoeci. It is difficult to quarrel with Brulé's approach (and Tuplin 1999, 333 has broadly approved of it: '... the terms of his analysis are largely unexceptionable'). Xenophon throughout the *Anabasis* remains a Greek looking at aliens.

After looking at how Xenophon describes the physical environment Brulé considers a number of cultural markers: grain, wine, oil, livestock (and especially meat-eating), cities and villages. He then goes on to look at Xenophon the ethnographer, with particular attention to the bellicosity Xenophon noted in several cultures, and to the Mossynoeci. Themes discussed by Brulé are then taken up again by Prestianni Gallimbardo (warfare) and Tripodi (food), whose papers, together with that of Brulé, make up the first section of the book: 'L'un et l'autre'. This approach calls for comment.

These writers are of course well aware that the Greeks had to fight many of the peoples whom they encountered, but they say relatively little about how Xenophon's cultural markers are conditioned by this military context. The Greeks wanted to pass through the territories of these peoples and were willing to fight their way if need be, and on their march the Greeks needed food and shelter. Later, when marching along the south shore of the Black Sea, they wanted other booty as well. Xenophon's account of the cultures the Greeks encountered from the upper Tigris until they left the Black Sea coast (especially in Books 4 and 5) therefore consists largely of marching, fighting, and finding food and shelter. The peoples of the area are presented as helping or opposing the Greeks' passage, and if they opposed it their warlike qualities emerge. Their dwellings and their food appear when the Greeks use them. These cultures are thus described from the viewpoint not merely of a Greek but of a Greek with certain very particular needs. This limited range of interests does not of course prevent Xenophon from showing how different the Cardouchi, say, or the Mossynoeci are from Greeks, but in general he makes little effort to explore other ways in which these cultures might differ from Greeks.

Even within these limited terms of reference what Xenophon says about particular cultures is often ambiguous (Tuplin 1999, 339: 'In *Anabasis*, as in *Hellenica*, ... little is ever black-and-white for long'). Brulé discusses for instance the warlike quality Xenophon saw in several peoples (see Brulé 1995, 15 on "bellicosité", a theme taken up also by Prestianni Gallimbardo). Brulé suggests that attributing an inherently bellicose nature to non-Greek peoples justified the use of warfare against them by the Greeks. Perhaps so, but the Greeks felt justified in attacking anyone they met. When the Greeks approached the Tibareni, the Tibareni offered gifts of hospitality (*xenia*) and clearly hoped to avoid warfare, but the Greek generals wanted to pillage the territory of the Tibareni and refused the *xenia*. It was only after numerous sacrifices had failed to produce favourable omens for an attack that the Greeks abandoned their plan of pillage and accepted the *xenia* (5.5.2–3). With that episode one can compare one of the last episodes of the *Anabasis*, an utterly unprovoked attack led by Xenophon himself on the family and property of the wealthy Persian Asidates (7.8.9–22). Xenophon also, by his own report (5.5.23), told ambassadors from the Greek city Sinope that if necessary the army would ally with Corylas of Paphlagonia against Sinope. In fact bellicosity is a quality Xenophon reports only in certain of the peoples whom the Greeks encountered, and in varying degrees. The Carduchi, for instance, who were well equipped to fight from a distance on their native mountains but could not face the Greeks hand-to-hand (4.2.27–28, 3.2), were warlike (*polemikous*, 3.5.16) and inflicted more suffering on the Greeks than did Artaxerxes and Tissaphernes (4.3.2), but the Chalybes, who did fight the Greeks hand-to-hand, were the most warlike (*alkimotatoi*) people the Greeks met

(4.7.15). Xenophon in fact appears to be recording a scale of bellicosity, measured by capacity to face the Greeks on equal terms.

Ungreekness is also a complex quality, as can be seen from the case of the Mossynoeci. They were not armed like Greeks, but had a weapon with a spearhead at one end and a ball at the other, an iron axe, and a wickerwork shield covered in white oxhide. They wore a tunic ending above the knee and a leather cap with a tuft on top. Before attacking their force lined up in two rows facing each other and sang (5.4.12–14). Left to their own devices, they did not manoeuvre in orderly Greek fashion: those friendly to the Greeks attacked a fort held by other Mossynoeci and were driven off with heavy losses, as were a number of Greeks who had followed them in disorder, whereupon the Greeks attacked in proper formation and captured the enemy position (5.4.14–26). The food of the Mossynoeci was ungreek: they used dolphin fat in place of oil, and made great use of chestnuts boiled or baked like bread. They even had bread reputedly handed down from father to son (5.4.27–29). The children of prosperous Mossynoeci were fed on boiled chestnuts so that they became fat, almost as wide as they were tall, and were very pale with flowers tattooed on chest and back (5.4.32). The Mossynoeci wanted to have sex in public with women (*hetaerae*) travelling with the Greek army, and generally did in public what men would do in private, and behaved in private as if they were in company, laughing by themselves and stopping anywhere to dance (5.4.33–34). All this has a satisfactorily ungreek quality, flagged much more explicitly than is usual in the *Anabasis*: these are, after all, the most ungreek of all the peoples encountered by the Greeks.

Yet the Mossynoeci have very close links to the Greeks of Trapezus. They have a proxenus, the Trapezuntian Timesitheus (5.4.1), which implies regular dealings with Trapezus on terms Greeks recognised. Indeed Timesitheus is able to manipulate the Mossynoeci. Among them two groups were evidently competing for power at the time when the Greeks arrived. Their king lived in a wooden tower at the highest point in what the Mossynoeci regarded as their metropolis, and whichever group controlled the metropolis was considered to have power over all the Mossynoeci (5.4.15, 26). (It may well be that Xenophon had not fully understood the situation among the Mossynoeci, or had failed to describe it fully, for there was another king in a fort in front of the metropolis (5.4.26), and "king" may not be a helpful term). At any rate Timesitheus exploited the division among the Mossynoeci. He first negotiated on behalf of the Greeks with the Mossynoeci nearer Trapezus, to see whether they would allow the army to cross their territory, but they refused. He then went to the others, presumably farther west, and brought their leaders back to the Greeks, who made an alliance with them against the first group. This alliance was successful, and the friendly Mossynoeci allowed the Greeks passage through their territory (5.4.2–5.1). It is notable that the Mossynoecan metropolis was apparently situated very close to the edge of their territory, near the frontier with the Greek city Cerasus, which was, like Trapezus, a colony and dependency of

Sinope (5.3.2, 4.8.22). We may also recall that those Mossynoeci allied to the Greeks first made a very unsuccessful attack on the others using their own methods of warfare (5.4.16), but then took part in a second attack with the Greeks drawn up in Greek formation (5.4.22). The Mossynoeci, however exotic, were under a good deal of Greek influence.

In that respect the Mossynoeci were not alone. When the Greeks reached the territory of the Colchians they dispersed a force of Colchians drawn up against them, and then pillaged Colchian territory from their camp at Trapezus (4.8.9–19, 23). The Trapezuntians however negotiated with the Greeks on behalf of the Colchians, who offered gifts of hospitality and oxen (4.8.24). The situation that resulted may have retained some tension, since Colchians who had been driven from their homes occupied heights above the Greek camp (5.2.1), but Xenophon claimed later (5.5.14) that the Greeks had spared the non-Greek friends of Trapezus. When the Greeks, while still camped at Trapezus, looked for communities from which they could seize provisions, the Trapezuntians in fact took care to direct them not against communities friendly to Trapezus from which it would have been easy to take supplies, but instead against the Drilae, who lived in mountainous and difficult terrain and were the most warlike of the peoples of the Black sea coast (5.2.2). (Here bellicosity seems to be mainly a measure of the Greeks' inconvenience). It is clear that the Trapezuntians and their non-Greek neighbours were heavily involved with each other.

The Greeks with Xenophon also showed a capacity to adapt to non-Greek conditions. On one occasion the Greek commanders entertained Paphlagonian ambassadors to dinner, inviting such other members of the army as they thought most fitting. Xenophon describes the evening at length (6.1.3–13). Oxen and other animals were sacrificed and there was copious food. The diners reclined on *stibades*, couches of straw or foliage, and drank from local horn drinking-vessels. Tripodi (1995, 52) sees these couches and horn vessels as in Xenophon's eyes degrading: given the good humour which evidently reigned during the evening, it seems better to regard them as makeshift local replacements accepted by the Greeks as approximating to what they would have used at home. The evening went well. As entertainment several of the soldiers danced. When two Thracians, in a dance, skilfully acted out a killing, the Paphlagonian guests cried out in alarm; but when Paphlagonians commented on the fact that all the dances were performed in arms, a dancing-girl (who had been bought by an Arcadian) also danced in arms. The Paphlagonians asked whether women fought with the Greeks, and were told that it was the women who had turned the Persian king out of the Greek camp. In this relaxed mood the evening ended. The following day the good humour persisted, and the Greeks and the Paphlagonians agreed that neither side would harm the other. This episode shows Greeks and non-Greeks mixing easily, as Tuplin has suggested (1999, 338), and in a setting as Greek as the army's resources would allow.

Earlier the Greeks had made themselves very much at home in villages in Armenia (4.5.7–6.1). They came on these villages at a time of heavy snow and bitter cold, and took refuge there for several days. Each commander took his men to a different village, and Xenophon notes that one of his officers went ahead with some men to secure their village with all its inhabitants; otherwise there is a remarkable absence of any mention of resistance or hostility to the Greeks, though the army must have been devastating the stores of the villagers. There seems to have been no local military force to threaten the Greeks. The alien nature of the villages is noted. The houses were underground, with an entrance from above like a well. There were also entrances for livestock, and in the houses were goats, sheep, cattle, and poultry. There was wheat, barley, and vegetables, and Xenophon also records barley beer (or wine, as he calls it) kept in large jars (which he calls kraters) with grains of barley floating on top and drunk from the jars through straws. Once installed the Greeks made the most of the occasion: Xenophon mentions going from one village to another and everywhere finding the men feasting, with meat of lamb, kid, suckling-pig, and chicken, and both wheat and barley bread. They had developed the habit of drinking the beer not through the straws provided, but by lapping it direct from the jar. In Cheirisophus' village Xenophon found the men feasting with garlands of dried herbs on their heads, served by young Armenians with whom they communicated in sign language. The setting is obviously outlandish, but the Greeks have made themselves very much at home there.

Brulé and others have been right to identify the ways in which Xenophon expresses the otherness of the cultures he came across during the *Anabasis*. Behind the Mossynoeci, the most ungreek of all the communities the Greeks met, were numerous other peoples all ungreek in some degree. Yet Xenophon and other Greeks show a readiness to adapt to these alien circumstances when opportunity offers. Of course the encounters with the barbaroi were often purely military and hostile, though the hostility came sometimes from the Greek side. Yet it was possible to come to terms with barbaroi, and find substitutes for the normal Greek life-style.

The march was intended to take the Greeks back to Hellas. It was long and hard, and Xenophon records several occasions when the Greeks find it difficult to make progress. Yet the cumulative fatigue of their march is not mentioned until the possibility of sailing rather than marching presents itself on the Black Sea coast. Then Leon of Thurii declares that he wants to sail home, lying comfortably like Odysseus (5.1.2), a phrase which evokes not only the *Odyssey* but also the theme of *nostos*, return, so important in the *Anabasis*. The intention of the Greeks had always been to return to Hellas (e.g. 1.3.14, 14.7, 2.3.26, 3.1.2, 3.1.26). Hellas is not defined in the *Anabasis*, but Xenophon evidently understood it in a geographical sense as the area of concentrated Greek settlement. Isolated communities outside the area of concentration were Greek but not did not form part of Hellas; at Harmene, the port of Sinope, with the Greek cities Trapezus, Cerasus, and Cotyora to the east of them, the Greeks were 'getting near Hellas' (6.1.17), and farther west near Calpes Limen, having also passed Heracleia, they were 'at the doors of Hellas' (6.5.23). Though Xenophon does not explicitly say so, the army was evidently back in Hellas when it came near to Byzantium. Expressions of a desire to reach Hellas or to go home (*oikade*) then disappear from the text, apart from references to Xenophon's personal return home (7.6.11, 7.6.33, and 7.6.57). The Greeks had reached the goal of their whole march.

Yet Hellas was not a happy place for the Greeks with Xenophon. They were a large and dangerous force, and were treated with suspicion by the Persian satrap Pharnabazus (7.1.2) and by various Spartan officials (e.g. Anaxibius, 7.1.7, and Aristarchus, 7.2.6). They took service with the Thracian ruler Seuthes, moving again beyond the fringes of Hellas, but had great difficulty in getting paid (7.5.1–7.7.56). They were then hired by the Spartan Thibron (7.8.24), at which point Xenophon chose to close his account. Hellas, as presented in Book 7 of the *Anabasis*, is the Greeks' home, but it is not a happy place.

In conclusion, Xenophon's interest in travel, as revealed by the *Anabasis*, can be summarised as follows. Naturally enough he pays great attention, particularly in Books 2–7, to military matters. He had of course military experience before he joined Cyrus' march, and may well have been already disposed to assess territory in military terms. That would account for his tendency to record settlements in very stereotyped terms, brief but sufficient to suggest their resources. However, it would not explain why, for instance, he takes such different views of mountains and rivers. Mountains are worth mentioning only if they matter for military purposes, and even then are not worth naming, apart from Mt. Theches. Rivers on the other hand are recorded and named, and their width is assessed, though they are seen from the viewpoint of a traveller by land, and not as waterways. Xenophon clearly had a perception of landscape in which rivers were inherently important while mountains were not. Xenophon shows only a very limited interest in the mythical and historical associations of the places he travels through, and shows strong ethnographic interest only when he is among very ungreek peoples, though even then his interest in their way of life is skewed towards military concerns. He is, however, willing to adapt and to make the most of what material comforts these alien communities can offer. He is in general a perceptive but highly selective observer. He is in fact little interested in the practical details of travel, except insofar as they take on military importance, but he takes a considerable but distinctly idiosyncratic interest in what travel reveals.

Acknowledgements

I am grateful for comments offered when this paper was delivered, and for assistance generously given then and later by Christopher Tuplin. Remaining faults are of course my own.

Bibliography

Briant, P. (ed.) (1995) *Dans les pas des Dix-Mille* (Toulouse) (= *Pallas* 43 [1995]).

Cartledge, P. (1993) *The Greeks* (Oxford).

Geysels, L. (1974) 'Πόλις οἰκουμένη dans l'*Anabase* de Xénophon', *Les Études Classiques* 42, 29–38.

Glombiowski, K. (1994) "The campaign of Cyrus the Younger and the retreat of the 'Ten Thousand': the chronology." *Pomoerium* 1 [electronic journal without pagination].

Lendle, O. (1995) *Kommentar zu Xenophons Anabasis* (Darmstadt).

Nielsen, T. H. (2000) 'Xenophon's use of the word *polis* in the *Anabasis*', in P. Flensted-Jensen (ed.) *Further studies in the ancient Greek polis,* 133–139 (Stuttgart).

Stronk, J. P. (1995) *The Ten Thousand in Thrace: an archaeological and historical commentary on Xenophon's* Anabasis *Books VI.iii-vi – VII* (Amsterdam).

Tuplin, C. (1997) 'Achaemenid arithmetic: numerical problems in Persian history', *Topoi* Supp. 1, 365–421.

Tuplin, C. (1998) Reviews of P. Krentz *Xenophon: Hellenika 2.3.11–4.2.8* and O. Lendle *Kommentar zu Xenophons Anabasis: Bücher 1–7, Classical Review* 48, 286–288.

Tuplin, C. (1999) 'On the track of the Ten Thousand', *Revue des Études Anciennes* 101, 331–366.

Travelling by Land in Ancient Greece

Yanis A. Pikoulas

What is travel in the ancient world?

It is necessary, by way of introduction to my paper, to offer a definition of the term *travel*, especially for the ancient world, because such a definition would be useful for the purpose of my presentation: the new evidence of land transportation, especially that of the carriage-road network, throughout the landscape of Greece. What, then, is travel in the ancient world (cf. Purcell 1999)?

I believe that travel in its most simple and basic meaning must denote the situation in which one leaves temporarily his permanent place of living and working to move somewhere else – independent of the reasons for this action. Of course we need to define the difference between simple moving and travel, in order to avoid misunderstandings. I think that the main difference between moving and travel lies in the fact that during travel one sleeps away from home in a distant location or a foreign land. So, he who spends the night far away from his permanent residence, is called a traveller. The need to spend a night in a distant location depends on the distance to be covered: the number of nights increases according to the distance, as more kilometres mean more nights away from home. However, moving from one house to another, i.e. to a cottage for the harvest or other agricultural activities – a practice very common in ancient but also in modern Greece until the middle of the 20th century – cannot be called travel, as the parameter of the distant location or the foreign land is absent. Travel, therefore, in its most simple version is any temporary move of a person from his home to another, remote place where he has to stay overnight – regardless of the reasons for such a move or the form of transport used by the traveller.

Having established what travel is, we may safely specify the reasons for travelling. Of course we refer to ancient Greece, although the basic reasons did not changed for centuries and survived up until the 19th century of our era. The causes that forced someone, willingly or not, to move temporarily from his home to a foreign place are mainly two: commerce and worship, to which tourism, *theoria* in ancient Greek, should also be included (LSJ s.v.).

Lionel Casson in his basic manual *Travel in the Ancient World* (Casson 1994) defined clearly and described vividly these causes of travelling, to which we could add one more, i.e. war. I am aware that this view may cause objections. Was participation to a military expedition actually travel? I believe that undoubtedly it was, and two examples may suffice: is it not a fact that the travelling experiences of the majority of the Spartans were gained during their expeditions all around Greece and Asia Minor? Moreover, how many men, mercenaries from Arcadia or Crete, were travelling to seek money and wider experiences by their spear and sword? It is noteworthy that the modern Greek word *taxeidion* is a diminutive of the ancient word *taxis*, a term mainly used for military affairs and denoting "order or disposition of an army, body of soldiers, post or place in the line of battle, etc." (LSJ *s.v.*).

Concerning the term for travel, there is the ancient Greek word, the same as the modern one, *Tax(e)idion*, already known since the 2nd c. AD (LSJ Suppl. *s.v.*); there is also the synonym *apodemia*, that means "going or being abroad" (LSJ *s.v.*).

The causes of travel are four: commerce, worship, war and tourism, and the ways to travel are two: by sea or by land.

Ways of travelling by land

By land a person could travel on foot, on pack animals or by cart. Already much has been written on the first two means of transportation and for this reason I have nothing more to add: from the remote past until the middle of the 20th c. walking and riding on pack animals – usually a donkey or a mule and rarely a horse – were the exclusive means of transportation.

There is, however, new evidence of land transportation by cart, especially that of the carriage- or cart-road network, throughout the landscape of ancient Greece. Since the '80s and in view of this new evidence I have been supporting a revision of our conceptions about the role of the cart in transportation and travel (Pikoulas 1995 and 1999).

The new evidence for wheel-cart roads and land transport

Today we know that a very dense network of carriage roads crisscrossed the Greek landscape and ensured communication even between isolated settlements: all around the Peloponnese (Pikoulas 1995, 1999 and 1999c), Attica, Central Greece (Pikoulas 1992–98b), Thessaly (Pikoulas 2002 and 2002c), Western Greece or the Cyclades (Kazamiakis and Pikoulas 1999, Pikoulas 2003) I have located and investigated roads for wheeled traffic. Thus, it is not an exaggeration to suppose that in ancient Greece the cart had a share equal to that of the ship as a means of transportation.

Transportation by land with various kinds of carts amounted to over three quarters of the whole volume of transportation; that means that only one quarter of transportation was carried out by pack animals or on very special occasions by men known as *achthophoroi* or *skeyophoroi* (LSJ s.v.). Of course, such a hypothesis is somewhat approximate, but, at any rate, I believe that it is close to reality and could be accepted as a rough estimate.

Today, having investigated wheel-ruts of ancient carriage-roads at every pass of Taygetus, Parnon, and Artemision mountains in the Peloponnese, I have come to the conclusion that our scholarly stereotypes which have prevailed for years in the bibliography must be revised. I intend to come back to this subject later.

In what follows, my main focus is on *extra muros* land-transportation by cart in ancient Greece from the Archaic period to Late Antiquity, a period when the whole system changed dramatically. After the collapse of the Roman empire and the inability of the state to maintain the road-network, the cart was gradually abandoned and was replaced by the pack animal, which was exclusively used from the 5th c. AD onwards. I do not intend to mention the technical details and problems of dating, or the creation and evolution of the road-network, since full information may be found in my relevant publications (Pikoulas 1995, 1998 and 1999). Nevertheless, I am going to present briefly the data of the ancient Greek carriage-road and its dating and, at the end, there is a map of Greece with an updated road-network (Fig. 3), to illustrate my suggestion that a revision of former opinions is long-overdue and imperative. What is then an ancient Greek carriage-road? And, after all these twenty years of research, what knowledge have we gained in the field?

What is an ancient Greek road? The road-network of ancient Greece

Known for their numerous technological achievements, the Greeks also made significant advances in the field of land transport and communication. Recent research (Pikoulas 1995 and 1999) has shown that the Greeks applied high-standard road-construction techniques. Basic principles of road-construction know-how must either have been inherited from the Mycenaeans, or – more likely – imported from the East. These principles were improved and used to create a dense road-network, innovative in its conception and realization, thus securing unimpeded wheeled communication over the greatest part of Greek territory. The Romans' reputation as pioneering and exceptional road makers is thus subject to reconsideration. Revision of modern bibliography is also necessary since it continues to ignore the subject of ancient Greek roads.

We have to focus on the cart-wheel road-network, i.e. the roads that were constructed exclusively for the operation of animal-driven carts. Obviously, there were also many pathways used by pedestrians and pack animals which constitute a separate category of roads; continuous use of these pathways, however, and the fact that their mode of construction always remained the same, does not permit secure dating. A different category is the *intra muros* roads of a city; urban roads were usually laid with condensed earth/dirt mixed with gravel or sherds. Stone paved roads were rare and seem to have been introduced in Roman times. In what follows I present my research data on the cart-road-network, that is, the *extra muros* roads that crossed the territory of different city-states.

The cart-wheel road was constructed for the use of carts regardless of the type

Fig. 3 Map of Greece.

and number (two/four) of wheels. The road's principal remains are the artificial bed with obvious traces of rock cutting, and the carved wheel-tracks with a standard gauge of 1.40m. (Pikoulas 1998).

By investigating the remains of ancient road-beds, and, more importantly, of wheel-tracks, it is possible to map the routes followed by the ancient road-network. Wheel-tracks are normally extant only on rocky surfaces since they were not bound to survive on exposed softer ground; recently however, wheel-tracks on soft earth have been discovered in the course of excavating activities for modern road construction (Schiza 2002; Pikoulas 2002). So, when constructing a cart-road, the Greeks used dirt mixed with gravel or sherds in order to form the road-bed on soft and flat soil whereas on rocky soil and especially at difficult spots, such as steep ground, curves and junctions, the Greeks carved the road bed and formed wheel-tracks. In other words, the cart followed a fixed course and moved with its wheels within the tracks without deviating. This was a noteworthy achievement of the Greek road-makers. In fact the Greek cart-road can be thought of as a "negative railway": just as modern trains run on the raised railway, in a similar way the Greek cart moved consistently in the wheel-tracks, that is, the ruts that were carved in the rock (0.05m. to 0.015m. wide and 0.01m. to 0.30m. or more deep, depending on the nature of the rocky surface). This is particularly evident at forks or branches, *ektropes* (LSJ s.v. 2) in ancient Greek, which are identical with the points of modern railways and were carved so that a change in the course of the cart would be possible.

Since the network allowed for the operation of only one vehicle at a time, there was no possibility of simultaneous use of a cart-road by two carts coming from opposite directions. In such cases one of the two carts had to come out of the wheel-tracks and give way to the other cart, an operation impossible on steep ground especially when the cart was loaded. If we recall the famous fatal dispute between Oedipus and Laius (Soph. *OT* 800–812), we can get an idea of how such disputes would commonly take place, as is the case nowadays, when two carts coming from opposite directions met in an extremely narrow street (cf. Pikoulas 1992–98b). Presumably, there must have been regulations concerning these matters, which have not survived in literature. I assume on the basis of the evidence that at the key points of a difficult route there must have stood individuals, "watchers", whose duty was to inform the driver from a distance (by either visual or sound signal) whether a particular section of the road was free. Obviously, things were much easier with roads running through the plains; besides, in some of the latter areas there is evidence of roads running in parallel courses. There were also some rare exceptions to the rule, e.g. the widening of the *Skironis* road, leading from Megara to Corinth, by Hadrian (Pausanias 1.44.6).

Furthermore, it should be stated that no ancient road in the Greek countryside was stone-paved. Stone-paved roads in Greece are only found in the urban parts of cities and belong to the Roman period. The only exception is the *Diolkos* of Korinth, which was basically a specialized stone-paved cart-road with a gauge of 1.50m.

(Raepsaet 1993). In general, Greek road makers would undertake to construct only what was absolutely necessary, e.g. bridges, great retaining walls, etc.; their building activities conformed to the peculiarities of the natural landscape.

On the contrary, the Romans established solidly founded stone-paved roads and engaged in large-scale public works that altered significantly the nature of the landscape. It should be noted, however, that on rocky surfaces Roman roads are neither built on specially constructed foundations nor paved with stone. The wheel-tracks were not artificially created but were formed over time by the continuous passage of vehicles. A typical example of a Roman road in Greek territory is the *Via Egnatia*.

I believe that the evidence now available of the road-network in mainland Greece alters the generally accepted picture. Specialized study of Greek roads only started in the 1980s, and is still largely ignored in the bibliography, which considers the Romans as the pioneers and the road-makers par excellence. Without wishing to underestimate Rome's contribution to the development – but not the invention – of road-making techniques, I think that the *opinio communis* about who laid the foundations in the field of road construction should now be revised.

In other words, I would like to point out that although the needs of Greeks and Romans that were met by the construction of road-networks were similar, Greek and Roman roads are very different from the point of view of construction technique. Since the Greek cart-road-network existed a few centuries before that of Rome, I think that the latter did not evolve independently of the former. The Romans must have inherited the relevant know-how from the Greeks and not from the Etruscans (Casson 1994, 163). In their turn, they developed and standardized it.

I note that the road-network covered almost the entire Greek territory. It is surprising to observe the boldness of Greek road-makers in creating roads on steep slopes, often exceeding 10–15%, or in the alpine zone e.g. the road running along the mountain crest of north Taygetus at an altitude of 1600m. (Pikoulas 1988, 151–153 and 221–224). In addition to remains of road-construction there are the remains of bridges, which are very few if one takes into account the density of the road-network. The poor evidence of river bridges should most likely be attributed to the fact that they were made of wood, a material that is not likely to survive (Pikoulas 1990–91b, 146–7; Pikoulas 1999, 311; Pikoulas 2002b). Finally, a unique piece of road-work is the artificial pass that was carved on a mountain crest in order to provide for the road from Sparta/Mantineia leading to Argos/Korinth. This artificial pass is located at a level of 300m above the tunnel of Mount Artemision of the new Korinth-Tripolis highway (Pikoulas 1995, 104–109 and 288–290, Figs 4–9).

Occasionally the literary sources offer valuable information for our knowledge of the Greek road-network. Significant gaps are covered by scanty archaeological evidence, especially by drawing inferences from the more complete evidence of the Roman world. Modern parallels can also at times be of some use but most important is the pursuit of the study of actual remains of ancient roads such as wheel-tracks, forks, supporting constructions, bridges and so on.

I shall not discuss here the complex subject of the different kinds of vehicles or of the draft animals that were used during antiquity, nor shall I address some other special themes, such as the medieval roads and system of land transportation, the *kalderimia*, or the horseshoe, as they fall beyond the scope of the present paper (Pikoulas 1999d).

Today, after two decades of investigation and study of ancient roads, we have gained a good idea of the road-network all around Greece. As you can see on the map (Fig. 3), my study has covered a large part of the Peloponnese, i.e. the whole of Argolis, Korinthia, Arkadia, Lakonia, and part of Messenia and Achaia; it has also covered part of Central Greece (Boeotia, eastern Phokis), Thessaly, Epirus, Macedonia (Pikoulas 1997 and 2002d), ancient Thrace (modern eastern Macedonia; see Pikoulas 2001, 189–195) and the Aegean islands (Anaphi, Kythera, Kea, Naxos, Tenos; see Pikoulas 1990–91, 1999b; Kazamiakis and Pikoulas 1999; Pikoulas 2003).

I have spent many pages of my earlier monograph trying to date a cart-road and I have especially re-examined this topic in a recent congress (Pikoulas 1999, 306–9 and 2001b). I shall present briefly the whole problem of dating the creation of the Greek road network.

The ancient Greek road system, beyond doubt, belongs to the historical period starting in the 7th c. BC and ending in the 4th to 5th c. AD

I would like also to point out the military character of the road-network. According to our data the soldiers were the first to use the road network, followed by the merchants. In any case, no-one, either individual citizens or groups of wealthy people, could afford the construction or maintenance of such a large-scale network, although they were always willing to take advantage of it. I have already stated that the construction of the road-network was actually due to a centralized powerful state. Assyria, Persia and Rome had similar networks and their study gives us convincing answers to many questions.

The remains of the ancient road-network in Greece suggest that it was a systematic operation undertaken by state authority: the roads were properly and regularly repaired and parallel routes were provided along central axes of communication. It is logical to assume that such a sophisticated and complete road-network would presuppose a powerful central authority that would be in charge of a project of this scale with a view to provide efficient transportation, communication and maintenance services. I have come to the conclusion that the Peloponnesian League, with Sparta as its motivating force, must have been the central authority that created and supervised the cart-road network in the Peloponnese. The evidence suggests that the creation of the network is to be dated to the seventh century (at the latest), with the middle of the 6th century, when the Peloponnesian League was consolidated, being a landmark for its later development; this is when the road-network is extended with the creation of new and alternative roadways and the practice spreads to the whole of the Peloponnese and the rest of Greece.

Attika, Central Greece and the Cyclades possessed a similar cart-road system. I have recently offered the hypothesis that possibly the "know-how" of constructing a wheel-road reached Lakonia, the Cyclades and Attika from Ionia as early as the Geometric or the early Archaic period. In these areas it was developed, and later spread out to the rest of Greece. Although we have as yet only indications but no proof, the extant evidence may suggest the following link: Mesopotamia–Assyria–Persia–Ionia–Greece.

In any case, basic skills in road construction must have been transmitted to the Romans by the Greek western colonies; the Romans in their turn developed this knowledge admirably.

In the Peloponnese, and in the rest of Southern Greece, there are no exclusively Roman road constructions, or at least I have not located any. Cases such as the *Via Egnatia* road in Northern Greece or the widening of the Skironis road by Hadrian (Paus. 1.44.6) are the exceptions. Obviously the sixteen known miliaria from the Peloponnese (Pikoulas 1992–98) or the twenty-four from Thessaly (Mottas and Decourt 1997) are a strong indication; however, they do not attest new road construction, but only the maintenance of the existing roads.

Revising Lionel Casson

In light of the foregoing presentation, I believe it is possible, if not imperative, to revise some of Lionel Casson's assessments and discussions in his manual on *Travel in the Ancient World* and to begin the process required for reevaluating the subject-matter of travel in antiquity. I present a few characteristic passages taken from Casson's manual about land-transportation that must perforce be revised:

> *'Even the Mycenaeans did not have carriage roads between the places involved, and there certainly were none in the dark age, or for that matter, throughout most of Greek history (46)*
>
> *'Until the coming of the railroad, the water was the only feasible medium for heavy transport and the most convenient for long distance travel' (65).*
>
> *'A traveller in Greece of the fifth and fourth century BC thought twice before taking along any vehicle, light or heavy, since roads that could handle wheeled traffic were by no means to be found everywhere. A unified network of highways could hardly be expected in a land diced up into tiny, fiercely independent states. What is more, few of them had the resources to go in for proper road-building even within their own confines;... Besides, Greece is so rocky and mountainous that the cost of laying good roads would have been prohibitive, no matter how wealthy a state was' (68).*

'The Romans learned the art of road building from excellent teachers, the Etruscans. ... They [sc. Etruscans*] taught Rome how to make sewers, aqueducts, bridges, and – more to our present point – properly drained, and carefully surfaced dirt roads. The Romans went one key step further: they added paving' (163).*

Conclusions

To conclude: revision and reevaluation of the commonly accepted scholarly view of ancient Greek land-transportation is not only necessary, but urgent as well. Carriage-roads had crisscrossed the entire Greek landscape from the end of the 7th c. BC until Late Antiquity. A fairly good impression of this is gained from the map of Greece with an updated road-network (Fig. 3). There is no question that the cart was the principal means of land-transportation used by ancient Greeks, whereas travelling on pack animals and on foot were only supplementary means. And in that sense, the cart in land-transportation paralleled the ship in sea-transportation.

Acknowledgments

There is an old friend at Nottingham, an Arcadian friend since 1982, Jim Roy, and I thank him for the invitation to speak at Nottingham. Let this paper be the *elachiston antidoron* to him for his friendship.

September, 2002.

Bibliography

Casson, L. (1994, 2nd edition) *Travel in the Ancient World* (Baltimore and London).
Kazamiakis, K. and Y. A. Pikoulas (1999) 'Αμαξήλατος οδός Κέας', *Ηόρος* 13, 177–188.
Mottas, F. and J.-C. Decourt (1997) 'Voies et milliaires romains de Thessalie', *BCH* 121, 311–354.
Pikoulas, Y. A. (1988) *Η Νότια Μεγαλοπολιτική Χώρα, από τον 8° π.Χ. ως τον 4° μ.Χ. αιώνα. Συμβολή στην τοπογραφία της*, *Ηόρος*: Η Μεγάλη Βιβλιοθήκη no 1 (Athens).
Pikoulas, Y. A. (1990–91) 'Αρχαιολογικές σημειώσεις από την Ανάφη, Ηόρος 8–9, 119–130.
Pikoulas, Y. A. (1990–91b) 'Το Τορθύνειον της Αρκαδίας', *Ηόρος* 8–9, 135–152.
Pikoulas, Y. A. (1995) *Οδικό δίκτυο και άμυνα*, *Ηόρος*: Η Μεγάλη Βιβλιοθήκη no 2 (Athens).
Pikoulas, Y. A. (1997) 'Η αμαξήλατος οδός στη Βόρεια Ελλάδα, in *Αφιέρωμα στον N. G. L. Hammond*, Makedonika Suppl. no. 7, 357–363 (Thessaloniki).
Pikoulas, Y. A. (1992–98) 'Miliaria Peloponnesi', *Ηόρος* 10–12, 305–311.
Pikoulas, Y. A. (1992–98b) 'Σχιστή Οδός', *Ηόρος* 10–12, 579–582.
Pikoulas, Y. A. (1998) *'Η αμαξήλατος οδός στον αρχαία Ελλάδα. Τεχνολογία και συναφή προβλήματα'*, in Proceedings of 1st International Conference Ancient Greek Technology, Thessaloniki 4–7.9.97, 615–621 (Thessaloniki).
Pikoulas, Y. A. (1999) 'The Road–Network of Arkadia', in T. H. Nielsen and J. Roy (eds.) *Defining Ancient Arkadia*, Acts of the Copenhagen Polis Centre 6, 248–319 (Copenhagen).
Pikoulas, Y. A. (1999) 'Κυθηραϊκά', *Ηόρος* 13, 71–80.
Pikoulas, Y. A. (1999c) 'Κλειτορία: διαβάσεις και άμυνα', *Ηόρος* 13, 137–154.
Pikoulas, Y. A. (1999d) 'Από την άμαξα στο υποζύγιο και από την οδό στο καλντερίμι [Δρόμοι και μεταφορές στο Βυζάντιο και την Τουρκοκρατία]', *Ηόρος* 13, 245–258.

Pikoulas, Y. A. (2001) *Η χώρα των Πιέρων. Συμβολή στην τοπογραφία της*, Municipality Piereon Kavalas and KERA-NHRF, Athens.

Pikoulas, Y. A. (2001b) 'Το οδικό δίκτυο της Λακωνίας. Χρονολόγηση, απαρχές και εξέλιξη', in V. Mitsopoulos-Leon (ed.), *Forschungen in der Peloponnes*, Akten des Symposions anläβlich der Feier "100 Jahre Österreichisches Archäologisches Institut Athen", Athen 5–7.3.1998, 325–330 (Athens).

Pikoulas, Y. A. (2002) 'Η "Βελεστινόστρατα". Συμβολή στο οδικό δίκτυο της αρχαίας Θεσσαλίας, in D. Karaberopoulos (ed.) *Acts of the 3rd International Congress "Φεραί–Βελεστίνο–Ρήγας"*, Velestino 2–5.10.97, *Υπέρεια* 3, 147–158 and 1009–1012.

Pikoulas, Y. A. (2002b) 'Ολες οι γέφυρες δεν ήταν λίθινες...', in Acts of Symposium "Ancient Greek Bridges", EMAET, Athens 20.5.02, 97–102 (Athens).

Pikoulas, Y. A. (2002c) 'Από τη Νικόπολη στη Θεσσαλία', in Acts of 2nd International Nicopolis Symposium, Preveza September 11–15, 2002, Preveza [forthcoming].

Pikoulas, Y. A. (2002d) 'Οι διαβάσεις της Πίνδου', in *Ancient Macedonia VII*, Papers read at the seventh International Symposium held in Thessaloniki October 15–20, 2002, Thessaloniki [forthcoming].

Pikoulas, Y. A. (2003) 'Αμαξήλατος οδός στη Νάξο', *Ηόρος* 14–16, 363–368.

Purcell, N. (1999) sv. Travel, in *OCD*^{3}.

Raepsaet, G. (1993) 'Le Diolkos de l'Isthme à Corinthe: son tracé, son fonctionnement', *BCH* 117, 233–266.

Schiza, E. (2002) 'Η αρχαία οδός Φερών – Παγασών', in D. Karaberopoulos (ed.) *Acts of the 3rd International Congress "Φεραί–Βελεστίνο–Ρήγας"*, Velestino 2–5.10.97, *Υπέρεια* 3, 173–187.

Representations of Means of Transport on Reliefs in the Collection of the National Archaeological Museum at Athens

Eleni Kourinou

The means of transport used by the ancient Greeks obviously depended on the modes of travel. The two possible ways to travel were by land and by sea and according to this criterion the means of transport fall into two categories: land and maritime.

In what follows I intend to present how these means of transport were depicted in ancient Greek sculpture. Since this is an extensive and complex subject, I am going to focus especially on reliefs housed in the National Archaeological Museum at Athens, which offer, nevertheless, a very representative sample of the relevant iconography.

In spite of the variety characterizing the iconographical themes depicted in ancient Greek sculpture – statues, funerary and votive reliefs – means of transport were not particularly favoured subjects. Representations of means of land transport in relief sculpture are extremely rare, with the exception of the representations of chariots or of horses, during the classical and hellenistic periods. When they were depicted, for example, on grave monuments, they were usually indicators of the deceased's social position.

Although representations of pack animals such as donkeys are not to be found on classical grave reliefs, and the oxen, which are often represented on votive reliefs, are always depicted as being led for sacrifice with no depiction of the cart or of the wagon that they might had once pulled, there exist, surprisingly enough, some representations of mules. In the National Archaeological Museum are housed two marble votive reliefs dated to the beginning of the 4th century BC on which mules are depicted. They both were found at the Athenian Asclepieion. The first relief [inv. nr. 1341], known as "the coachman's dedication"[1] dated to the first decades of the 4th century BC, is a unique piece, especially for the classical and hellenistic periods, with the representation of a coachman by his cart, led by mules (Fig. 4). On the second relief [inv. nr. 1358] two mules are represented. According to Svoronos' interpretation, followed by Beschi (1969, 94, fig. 4), they were led by Telemachos and pulled a cart on which the sacred serpent of the God Asclepius was transferred to Athens.

Concerning especially the Roman period, it must be noted that the National

Fig. 4 National Archaeological Museum (NM) inv. nr. 1342, 'the coachman's dedication'.

Archaeological Museum of Athens has no reliefs, votive or funerary, which show means of land transport, such as pack animals, carts, or wagons. In North Greece also, as far as I know, the number of such reliefs is very limited.

The case is slightly different for maritime means of transport. This paper deals with these and focuses on their representation on reliefs housed in the National Archaeological Museum at Athens.

The representation of the ship has a very long history, as it was a favourite pictorial theme from the Bronze Age. Despite the fact that ships were often depicted on vases from the Geometric and Archaic periods onwards,[2] although always in the context of a myth, as for example the Argonauts and the Argo, episodes of the epic circle etc., they were very rarely represented in sculpture and least of all in funerary and votive reliefs.[3] It seems that during the early period ships were connected in men's minds with the long-distance travels and expeditions of the heroic period, and not with the fate of simple men.

Considering the rarity of ships' representations on reliefs throughout antiquity, it is rather indicative that among 15,000 pieces of sculpture kept in the National Archaeological Museum at Athens only about 20 reliefs have ship depictions and these date to the 4th, 2nd and 1st century BC and to 2nd century AD. Their provenances are Athens, Rheneia in the Cyclades, and the Piraeus. Of course they are not the only representations of ships to be found in Greece but, on any reckoning, the total number seems to be rather limited. Covering such a long period the reliefs of the National Museum allow us to make some interesting observations about the maritime means of transport used by Greeks during the above mentioned periods.

They also give us the opportunity to realize what a ship actually meant when depicted on the funerary relief of an average person.

Reliefs of the 4th c. BC

On the well-preserved grave stele of Demokleides [inv. nr. 752], the son of Demetrios, which is dated to the beginning of the 4th century BC, a ship is depicted.[4] The deceased Demokleides is depicted seated on the prow of the ship with his shield and helmet by his side (Fig. 5). The ship is easily identified as a *trieres* (a trireme). The ship's bow, the contour of the *embolon* (the ram), and the *proembolion* (the foreram) are in low relief, while the rest of the details and the landscape were painted in colour. The stempost inclines inwards. The representation of the trireme and the young man's armour implies that he might have been killed during a naval battle.

A prow of the same kind is depicted on the very interesting funerary relief inv. nr. 1488, from the Athenian Kerameikos, dated to the second half of the 4th century BC. According to the bilingual inscription engraved over the relief and the epigram under it, the stele was erected on the grave of Antipatros, son of Aphrodisios from Phoenike, by a certain Domsalo, son of Domano, from Sidon (Fig. 6).[5] The epigram informs us about the after-death adventure of Antipatros' corpse, which was snatched by a lion from his ship; his companions had to fight to regain his body in order to bury him properly. On the relief there is the representation of the event: the deceased is represented on a *kline*; a lion is attacking him, while a man is trying to push the animal back. Behind this man's head the prow of a ship is depicted which according to the inscription was a sacred ship, a *Hiera Naus*. Since the ancient term *naus* usually means a trireme and since the prow of the ship is identical to the prow depicted on the above mentioned stele of Demokleides, I believe that it is safe enough to identify this ship as a trireme (Herodotus 7.1.68; see Morrison and Williams 1968, 128, 244, 248). Behind the stempost of this trireme the most interesting aspect of this ship is clearly visible: a deckhouse on which a pole is erected. The depiction of a deckhouse on this relief is of great interest, since the deckhouse [a cabin], being a very useful structure already known from ship-representations of the prehistoric era, is not, according to modern scholarship, attested thereafter, at least until Roman times. In my opinion, the upright pole originating from the deckhouse should be interpreted as a *stylis*, symbolizing the guardian deity of the ship; anyhow it must be noted that it is generally accepted that a *stylis* was set up alongside the *aphlaston*, the ship's sternpost (Svoronos 1914, 81–120; Casson 1971, 116, 147, 247, 345–6). The depiction of a *stylis* on the prow of the triereme on the stele of Antipatros is evidence that a stylis could also be set up at the prow of a ship, at least during the 4th century BC. It is noteworthy, for example, that on the coins of Demetrius Poliorketes a prow of a ship was depicted on which a Nike stood holding a stylis. If the depiction of the stylis on the prow of the trireme on the Antipatros stele is not to be connected with the sacred character

Fig. 5 NM inv. nr. 752, grave stele of Demetrios.

Fig. 6 NM inv. nr. 1488, funerary relief of Kerameikos.

of the ship, it is at least evidence that the stylis of a trireme could also be erected on the prow.

On the marble lekythos inv. nr. 9167 dated by its shape and iconography to the 4th c. BC, the prow of a trireme is represented on which a full-armed warrior is depicted attacking to the right (Fig. 7) (Τζάχος 2001, 370–9). The trireme is depicted from the lower level to the outward-curving stempost. The *zoster* (gunwale) ends in front at a two-stepped *embolon*, and at an upper level the foreram, *proembolion*, is clearly visible. Most of the details concerning the construction of the trireme are represented: the *parexeresia* (outrigger), the apotropaic eye, three of the oars, of which two belong to the level of the *parexeresia* etc. As far as I know, this is one of the most detailed representations of the prow of a trireme on relief.

To the group of the 4th century BC grave reliefs may be added the marble grave stele inv. nr. 887 (Fig. 8), on which a loutrophoros is depicted (Clairmont 1993, nr. 3371; Τζάχος 2001, 374). On the belly of the loutrophoros is a scene of *dexiosis* between an old seated man and a young one. Behind the young man the

Fig 7 NM inv. nr. 9167, relief of the trireme Paralos.

stern of a boat is represented. There are two possible interpretations concerning this boat: either it was somehow related to the cause of the man's death, or even to his profession during lifetime, or, and I incline towards this view, this boat was a symbol of the *porthmeion*, the boat used by *Charon* to transport the deceased to the underworld; it is noteworthy that this theme is very popular on white lekythoi.

The above mentioned representations of triremes on funerary reliefs can be added to the very few representations of this type of ship on other reliefs of the 5th/ 4th century BC in other collections as, for example, on the famous Lenormant relief dated to the end of the 5th century BC,[6] or on a fragmentary relief depicting part of a trireme in the Museum of Eleusis (Basch 1987, 288–293; Τζάχος 2001, 366–7), dated to the middle of the 4th ccentury BC.

The following remarks emerge from the survey of the 4th century BC representations from the National Archaeological Museum: first, it can be confirmed that the form of trireme was stable during the 4th century BC. It is evident that identical or closely similar forms of triremes are represented on the stele of Deimokleides [inv. nr. 752], dated to the beginning of the 4th century BC, on the stele of Antipatros [inv. nr. 1488], and on the lekythos of the warrior [inv. n. 9167], dated to the second half of the century.

Fig. 8 NM inv. nr. 887, grave stele with loutrophoros.

Second, it seems that the ram used on the triremes during the 4th century BC belongs to two contemporary types. It is known that the 6th ccentury BC ram, in the shape of a boar's head, well known from vase painting, was replaced by a two-pronged ram, the *embolon,* reinforced by a bronze casing. The embolon, more elongated and three-stepped on the stele of Demokledes, is shorter and two-stepped on the marble lekythos of the warrior. An unpublished classical bronze embolon, on display at the Piraeus Museum, is three-stepped, but shorter than the embolon on the stele of Demokledes. The representation of the three-stepped embolon on the stele of Demokledes, and of the two-stepped one on the marble lekythos of the warrior, might be an indication that during the 4th ccentury BC the two types existed in parallel. The evidence implies that it was the three-stepped type that survived through the hellenistic period.

Third, the stele of Antipatros might be an indication that a deckhouse was actually constructed at least on some triremes of the 4th century BC. And last, the representation of a stylis on the prow of the same trireme might be an indication that some triremes of the 4th century BC could actually have a stylis on the prow.

Concerning the meaning of the representation as a whole, it is noteworthy that the ships depicted on grave reliefs of the classical period were mainly related to the causes of a man's heroic death in battle (e.g. the representations on the stele on Demokleides and on the lekythos of the warrior).

Reliefs of 2nd and 1st century BC/1st century AD

Maritime means of transport of the second and first centuries BC are represented on four grave stele found at Rheneia and one votive relief from the Piraeus.

The front half of a ship is depicted on the small grave stele of Nikephoros from Rheneia [inv. nr. 1294] (*IG* XII 5, 690; Couilloud 1974, 176 nr. 354, pl. 69), which is dated, according to stylistic criteria and the inscription, to the latter years of the 2nd century or early 1st century BC (Fig. 9). On the deck of the ship Nikephoros clad in a short chiton is represented fighting, holding a shield in his left arm and a sword in his raised right arm. Since Nikephoros is represented fighting and the ship is equipped with a three-stepped embolon it seems likely that the ship is a warship. Although the scale of the ship is disproportionate in comparison with the scale of the human figure and it is obviously a supplementary element of the motif, it is also a decisive one for the interpretation of the representation: there is no doubt that the man was killed in action. The same or a very similar motif is repeated on at least six more contemporary grave stelai from Rheneia, housed in the Museum of Mykonos and the Museum of Delos (Couilloud 1974, 176–7, 292–4).

The next three grave stelai from Rheneia in the National Museum give a good picture of what a merchant ship in the Aegean might have looked like during the same period.

On the badly weathered marble grave stele inv. nr. 999, the deceased is depicted sitting on a rock by the coast and, at a lower level, a ship is depicted from prow to stern (Fig. 10).[7] The hull of the ship is rounded and the lower part of the prow is concave, ending in a cutwater that projects forward into a ram-like point. This feature indicates that the ship is a merchant galley, perhaps an *akatos* or a *lembos*. At the stern of the ship the steersman, *pedaliouchos*, is depicted holding the steering oar. The man in front of the seated dead man is making a gesture honouring him or saying goodbye to him. It is obvious that the representation of the ship is related rather to the deceased's profession (it seems that the stele was erected for a mariner) than to the conditions of his death.

On his marble grave stele [inv. nr. 2106] Zenon, the son of Artemidoros, is depicted seated on a rock (Fig. 11) (*CIG* II 2373). In front of him the stern of a merchant ship with sail is depicted in the same form as that on the grave stele inv. nr. 999. Since a steering oar is depicted, but the steersman's seat is empty, it can be assumed that Zenon held this office during his lifetime. The strange position of the ship might also imply that he died on duty, perhaps in a shipwreck.

Fig. 9 NM inv. nr. 1294, grave stele of Nikephoros.

Fig. 10 NM inv. nr. 999, grave stele.

Fig. 11 NM inv. nr. 2106, grave stele of Zenon.

Fig. 12 NM inv. nr. 1313, grave stele of Sporios Granios.

Fig. 13 NM inv. nr. 1409, votive relief.

A similar and very vivid scene is represented on the grave stele [inv. nr. 1313] of Sporios Granios (Fig. 12) (*IG* IV 160; Couilloud 1974, 173–4 nr. 343). The deceased is seated on a rock. At a lower level a ship is depicted during a storm, in a very rough sea: the crew is shown in great agony and exhausted from the adverse conditions. Although the ship looks very much like the one represented on the famous Althiburus mosaic and named as a *keles* (Basch 1987, 482), I hesitate to identify it as such, because of the concave prow with the pointed cutwater (see Casson 1971, 163 for the differences). Anyhow, the motif indicates that Sporios drowned in a shipwreck during a storm, while the fate of his colleagues seems to have been the same.

Although the ship is obviously a motif to be expected on the grave stelai of an island, its fate being firmly connected with the sea, those funerary reliefs from Rheneia with representations of ships form only a small proportion of all Rheneian funerary reliefs (for the funerary reliefs of Rheneia, see Couilloud 1974).

The grave stele of the warrior Nikephoros, as well as the similar and contemporary stelai in the Mykonos and Delos Museums, might imply a period of disturbance in the Aegean sea, caused probably by pirates. In 1921 Durrbach associated these stelai with a decree [*ID* 1506] by which the Athenians, who had the protection of the island after 166 BC, honoured a certain Dioskorides for undertaking to equip some *triemiolia*, a kind of fast galleys, in order to patrol the sea around Delos (Durrbach 1921, 247–8, nr. 158; Couilloud 1974, 292–3). Although I follow Durrbach, who supposed that those ships, the *triemioliai* of the inscription, were used against pirates, I hesitate to recognize a triemiolia on the grave relief of Nikephoros. I simply note that these stelai from Rheneia could be an indication that the Rheneians owned their own small fleet to protect their island against piracy. On the other hand, the rest of the grave stelai provide evidence not only for the commercial activities of the islanders and the preferred types of vessels, but also for the dangers that a mariner regularly faced. Besides storms he also had to confront pirates. Otherwise, how else are we to explain the ram–like projection on the prow seen on two of these reliefs?

The last relief dated to the 2nd century BC is the votive relief [inv. nr. 1409] from Piraeus (Fig. 13) (Καλτσάς 2001, 277 nr. 580). An adorant is depicted standing on a boat, his right hand upraised in a typical religious gesture, honouring the

Dioskouroi, who are represented on the shore with their horses. It seems that the man was a mariner and honoured the deities for his salvation, or that he was praying for a safe journey. It is well known that the Dioskouroi were worshipped especially by mariners; their shrine on the small island of Prote, on the Ionian Sea directly opposite the Messenian cost, is well known thanks to a number of inscriptions.[8]

Reliefs of the 2nd and 3rd centuries AD

Some types of merchant and war ships, which were in use during the 2nd century AD and at the beginning of the 3rd century AD are depicted on grave stelai and ephebic lists from Athens.

As far as it concerns the grave stelai, the ship is a supplementary motif. It is usually depicted on the pediment of the stele or under the main representation. It is not easy to draw a conclusion about the meaning of the depiction of the ship in most of cases – that is whether it is an allegoric representation of the deceased's navigation to the Underworld or a realistic depiction of his activity during his lifetime. The three funerary reliefs, which are going to be briefly presented, illustrate well the above-mentioned difficulty. At the same time they offer a relatively clear picture about the types of ship were in use during this period in the Aegean Sea.

On the shaft of the grave monument of Zosimos and his family [inv. nr. 2587] a man, a little girl, and a woman are depicted. Their names are engraved on the entablature: Zosimos, Flavia Zosime and Flavia Charmosyne (Fig. 14) (*IG* II^2 10368, see Moock 1998, 143 nr. 304). On the pediment of the same stele a ship is depicted with two persons handling oars and the steersman at the rear. The

Fig. 14 NM inv. nr. 2587, grave monument of Zosimos.

Fig. 15 NM inv. nr. 3240, grave stele.

sternpost is finished off in a *cheniskos*, the goose-head, a feature as Casson remarks, although 'sometimes it appears on galleys, including war galleys, it was the decoration par excellence of merchantmen, often gilded for added effect' (1971, 347–8). It is possible that this vessel, which is armed with a ram-like projection on the strongly concave prow, is a *lembos* of small size. Concerning the interpretation of the representation of the ship on this stele, it seems reasonable that it is not related to the cause of death of the whole family. It is also difficult to accept the hypothesis that on the pediment of the stele is actually depicted the journey of the deceased to the Island of the Blest,[9] because the ship represented seems to be a merchant one. I think that a more plausible explanation is that Zosimos during his lifetime was a mariner and that the ship on the pediment of the stele is actually connected with him, depicting his occupation during his lifetime. Even in such a case the presence of the woman and the girl on the stele is not strange: the depiction on a grave monument of the deceased along with other members of their family still living, especially their close relatives, was actually a very common practice.

A similar kind of vessel is presented on a fragment coming from the pediment [inv. nr. 3240] of a grave stele dated to the same period (Fig. 15) (Moock 1998, 147 nr. 323). Although nothing can be said about the interpretation of this representation – due to the absence of the shaft of the stele – it seems that this type of ship was widespread in the Mediterranean Sea and had been in use since the 1st century AD: it is depicted, for example, on a funerary relief and by a number of graffiti from Pompeii, and on a relief from Avezzano in Italy (Casson 1971, pl. 139). In addition, the existence of the ram-like projection of the prow implies that the conditions of travelling were not totally safe.

A different kind of vessel is depicted on the grave stele of Dieuchis [inv. nr. 1246] travelling surrounded by dolphins (Fig. 16) (*IG* II^2 11143. v. Moock 1998, 129 nr. 240). It can be identified as a *keles*, which had four oars – it was *diskalmos* – as the depiction of the two mariners implies. The *pedaliouchos* is seated at the back of the vessel. Although it is more likely that the deceased, depicted with his wife and members of his family, was a mariner, in this case the hypothesis that this is an allegoric representation of the journey towards the Islands of the Blest cannot be excluded (Kritzas 2002, 71).

On a different category of monuments, some ephebic lists dated to the 2nd and 3rd centuries AD, there are representations of ships that look very similar to contemporary Roman galleys. The fragmentary stele inv. nr. 1470 is dated on epigraphic evidence to 192–3 AD (*IG* II^2 2130). Under the list a ship is depicted with an *aphlaston* (sternpost) at the stern, meaning that this was a warship. Although the stele is broken at that point, it is reasonable to assume that the ship had also an *embolon*, as this element is represented on other stelai of the same category. The inscription mentions the ephebic competition in which the ephebes won, namely the *naumachia*. Since the hypothesis that those ships were constructed *ad hoc* cannot be supported, and it seems that war galleys were used for such occasions, I simply note that they offer a picture of what a warship looked like more or less during the 2nd century AD in Greece.

Fig. 16 NM inv. nr. 1246, grave stele of Dieuchis.

Among the various above–mentioned representations of ships on reliefs housed in the National Archaeological Museum, the hitherto unpublished relief inv. nr. 6031 deserves a separate analysis.

The relief inv. nr. 6031

It is a marble slab, broken all around. It is 43 cm high, 80 cm long and 8 cm deep. The provenance is unknown. The surface is so weathered that the details of the figures represented are not easily discernible.

In almost the centre of the decorated surface a small sailing vessel is depicted (Fig. 17). The hull is rounded and the sternpost seems to incline inwards; the form of the stempost is not recognizable due to the condition of the surface. The vessel had a square sail on its mast, of which only the lower part is preserved. Two persons are seated on the deck. The one seated at the sternsheets must be recognised as the *pedaliouchos* because he is depicted holding the steering oar. Although the surface is very damaged at this spot, he seems to wear a *pilos* on his head. The other, seated on the prow, raises his right hand: if his gesture is to be interpreted as meaning that he is giving orders for the sail, then he must be identified as the *kybernetes* (captain) of the vessel. The two holes depicted on the visible side of the vessel might be oar ports, suggesting that the vessel had four oars.

Two strange figures are depicted on both sides of the ship. Both of them are stepping on rocky projections. The figure on the left does not look like a human one. In spite of the bad condition of the surface in this area I think that it can be safely identified with a siren (for the iconography of the sirens, see Hofstetter 1997). She looks to have an animal form for the largest part of her body (more precisely, the feet and body of a bird) but her head and the details of the figure are not discernible. Between her head and the stern of the vessel there are two long projections that might be the double pipe she was playing (Fig. 18). Although the figure on the right is more weathered I think it is safe enough to recognise here a second siren, represented with open hands. The rendering of the two human figures and the representation of the landscape, I believe, suggest a date around the end of the 4th century BC.

The interpretation of the scene and the defining of the function of the relief present difficulties. Although the presence of the two sirens on the rocky promontory-like projections and of the vessel, which sails between them, recalls the famous scene from the *Odyssey*, namely the scene of Odysseus's navigation past the island of the Sirens, such an interpretation must be rejected since it is not supported by a very significant iconographical detail: neither of the two human figures on the vessel can be identified as Odysseus and there is no trace of him ever hanging from the mast, at least according to the known iconography (for the iconography of this scene, see Touchefeu and Meynier 1992, 962–4). Anyhow, it must be noted that the motif

Fig. 17 NM inv. nr. 6031, marble slab.

presents a striking similarity with the later wall–painting from Pompeii in the British Museum representing the scene from the Odyssey (British Museum, GR 1867. 5–8.1354; Touchefeu and Meynier 1992, 962 nr. 159). On the other hand, the representation of the two sirens on the rocky promontories, and of the ship between them on the relief inv nr. 6031 recalls representations of harbours on Roman mosaics or on Roman wall paintings: the sirens seem to "frame" the entrance of a harbour exactly like the statues "framed " the entrance of various harbours (Lehmann-Hartleben 1963, 217–239). So they become the main iconographical element for the interpretation of the representation. I think that the depiction of the sirens on the relief at the National Archaeological Museum actually suggests a funerary character for it. Sirens were, according to Homer (*Od.* 12.39ff), sea creatures living on an island in the Ocean, which, according to mythology, was the Island of the Blest. They become prominent in Attic and East Greek funerary art in the 4th century BC in relief and in the round, represented either as mourners or as musicians, playing the double pipes or the lyre. Although it should be noted, concerning the representation of vessels on funerary reliefs, which according to Cumont (1942, 53, 166–9, 306, 328) symbolize navigation to the Island of the Blest, that such a general conclusion is not supported by the examples in existence, it seems that on the relief inv. nr. 6031 this unique scene is depicted, as the combination of the two special iconographical elements suggests: the sirens and the ship. If this interpretation is correct, the relief was part of a grave stele, perhaps forming a separate panel on it, as occurs, for example, on East Greek grave stelai.[10]

Fig. 18 NM inv. nr. 6031, detail, the left figure.

Finally, it should be noted that independently from the interpretation of the scene and the defining of the function of the relief, the representation on the relief inv. nr. 6031 gives also a very good picture of how a harbour would look at the end of the 4th century BC.

Conclusions

The representations of ships on funerary reliefs are not numerous. Nevertheless, they offer a picture of the evolution of maritime means of transport used by the Greeks for several centuries, from the classical period to 2nd/3rd centuries AD. In any case we must keep in mind that the National Museum collection consists of sculpture mainly from Athens and Attica and to a lesser degree from the rest of southern Greece. Therefore, the data are representative mainly of Attica and the Cyclades. As for Classical, Hellenistic and even Roman Attica, in my opinion the rarity of the representations of ships on funerary reliefs can be explained by the 'insistence' of the Athenians on the depiction of the predominating value of the common people's lives: the family. The causes of death and the dead person's profession were not so important as to become the main iconographical theme represented on funerary reliefs in comparison with the human feelings for the eternal separation.

Acknowledgments

I owe my warmest thanks to Jim Roy not only for his kind invitation to participate in the Conference but also for his generous and warm hospitality and his advice on the preparation of this paper. The photographs are by Dr. K. -V. von Eickstedt.

September, 2002.

Notes

1 *IG* II² 3456. Beschi 1969–70, 86–101, fig. 1. Καλτσάς 140, nr. 267 with the previous bibliography. The photograph of the relief inv. nr. 1341 as well as of all the reliefs presented here were taken by Dr. V. von Eickstedt.

2 For a survey of the Greek representations of oared ships see Morrison and Williams 1968. Basch 1987, 156–264; Casson 1971, 49–76

3 The ship Argo was represented on two limestone metopes of the Sicyonian Treasury at Delphi. The monument is dated ca 560 BC, Boardman 1978, fig. 208. 1.

4 *IG* II² 11114. Basch 1987, 299; Clairmont 1993, nr. 1.330; Καλτσάς 2001, 163 nr. 320.

5 *IG* II² 8388; Clairmont 1993, nr. 3.410; Καλτσάς 2001, 190 nr. 376.

6 The trireme on this relief is usually identified as *Paralos*, the famous sacred Athenian ship, Morrison and Williams 1968, 170–173; Beschi 1969, 117–132; Basch 1987, 279–283; Τζάχος 2001, 365– 6.

7 Couilloud 1974, 174 nr. 344. For the various aspects concerning the motif of the dead person seated on a rock, Couilloud 1974, 294–6, 297–8.

8 *IG* V1, 1548–1551. Dioskouroi were worshipped as maritime deities also at Lesbos, Αχειλαπά 2001.

9 For the representation of ships and boats on Roman funerary reliefs, as an allegorical representation of navigation towards the Island of the Blest, Cumont 1942, 166–7, 306. Kritzas 2002, 71.

10 It must be noted that the marble is non-Attic. For similar arrangement of panels on East Greek grave stelai, see Pfuhl and Mobius 1977, 30–1 nr. 73, 113 nr. 282, 188 nr. 687).

Bibliography

Αχειλαρά, Λ. (2001) *Η λατρεία των Διοσκούρων στη Λέσβο*, στο ΑΓΑΛΜΑ, Μελέτες για την αρχαία πλαστική προς τιμή του Γιώργου Δεσπίνη, 205–210.

Basch, L. (1987) *Le musée imaginaire de la marine antique* (Athens).

Beschi, L. (1969) *'Relievi votivi attici ricompositi'*, ASAtene 47/48, 86–101.

Boardman, J. (1978) *Greek Sculpture: The Archaic Period* (London).

Casson, L. (1971) *Ships and Seamanship in the Ancient World* (Princeton).

Clairmont, C. (1993) *Classical Attic Tombstones* (Kilchberg).

Couilloud, M.-T. (1974) *Les monuments funéraires de Rhénée*, Délos XXX (Paris).

Cumont, F. (1942) *Recherches sur le symbolisme funéraire des Romains* (Paris).

Durrbach, F. (1921) *Choix d'inscriptions de Délos* (Paris).

Hofstetter, E. (1997) *Seirenes*, LIMC VIII, 1093–1104.

Καλτσάς, Ν. (2001) *Εθνικό Αρχαιολογικό Μουσείο. Τα Γλυπτά* (Athens).

Kritzas, C. (2002) *A Roman funerary stele with a representation of a ship from the Tymbaki area in Crete*, ΕΝΑΛΙΑ 6, 66–71.

Lehmann–Hartleben, K. (1923) *Die antiken Hafenanlagen des Mittelmeeres* (Leipzig).

Moock, D. W. von (1998) *Die figürlichen Grabstelen Attikas in der Kaiserzeit* (Mainz.)

MorrisonJ. S. and R. T. Williams (1968) *Greek Oared Ships*, 900–322 BC (Cambridge).

Pfuhl, E. and H. Mobius (1997) *Die Ostgriechischen Grabreliefs*, vol. i (Mainz).

Svoronos, J. N. (1914) *Stylides, ancres hierae, aphlasta, stoloi, acrkostolia, embola, proembola et totems marins*, Journal International d'Archéologie Numismatique 14, 81–152.

Touchefeu-Meynier, O. (1992) *Odysseus*, LIMC VI, 943–970.

Τζάχος, Ε. (2001) *Μία επανεκτίμηση της αθηναϊκής τριήρους*, in ΚΑΛΛΙΣΤΕΥΜΑ, Μελέτες προς τιμήν της Όλγας Τζάχου-Αλεξανδρή, 357–384.

Woysch–Méautis, D. (1982) *La représentation des animaux et des êtres fabuleux sur les monuments funéraires grecs*, PhD Thesis, Université de Neuchâtel.

Pausanias in Arkadia: an Example of Cultural Tourism

Madeleine Jost

My subject is a traveller of the second century of our era, Pausanias, who wrote a *Description of Greece* or *Periegesis*. Pausanias' journey in Greece was not linked to any professional requirement, as was most often the case in the Hellenistic period (André and Baslez 1993, 72); what dominates is the idea of satisfying personal curiosity, of going to see with his own eyes. But this is the tourism of a man of letters; in the course of his account of his journey, Pausanias brings to life the history and the myths that define the cultural identity of the region that he is visiting.

We shall begin with a few words on the author and his background (see Bowie 2001, 21–32). Pausanias was a Greek from the east, no doubt born near Magnesia on the Sipylus around A.D. 110. He drew up the *Perigesis* in the third quarter of the second century of our era (between 165 and 180). He lived in the brilliant period of the century of the Antonines, in particular under Antoninus Pius, to whom he pays tribute at 8.43.1–6, and Marcus Aurelius. The work that he has left was intended to appeal to people of means who, on the model of Hadrian, traveller and philhellene, took an interest in Greece, went to visit its principal sites, and felt curiosity about ancient Greek civilisation. Nonetheless, the author is little known, save through his work.

The *Perigesis* is a description of Greece according to the taste of the age; it does not claim to give detailed and complete information on each site and monument, but brings together, for each region, the sights "which are worth seeing" (Θέας ἄξια 1.17.5; 2.15.2; 10.32.1): Pausanias makes a selection of the facts which "are worth mentioning" ἄξια μνήμης 3.11.1; cf. 1.39.3; 8.54.7). From this point of view, it is a work by a consciously literary writer, and attention has often been drawn to the influence of the Second Sophistic (Porter 2001, 90–92). Yet the *Perigesis* is far from being the product of a scholar working in a library. Pausanias is above all a traveller and he declares that he wants to describe the whole of Greece (1.26.4). In fact only ten books have come down to us; I shall fix my attention on Book 8, which describes Arkadia, because we know, since the researches of Heberdey (1894, 11–18), taken up again by Pritchett (1999, 13–16), that it is the book in which there is the greatest number of expressions that refer back to personal observation by the traveller, i.e. to "autopsy", such as ἐπ᾽ ἐμοῦ, κατ᾽ ἐμέ, ἔλεγον. His procedure is topographical; he describes Arkadia arriving from the Argolid and thus begins with the Mantinike and northeastern Arkadia; he continues towards the northwest and west; he arrives at Megalopolis, whose territory he describes; and finally he sets off again for the Tegeatis and returns to the Argolid.

His account of his journey is first and foremost the account of ground covered, of a circular route, and he bears witness to what he has seen himself, to what survived in his day (hence the title of a chapter of Casson 1974, 292–299, following others: "Baedeker of Ancient World"; cf. Habicht, "Pausanias as a Guide", 1985, 28–29 and Arafat 1996, 33–36). He likes to underline the quality of personal observation in his work: he has seen or he has learnt on the spot. He makes this clear regarding the sources of the Lymax: "There is on Mt. Kotilion a spring of water, and, if a writer has already written that from there began the course of the river Lymax, he did so without having himself seen the course of the water and not in accordance with the statements of a man who would have seen it. I myself had both procedures available to me" (8.41.10), that is to say autopsy and enquiry from the local inhabitants. When he has not seen what he is talking about, he sometimes points that out explicitly (8.41.6: "I have not seen the statue of Eurynome"). The *Periegesis* is therefore an account of the slow discovery and absorption of the landscape made possible by a journey. Admittedly, it sometimes happens that he has moved rather too quickly, as at Gortys where, having no doubt chosen the direct route, along the northern ravine, towards Megalopolis, he saw only one of the two sanctuaries of Asklepios revealed by excavation, the lower one (Jost 1985, 209–210). But, most of the time, he combs the region, and archaeologists have often underlined the precision of his descriptions (cf. Habicht 1985, 28–63 and Arafat 1996, 18–22).

To the topographical framework are added explanatory passages, often fairly long. Several of these passages are in the tradition of Hellenistic *Periegeses*: for example, the interest that Pausanias shows for special features of the soil, for hydrography, for fauna and flora. Other digressions are due to a classical humanism entirely typical of the time of the Antonines: Pausanias belongs to the literary tendency which endeavours to maintain classical culture in the East and to pass on the Hellenic heritage; in these passages Pausanias likes to cite earlier authors, in particular Homer, and he uses the chronicles and works available to him. His accounts of the historical past in Greece are numerous, but Pausanias' favourite theme is Greek religion. Regarding sacred monuments he reports religious traditions and describes the rites that he has celebrated (8.42.11) and the ceremonies in which he has taken part, save for the mysteries whose secret he respects (8.57.9).

It is Pausanias' method of tackling his subject that we shall examine, dealing first with his actual experiences on his travels and then the intentions behind his account.

The experiences of a real journey

The elements of descriptive vocabulary for the landscape

The descriptions are restrained. Several features attract Pausanias' attention: roads and their layout, watercourses and mountains, together with towns, villages, and sanctuaries. For each city (the structural division of the work, to which I shall return later, is in fact by cities) Pausanias mentions the road by which he arrives from the previous city, the urban layout of the town in question, its territory, which he describes according to itineraries radiating from the the city, then the line of the roads leaving the city. On roads he gives distances in stades. The latter can be converted only approximately into kilometres for, as was demonstrated long ago, on main roads Pausanias uses, it seems, the Olympic stade, but, in hilly areas, a stade is used which is less long and probably based on the time taken to cover the distance (Jost 1973, 242 n.3, following Puillon de Boblaye 1836, 6–7; see also Pritchett 1999, 22). Distances are thus given in terms of the walker's speed, and moreover are often accompanied by expressions that note their approximate character (Pritchett 1999, 20–22, according to whom Pausanais seems not to have had a map available nor to have met with Roman milestones). On occasion some information is given on the importance or the condition of the road: "The road from Tegea to Argos is entirely suitable for a carriage" (8.54.5); on the other hand the sanctuary of Eurynome is "difficult to reach" (8.41.4) and we must suppose a simple track. In addition Pausanias indicates explicitly when he leaves the main road: he makes clear, for instance, regarding Zoitia that it "is situated about fifteen stades from Trikolonoi – *not in a straight line, but to the left of that town*" (8.35.6). On the other hand information concerning the practical organisation of his journey is totally absent.

As he makes his way along the road Pausanias gives an idea of the physical relief by indicating rises and descents. Thus the expression e)stin a)/nodoj in the description of the road between Lykosoura and Phigalia (8.39.1) refers to the climb towards Mt. Tetrazi. It has the same meaning when the Periegetes describes the section of road between Asea and Tegea to the east (8.44.4): ἔστι δὲ ἄνοδος ἐξ Ἀσέας ἐς τὸ ὄρος τὸ Βόρειον καλούμενον, "from Asea you go up to Mt. Boreion, and at the summit of (or, high on) the mountain there are traces of a sanctuary." Indeed, if one advances from Asea towards the east, beyond the springs of the Alpheios, one rises gradually above the plain, and then on the slopes of Mt. Kravari, which is the ancient Boreion: it forms a rocky barrier between the two basins of Megalopolis and of Tegea. One arrives at a pass, which shows as a notch in Mt. Boreion. Thereafter the road descends again towards the Dyke ("Choma") which marks the boundary of Megalopolis, Pallantion, and Tegea (8.44.5–7). At the highest point of the road, in the pass, there are the traces of a temple once excavated by Rhomaios (1957, 114–163; Jost, 1985, 195–197). From there one has a view towards Asea before going down again towards the plain of Tegea. For Phigalia, Pausanias arrives from the east by

Fig. 19 One of the roads of the Periegesis: the pass above Sanga, between the Argolid and Arkadia.

the enclosed valley of the Neda; he has first to climb above the river on very steep slopes: then, "once over these escarpments" (8.39.5: ἀνελθόντι δέ, he arrives on the hillocky platform where there are various ancient remains, including the temple dug by X. Arapoyanni (Arapoyanni 2001). Ἀνελθόντι refers to the precipitous slopes that overlook the Neda and which caused misadventures when climbed by certain travellers of last century.

Rivers large and small occupy a place almost equal to that of roads in the topographical references of the *Periegesis*. The description of the territory of Thelpousa, for instance, follows the course of the Ladon and it is in relation to that river that the sites are located (8.25.1–12). Its descriptions are precise and are borne out by the facts. In his description of Megalopolis, he uses the Helisson for the precise localisation of the agora. He begins his description with the northern sector, where the agora and the buildings linked to the life of the city are located. The expression δεξιῷ δὲ κατὰ το μετέωρον τοῦ ποταμοῦ (8.30.2) for the northern sector of the agora cannot mean, as the dictionary of Liddell, Scott, and Jones suggests, to the right "as one looks up the river": that would be at odds with the topographical reality (the northern sector of the agora is not on the right but on the left if one looks upstream). In fact δεξιῷ certainly means the right bank of the river in relation to direction of its flow (as is the case at Heraia, 8.26.1), and in the expression κατὰ τὸ μετέωρον τοῦ ποταμοῦ it is necessary to take μετέωρον in the sense "variation in height" (as at Phigalia: 8.39.5), giving the translation "to the right [i.e. on the right bank] overlooking the river": the agora is indeed on a small plateau overlooking the Helisson: the bank, especially to the east, was fairly high and the monuments extended as far as the drop to the river.

For the mountains the geographical classifications may have a written source: Mount Lampeia is part of Erymanthos (8.24.4) and Mount Kerausion part of Mount Lykaion (8.41.3) etc. But beside the mountain as a simple element in the topographical definition of the countryside the designation as ὄρος or λόφος and the evaluation of the height of the mountains derive more from a descriptive vocabulary whose subjective character will be seen later. On arriving at the culminating point of Mount Lykaion Pausanias points out the view that opens before him over "almost all the Peloponnese" (8.38.7).

As for description of urban landscapes it is, save for Megalopolis, generally succinct, and the same comments might be made as for Athens or Corinth. City walls are mentioned only incidentally and as topographical references (e.g. 8.30.7). Monuments of civic architecture (porticoes, like the Stoa Philippeios at Megalopolis, and rooms for meetings like the Bouleuterion in the same city) appear above all as 'markers' in the description (8.30.2–31.8). Sanctuaries attract the Periegetes' attention more; but it is essentially cult statues and the rites themselves that, as we shall see, he likes to describe.

Descriptive elements: the example of the vocabulary for mountains

A study of the vocabulary that serves to designate mountains shows that the use of descriptive terms does not obey fixed rules, but depends on the physical environment of the sites mentioned (cf. Jost 1996, 719–738): in brief, the landscapes described by Pausanias are, in most cases, landscapes perceived and experienced subjectively in the course of his travels.

The term *kolonos* (κολωνός) is used by Pausanias for the description of the village of Methydrion. The text of the three primary manuscripts of the *Arkadika*, V, F, and P, explains that Methydrion is a κολωνός ... ὑψηὸς Μαλοίτα τε ποταμοῦ καὶ Μυλάοντος μέσος, that is to say, word for word, "an elevated hill, situated between the rivers Maloitas and Mylaon" (8.36.1) The site has been identified since the *Arkadische Forschungen* of Hiller von Gaertringen and Lattermann (1911, 31–32 and pl. III) with a small hill situated in the triangle formed by two streams, in a winding valley north of Megalopolis, on the route proposed by Pausanias towards the interior of Arkadia. The remains of a fortified wall-circuit guarantee that this was a settlement. In what respect does it merit the description of κολωνός... ὑψηλός? In Pausanias, as already in Herodotus (7.225) *kolonos* is applied to a small isolated hill; thus in Attika the Kolonos Hippios was a small isolated hill ten or so metres high (Paus. 1.30.4). It therefore signifies a limited elevation. In that case how is the qualification ὑψηλός, "elevated", to be understood? In my opinion it indicates only that this hill is elevated *in comparison to* the level of the two rivers between which it is situated and which it dominates; in fact, even if the hill is limited in height, it nonetheless falls away steeply to the north and west. Consequently I do not follow the correction οὐχ ὑψηλός arbitrarily imposed by Leake (1846, 200–210; cf.

Fig. 20 Orchomenos from the south.

Pritchett 1999, 129–131). I shall keep the reading of the manuscripts, and consider that ὑψηλός is to be understood in relation to the surrounding relief and serves to contrast the valleys of the rivers and the raised ground between the two.

The term *lophos* (λόφος), which is translated 'hill', signifies in its turn rising ground, a slight elevation whose appearance may vary. Several sites of this sort are easy to identify. At Asea, "whose hill," according to Pausanias (8.44.3) "was formerly the acropolis," the form is clearly that of a hill that stands isolated in a basin, detached from any mountain chain: it is a rocky platform, small (240m. by 120m.), of no great height (54m.), with steep sides: it is still surrounded by a fortification wall (Jost 1985, 194–195 and pl. 52,2). Corresponding no doubt to the hill (*lophos*) Akakesion (Paus. 8.36.9), a small isolated hill stands out in front of Lykosoura (Jost 1985, 171). As for *oros* (ὄρος), that word is applied to imposing mountains like Mt. Lykaion (Paus. 8.38.2) or Mt. Kyllene (Paus. 8.17.1).

That being said, the use that Pausanias makes of *lophos* ('hill') and *oros* ('mountain') is sometimes disconcerting, as Pritchett for his part (1982, 66 and 1999, 125) has noted. The choice between the two words seems to be dictated by the perception that Pausanias has of the site in relation to the surrounding landscape. Why, when Phigalia is a *lophos* (Paus. 8.39.5), is Orchomenos or Nestane an *oros* (Paus. 8.13.2 and 8.7.4)? Phigalia and Orchomenos, both enclosed in a fortified wall-circuit, cover the same area of 20 ha., and the variation in height in both cases is of the order of 200m. (Nestane is smaller). Yet the impression produced by the two sites is very different. The site of Phigalia is made up of a rocky platform cut off on the south by the deep valley of the Neda and dominated by a steep-sided acropolis;

but all around the site is surrounded by higher mountains (Jost 1985, 82–83 and 86): "To the left," explains Pausanias, "it is dominated by Kotilion, to the right another height, Elaion, forms a rampart in front of it" (8.39.5). The presence of these heights means that, in comparison, Phigalia gives the impression of a hill, *lophos*. The site of Orchomenos is entirely different: an imposing conical hill rises at the meeting-point of the two plains that make up the Orchomenian basin (Jost 1985, 113–114 and 116–117). The northern plain in the time of Pausanias is, as he writes (8.13.4), "for the most part a marsh"; in the other plain the water is drained by a channel at the foot of Mt. Trachy. In other words, in the eyes of Pausanias, though equal in size and fairly close in their shapes, the height at Phigalia looks like a hill while the height at Orchomenos, whose mass stands out from a high and perfectly uniform plain, appears as a mountain. The impression created by the surroundings, reinforced perhaps by local names, must explain the choice of one word rather than the other to describe one or the other of two sites that are nonetheless intrinsically identical. The *Argon Pedion*, the Barren Plain, at the edge of which Nestane was set (Paus. 8.7.1 and 4; Jost 1985, 135), allows us to understand in the same way its description as *oros*: it stands out on a uniform surface, a surface which, moreover, in Pausanias' day was enlivened only by rare crops snatched from the earth at the cost of careful maintenance of the katavothres.

The location of the sites in the mountains calls for some comments. There are cases where ἄκϱα unambiguously means the summit (as for Mt. Lykaion: ἔστι δὲ ἐπὶ τῇ ἄκϱα τῇ *ἀνωτάτὼ* τοῦ ὄϱους γῆς χῶμα, i.e. "at the culminating point of the mountain there is a mound of earth": it is the altar of Zeus Lykaios, Paus. 8.38.7). Yet on several occasions κοϱυφή or ἄκϱα means not the summit but the highest point on the road crossing the mountain. Thus the temple near Asea (Paus. 8.44.4) is not "at the summit of the mountain" but "at the highest point" of the route set out by Pausanias across Mt. Boreion: it is the point on the road where, after a rise (ἄνοδος), one overlooks the two basins of Asea and Tegea. The expression "at the summit" designates the highest point of the Periegetes' passage and is to be explained in strict relation to the terrain crossed. The same comment could be made about Orchomenos. For Orchomenos Pausanias writes: "The former town was ἐπὶ ὄϱους ἄυϱᾳ τῇ κοϱυφῇ and there remain the ruins of an agora and a wall" (8.13.2). And yet, the summit of the acropolis has yielded no trace of antiquity, and the agora, like the sanctuary of Artemis Mesopolitis, is situated on the south slope of the acropolis, at an equal distance from the wall-circuit and the summit (Jost 1985, 116–119). In fact the road has already covered a rise in height of nearly 100m. from the plain when it reaches the agora; no doubt it stops there and Pausanias refers to this as the highest point. Thus, despite the Periegetes' very stereotyped vocabulary, the details revealed are those experienced on a real journey.

The "sights to see" in nature

Fig. 21 The cult group at Lykosoura, bronze coin of Megalopolis (Julia Domna).

Another aspect of Pausanias' description interested his readers, namely the mentions of natural curiosities encountered: these mentions make up one of the characteristic elements of his *Periegesis* (Jacquemin 1991, 123–130; Jost 1998b, xxxvi–xxxviii). They are often facts that he has observed himself, or wanted to observe: at Kleitor (8.21.2), where he had been informed that the "spotted" fish sing like thrushes at nightfall, he himself waited, in vain, at the edge of the river (the report was given also by Mnaseas of Patrai: see Athenaeus 8.331d); elsewhere he reports white hinds that he saw personally at Rome (8.17.4). Equally he has recourse to paradoxographical literature (cf. André and Baslez 1993, 65–66), in particular when he cites parallels taken from other regions. The courses of rivers large and small, with their disappearances and resurgences, are the subject of several observations (as, for instance, on the subject of the Alpheios, 8.44.4 and Pritchett 1999, 136–141; or, on the katavothres of Pheneos attributed to Herakles, 8.14.1–2). The quality of their waters also attracts his attention: the cold waters of the Gortynios call forth comparisons with the Danube, the Rhine, the Hypanis in the land of the Sarmatians, and the Borysthenes in Scythia (8.28.2). The water of the Styx has harmful effects (8.18.4–6): "Glass, crystal, porcelain, the objects that men make in stone and dishes in pottery, all that is broken by the water of the Styx; and objects in horn and bone, iron and bronze, as well as lead, tin, silver, and electrum are dissolved by this water. Gold suffers in the same way as all other metals ... In truth the water of the Styx is unable to attack only a horse's hoof: if you pour it on it, the hoof holds it and the water does not destroy the hoof" (cf. earlier Strabo 8.8.4). On the other hand, the water of the spring Alyssos near Kaphyai is beneficial: its waters cure rabies (8.19.2–3: "drinking this water is a remedy"). Plants and animals also give rise to several passages. Pausanias shows interest in the species of trees in the Arkadian forests: at 8.12.1 he describes different varieties of oaks: oaks "with wide leaves", "with edible acorns"; "a third species has bark which is porous and so light that it is used to make floats for the sea to mark anchors and nets". *Mirabilia* particularly draw his attention: at Lykosoura he mentions an olive-tree and a green oak sprung from a single root (8.37.10). Besides the singing fish of Kleitor the Periegetes points out birds, the white blackbirds of Kyllene, à propos of which he lists various white animals (8.17.2–4: cf. also Aelian *Hist. Anim.* 5.27 and 12.28). Tortoises are mentioned several times, near Psophis, after the wild boars and the bears (8.23.9), then on Mt. Parthenion (8.54.7); and he refers to the making of lyres for which they could be used. If the "sights" collected by the Periegetes vary in their degrees of interest, his method on the other hand seems very modern: he proceeds by citing "parallels" which should support the truth of the reported *mirabilia* (8.17.4). The examples in question bear witness to the breadth of his enquiry and to a clear taste for the exotic: they range, for the white animals, from Boeotia to the Sipylos, Thrace, Libya, and Rome. Thus the "sights" mentioned by Pausanias furnish the opportunity to set his enquiry in a cosmopolitan framework.

Nonetheless the regional, or even 'micro-regional', character of the *Periegesis* is its most striking trait: above all he is interested in local particularisms, in landscapes, but also in traditions. Indeed, the account of Pausanias' journey is not put together solely to offer the reader a substitute for seeing with his own eyes. His record of his travel serves as a support for long passages on history and local traditions, with a particular predilection for religious traditions rooted in the past.

The aims of the text

A 'political' view of travel

The composition of Book VIII testifies to a 'political' reordering of how the journey progressed. On the topographical order that governs the composition of the book is superimposed a division by cities (*poleis*), and therefore political in character. In all probability the Periegetes visited Arkadia without halting his progress at each frontier, and then composed his work by regrouping according to the organisation by cities the itineraries which he had followed.

The organisation of the *Periegesis* by cities is all the clearer because, for the most important among them, description is preceded by a historical introduction which recounts the striking events of its history from its foundation up to the time of Pausanias. The history of the cities unfolds the themes of their foundations and names, legendary events and major conflicts, most often with Sparta. We note several times over the Periegetes' concern to collate the different versions before giving his personal opinion: Psophis, for example, "according to some would have had as founder Psophis son of Arron ...; according to others, Psophis would have been a daughter of Xanthos .... But the truest version is that Psophis was a child of Eryx" (8.24.1–2). Elsewhere, when it is not disputed, Pausanias reports only the local version (cf. Alcock 1996, 261–265).

Megalopolis gives rise to the most fully developed treatment. The report of the foundation of the town in 371/0, with the list of cities which took part, is an indispensable document for the historian, even if it is not always easy to interpret (8.27.3–4: see most recently Nielsen 2002, 413–510). After a fairly detailed account of the synoecism of Megalopolis Pausanias passes more quickly over the periods that follow (8.27.9–16). He adopts a chronological approach, while organising events according to some governing ideas. First of all he is interested in the city's relations with Sparta, and then with Macedon. From Megalopolis' external politics he passes to the internal political life of the city with the tyrants of Megalopolis: Aristodemos and Lydiades. He omits to mention Megalopolis' entry into the Achaian Confederation, for his approach owes more to chronicling than to the comprehension of a historical evolution, and he limits himself to noting the succession of tyrants. After the tyrannies come the successive sieges of Megalopolis (an attempt at a siege is assigned to Agis IV, the sieges of Megalopolis by Kleomenes in 227 and then 224: he wrongly ascribes the death of Lydiades and the evacuation of the town under the leadership of Philopoimen to the same campaign). Whatever its real historical value, this long passage bears witness to the Periegetes' interest in the city's historical past. Finally, the description of Megalopolis and the notice of its ruins (8.30.1–32.5) ends with a moralising chapter on the role of Fortune in the prosperity and misfortune of cities as in all things (8.33.1–4).

As important as the mention of a town, and – where appropriate – of the villages, the demarcation of the frontiers serves to define the city's territory, and Pausanias is careful to show their position. When the frontier is made up of a succession of points, as can be seen for instance in a settlement of a frontier known from epigraphy for the fourth century (Dubois 1986, 133–146), the Periegetes cites the precise landmark which occurs on the road he is describing: it may be an inscription (between Psophis and Thelpousa: 8.25.1), an altar (between Mantinea and Tegea: 8.11.1), a sanctuary (between Kleitor and Thelpousa: 8.25.3), *Hermaia* (on the roads southwards from Megalopolis: 8.29.1 and 8.35.2), or a tomb (between Heraia and Elis: 8.26.3); Pausanias thus identifies the point on the frontier crossed by the road which he is following. But beside linear frontiers there appear several frontier zones: a *pedion* (between Thelpousa and Heraia: 8.25.12) or a mountain (Mt. Artemision between Argos and Mantinea: 8.6.6; Mt. Anchisiai between Mantinea and Orchomenos: 8.12.9): these are cases of *eschatiai*, which were often undivided, as is the case for the sanctuary of Artemis Hymnia situated on Mt. Anchisiai (8.13.1). Once these frontiers are defined it is the territory of each city that serves as the framework for the description of the sights to see. For S. Alcock the concern to indicate the territorial limits of the cities is something "intriguing" (Alcock 1995, 335; cf. also Alcock 1993, 118–120, and 1999, 171–173): Pausanias is indeed writing at a period when the notion of the frontier must have been somewhat relaxed by reason of the common inclusion in the Roman province of Achaia and of constructions which transcended the framework of a city, like the aqueduct built in the time of Hadrian (c. 125) that carried water from the springs of Stymphalia as far as Corinth (8.22.3).

It is therefore necessary to pose the question whether the *Periegesis* of Pausanias reflects the situation in his own time (the Roman province of Achaia) or an older state of affairs. S. Alcock (1995, 326–344) has rightly drawn attention to the fact that in general he describes the Greece of his own day. But, for Arkadia, the reference to the past is sometimes explicit. For the cities of Stymphalos and Alea that in his day entered an Argive confederation (8.22.1 and 23.1) Pausanias chooses to integrate them into his description of Arkadia with a reference to the past: for Stymphalos he cites as evidence of its original adhesion to Arkadia the Homeric Catalogue of Ships and the genealogy of the Arkadian kings, among whom appears Stymphelos, grandson of Arkas and founder of Stymphalos (8.22.1). For the territory of Megalopolis he sets out in chapter 8.27.3–4, à propos of the foundation of Megalopolis, the list of the 39 cities that participated in the synoecism of 371/0, and the same names reappear in identical form in the descriptive chapters. Then the Periegetes gives the ultimate fate of these settlements: "Among the cities (*poleis*) listed", he says, "some are entirely deserted today: others are villages (*komai*) subject to Megalopolis". The terms *polis* and *kome* are here not derived from his descriptive vocabulary; as at Book 10.4.1, on Panopeus (where the city is defined by material criteria); they reflect political realities (Jost 1986 [1990], 145–158).

The overwhelming impression is thus that, if Pausanias describes the cities of his day and their ruined state, he does so according to a division by cities that is inherited from the traditional conception of the region as a juxtaposition of political entities. Moreover, the changes in status (*polis* or *kome*) between the classical period and the the Antonine period hardly seem important (the continued existence of cities in the imperial period is well known: Alcock 1993, 18): coinage and texts allow us to say that the cities of which Pausanias speaks were already more or less those of the classical period. Thus the Periegetes restructures his itineraries according to a contemporary political reality, but one that sinks its roots in the past: this is what is brought out by the importance of the historical chapters through which Pausanias attaches what he sees to Arkadia's past. We can thus conclude that the organisation of the text derives from something other than the landscape: it reflects a political reality anchored in the past. This interest in the past of the life of the cities is still evident in the favoured place that Pausanias accords in his account to sanctuaries and religious traditions. Speaking of Phigalia, for instance, he does not hesitate to say that seeing the old sanctuary of Demeter Melaina was the essential reason for his visit (8.42.11).

Special interest in local religious traditions

The description of sanctuaries themselves is seldom detailed: it even happens that Pausanias offers only a random mention of the temple: for instance at Lykosoura à propos of the altars which are "in front of the temple" (8.37.2), and then "as one comes out of the temple" (8.37.7). This is so much the case that when he mentions a statue without locating it explicitly in a temple, the cult statue may be meant or an ex-voto outside a temple; only a comparison with archaeological data makes it possible to decide (for instance, at Megalopolis we know that the statue of Zeus Soter mentioned is that of the temple; at Alipheira, a base situated outside must correspond to Pausanias' reference: see Jost 1985, 225–226 and 81). In his description of cult statues Pausanias does not generally go beyond the name of the sculptor and a statement of the pose and the attributes of each of the deities. A particularly favourable case for appreciating his reliability is provided by the group at Lykosoura showing Despoina and Demeter seated between Artemis and Anytos. With the text of the *Periegesis* (8.37.3–6) can be compared important fragments of the group, 5m.80 high, found at the site in association with a colossal base, and also the coin-type of a large bronze coin of the very end of the second century found at Lykosoura and portraying Julia Domna, wife of Septimius Severus (Jost 1985, 327). The two central goddesses were sitting on a throne: the left hand of Demeter is resting on Despoina, observes Pausanias: "Despoina has a sceptre and on her knees what is called the cist [a small box for sacred objects] which she is holding with her right hand" (8.37.4). The Periegetes' description is borne out by the coin and the physical evidence. Thus, for the cist of Despoina, we possess a colossal right arm, bent at the elbow, which grips a fairly low object round in shape, the cist, which rested on her right thigh where it has also left traces (Levy-Marcadé 1972, 280–283). The pre-eminence of the daughter over the mother, manifest in the text from the assignment of the attributes, is confirmed by the facts. "Artemis was standing near Demeter" with a deerskin as garment and a quiver on her shoulder. With one hand she holds a torch, with the other two snakes" (8.37.5). Finally Anytos, the foster-father of Despoina according to a strictly Arkadian tradition, was standing to the left of Despoina, "in the guise of an armed man" (8.37.5). His head is preserved as well as some fragments; the coin confirms the pose.

Old statues have a very particular interest for Pausanias and there is no reason to raise doubts about his description when he mentions the *xoanon* with a horse's head of Demeter Melaina. Pausanias did not see the statue, but he retraces its vicissitudes very credibly. An old statue in wood that represented Demeter had "the appearance of a woman, save for the head: it had the head and the mane of a horse and representations of snakes and other wild animals were added on the head. She was clad in a tunic down to the very tips of her toes; she held a dolphin on one hand, a bird, a dove, on the other" (8.42.4). The statue was burnt; it was not at first replaced by the Phigalians, who neglected the sacrifices and the festivals. The land was made barren and the inhabitants of Phigalia found themselves advised by the Pythia to "pay the ancient honours" to the goddess. They appealed to the sculptor Onatas of Aigina who, in the first half of the fifth century, made for them a bronze statue that reproduced the ancient form: indeed he was working "having found a drawing or a copy of the old image and guided above all, from what they say, by a vision that he had in his dreams" (8.42.7). The statue of Onatas no longer existed in Pausanias' day and some of the Phigalians had even lost any memory of it. "At any rate," he adds, "the oldest of those I met told me that, three generations before him, stones fell on the statue from the roof of the cave, that it was broken by their fall, and that it had, so he said, completely disappeared." Pausanias confirms that he had seen in the roof "the place from which the stones had come free" (8.42.13). The antiquity of the representation and its theriomorphic aspect, peculiar to Arkadia, are the two points that attract the attention of the Periegetes. We thus see the care taken by Pausanias to record particular local features.

So far as concerns divine personalities, their cult and the legends attached to them, the chief originality of the *Periegesis* is in emphasising regional particularities. Pausanias gives the local name of deities and in this respect is very often our only source: for instance, for a number of epicleses derived from toponyms like Artemis Lykoatis (8.36.7) or Skiatis (8.35.5), that he learnt of on the spot, or of deities that have a strictly Arkadian personality like Demeter Erinys (8.25.6–7) or Athena Alea (8.45.4–47.4 and Jost 1985, *s.v.*). The interest of the text of the *Periegesis* resides in the fact that Pausanias does not yield to the temptation to assimilate local deities to those of the Greek pantheon: at Lykosoura for the daughter of Demeter he keeps her Arkadian name of Despoina (8.37.9) and, for the Great Goddesses of Megalopolis, he interprets them as Demeter and Kore but he takes care to note that the people of Megalopolis in fact call the second Soteira (8.31.1); near Megalopolis, he points out the existence of goddesses Maniai ('Mad'); "it is in my opinion," he says, "an epiclesis of the goddesses Eumenides" (8.34.1); this reference to a 'common' Greek name does not dispense him from relating a legend (8.34.2–4) which, while referring to Orestes, gives a purely local version (see Pirenne-Delforge 2001, 126–127 on this legend). The objectivity of Pausanias' account is a "sort of non-interference in the public truths of others" (Veyne 1983, 107). The systematic study of the divine epicleses that Pausanias cites allows us not only to be acquainted with strictly Arkadian deities but also to cast light on the particular content of apparently ordinary designations: for instance, Athena Poliatis at Tegea (8.47.5–6) offers, by means of a talisman, a magical order of protection to the city (see Jost, in press). Concerning Arkadia, I remain sensitive to the local diversities rather than the "cultic consensus of the Greeks" (Pirenne-Delforge 1998, 135, and article in press).[1]

The facts about cult and the legends are reported with the same obvious desire to throw light on what is peculiar to each sacred place; Pausanias specifies elsewhere on occasion that he has taken part in the rite: for instance, at Phigalia he offered "the produce of cultivated trees" (8.42.11). At Lykosoura he mentions two different sacrifices in front of the temple and in the *Megaron* (8.37.7–8). In front of the temple, "the Arkadians bring fruit from all cultivated trees, with the exception of the pomegranate" (8.37.7). The offering of the fruits of every sort is banal: the exclusion of the pomegranate recalls the disastrous part played by this fruit in the kidnapping of Kore-Persephone (*Homeric Hymn to Demeter*, 372); it thus offers evidence of an Eleusinian element at Lykosoura. In the *Megaron* "the Arkadians celebrate the initiation ceremonies and sacrifice to Despoina victims as numerous as they are abundant. Each of them sacrifices whatever animal he possesses; instead of cutting the victims' throat, as in other sacrifices, it is a limb chosen at random that each cuts off from the animal offered" (Paus. 8.37.8). The rite must not have been a part, strictly speaking, of the mysteries. It is remarkable for the freedom in choice of victims and for their abundance, but above all for the manner of rending the victims that recalls the orgiastic cult of Dionysos. The sacrifice, the dances with animal masks that can be supposed from small figures represented on a panel of the veil of Despoina, Kouretai and Korybantes shown on the steps of the goddesses' throne, take us to an unbridled setting that belongs peculiarly to Lykosoura (Jost 2002, 157–164 and fig. 6–8). At Pheneos the Periegetes describes yet another strictly local rite: "There is, on the Petroma [two large stones fitted one to the other that contain writings relating to the mysteries], a round coping that contains a mask of Demeter: the priest puts on the mask during the initiation known as 'major' to strike with rods, in conformity with some tradition, the inhabitants of the underworld" (8.15.3). In the course of the mysteries, during a ceremony which no doubt was not protected by secrecy, the priest of Demeter Kidaria puts the mask of the goddess on his face and strikes the "inhabitants of the underworld" with rods. Ὑποχθονίους, which is a correction of ἐπιχθονίους, designates the chthonian forces that the priest summons by exercising over them a form of magical compulsion. Behind the priest it is the goddess herself whose mask he wears who orders the sleeping forces to wake to a new life. The rite described by Pausanias thus invites us to see in the goddess an ancient deity of vegetation (Jost 1985, 319–322).

"The Greeks," observes Pausanias (9.16.7), "have legends of which the versions most often differ from each other." For these legends Pausanias knows the 'panhellenic' versions, those that refer back to a common substrate, to a vulgate (τά γνωριμώτατα) transmitted from Homer and Hesiod through Greek literature down to the compilation of a Pseudo-Apollodorus in his *Bibliotheca* and that "everyone knows by word of mouth" (9.33.2). But he makes efforts to give the local traditions on the occasion of his visit to the sites. Thus for Kallisto he cites in the introductory chapters (8.3.6) the Homeric tradition on the heroine's transformation into a constellation (the Great Bear or the Wain); but he notes the contradiction between that version and the Arkadian tradition that showed a tomb of Kallisto, and in fact on the road that leads from Megalopolis to the localities of the Arkadian interior he cites Kallisto's tomb (8.35.8). The account of the divine birth of Zeus even allows us to distinguish between local versions and regional version. À propos of the place known as Kretea Pausanias contrasts the Arkadian claims to have been the birthplace of Zeus with the better-attested version which set his birth in Crete (8.38.2). According to the official version of Megalopolis Rhea when pregnant with Zeus was supposed to have gone on to Mt. Thaumasion (beside Methydrion) in order to escape from Kronos; she would have given birth somewhere on Mt. Lykaion, and then it is again on Mt. Thaumasion that she would have cheated Kronos' voracity by giving him a stone wrapped in swaddling-clothes to devour (8.36.2–3 and 38.2). Manifestly the tradition of Methydrion and that of Mt. Lykaion have been 'manipulated' in such a way as to be, if not coherent, at least mutually compatible: the regional Arkadian version is the result of contamination of two local versions. It may be a consequence of the effort at political unity evidenced by the Arkadian Confederation (see Jost 1998a, 239–240 and, for the entry of Methydrion into the Confederarion, Nielsen 2002, 449–452).

For legends linked to cult there are numerous examples of local traditions: for instance, the story of Artemis the Hung (Apanchomene), formerly called Kondyleatis, at Kaphyai (8.23.7). The goddess reputedly changed epiclesis for the following reason. Children had knotted a rope around the neck of the goddess (meaning her image) and were saying that she was "hung"; the inhabitants of Kaphyai stoned them; a disease fell on the pregnant women who lost their children; the oracle at Delphi ordered them to carry out annual sacrifices to the children who had died unjustly and to call the goddess of Kondylea Apanchomene. The interpretation of the aetiological legend is not certain (cf. Jost, 2005); from it we can at least accept the original quality of Artemis Apanchomene. Another exemple: divine theriomorphism forms the starting-point for local legends that explain, at Thelpousa, the cultic epicleses of Demeter (Erinys and Lousia) and, at Phigalia, the form taken by her *xoanon* with a horse's head. "When Demeter was wandering," reports Pausanias (8.25.5–7), "at the time when she was looking for her daughter, Poseidon, according to the legend, starts to chase her, seized by a desire to mate with her; then, transformed into a mare, she goes to graze mingling with the mares of Onkos, but Poseidon realises that he has been tricked and mates with Demeter after himself taking the form of a stallion. At first Demeter was apparently furious at what had happened; but later, they say, she dropped her anger and wanted to bathe in the Ladon. As a result of which the goddess received two epicleses: because of her resentment, that of Erinys (because "to nurse one's anger" is *erinuein* in Arkadian), and then that of Lousia (bathing) because she "bathed" in the Ladon ... Demeter, so they say, had by Poseidon a daughter whose name it is not the custom to tell to those who are not initiated, and the horse Arion." The *logos* of Thelpousa also explained the epiclesis Hippios borne by Poseidon in all Arkadia. The legend of Demeter and Poseidon was found also at Phigalia with a variation that allows us once more to throw light on the local differences within a single region. "All that they say at Thelpousa about the intercourse that Poseidon had with Demeter is entirely accepted by the Phigalians; however the creature to which Demeter gave birth, according to the Phigalians, was not a horse but the deity that the Arkadians call Despoina" (8.42.1). The transformation of Poseidon and of Demeter is echoed here in the wooden statue of the goddess with a mare's head (8.42.4). The epicleses and the appearance of the cult statue are thus linked to local legends, which should not be overlooked by historians of religion (Jost 1985, passim).

Political history and an account of religious traditions combine to bring out a common 'Arkadian identity' in Pausanias' *Arkadika*: the land of Arkadia has a collective name and a common myth of origin, common historical events that Pausanias takes pleasure in listing, and a common culture with deities of its own, like Alea, elements of cult of its own, like divine theriomorphism, and national legends like that which claims the birth of Zeus (Jost 2002b). Was Pausanias' intention as J. Elsner thinks to define "the Greek identity" (1994, 224–254; 1995, 126–155; and 2001, 3–20)? The sum total of his descriptions by regions would amount, according to this scholar, to giving *a* unified image of *the* Greece that defined itself by its otherness in relation to Rome. The *Periegesis* would be a "programmatic" discourse of Pausanias on his "ideal of a 'Greece' that … was …" (Elsner 2001, 18)[2]. In truth I do not believe so. The various texts that are invoked to support a supposed 'panhellenism' of Pausanias are not decisive. Admittedly the list of "benefactors of Greece" (8.52.1–5) who have served well not "each his own homeland alone" but "Greece as a whole" recalls the idea of a Greek community. But one could readily cite, as a parallel, the list of exploits achieved in common (κοινῇ) by the Arkadians as a whole (8.6.1–2): in both cases the idea of community is central (Bearzot 2001, 93–108), but it is applied in the same way to all Greece or to a particular region. As for the epigram engraved on the statue of Epaminondas that boasts of a Greece "autonomous" and "free" (9.15.6), it refers not to a Greek unity but to the freedom recovered, thanks to Epaminondas, *from Sparta*. Finally, the passage of Book 7.17.1–2 on the misfortunes of Greece examines them κατά μέρη, "by region", and the regional framework is that which structures all the *Periegesis*. Does the interest of this work not reside precisely in the fact that the emphasis, far from being put on what is common to all the Greeks, is laid on what differentiates the customs, the gods, and the myths from one region to another? Moreover Pausanias' allusion in Book 1.26.4 to "all things Greek" is not associated with any idea of unity. After a digression on Artemis Leukophryene at Magnesia Pausanias picks up the thread of his discourse: "But I must continue my account, if I want to describe all Greece in this manner" (πάντα ... τά Ἑλληνικά): this is not, as J. Porter (2001, 68–69) thinks, the *hellenikon* of Herodotus (8.144.2). Pausanias is simply aware of the vastness of the subject and of the need to choose and to be brief, if he wants to succeed and to "cover in the same way all that concerns Greece".[3] In sum, the sense of regional diversities seems to me to prevail over that of Greek identity.[4] It corresponds to a wide-ranging curiosity about local particularisms, with a marked predilection for religious traditions.

Should Pausanias' interest in religion lead us to follow J. Elsner in seeing Pausanias as a "pilgrim" (Elsner 1992, 3–29; cf. earlier Hunt 1983, 400–401)? The notion of pilgrimage implies a personal piety and the celebration of rites, which can be applied to Pausanias. On the other hand, the dimension of spiritual quest that is found in the pilgrims at Eleusis is lacking in the *Periegesis* (Siebert 1974, 50–53; André and Baslez, 248–249, 260, and 558).[5] Moreover, and above all, the periegetic literature of Pausanias is not centred only on religion: his geographical and cultural horizon is wider than that of a pilgrim. That is why the expression 'cultural tourism' seems to me more suitable to define the *Periegesis*[6]: in it Pausanias satisfies curiosities of all sorts. Among these curiosities matters of religion occupy pride of place, but still leave space for other interests.

Acknowledgements

Je remercie de tout cœur Jim Roy d'avoir apporté tant de soin amical et de scrupuleuse exactitude dans la traduction de mon texte.

Notes

1 For the existence of a 'panhellenic' viewpoint in the approach to the gods, besides the mentions of literary epithets and local appellations, see the passage 7.21.7 in the *Periegesis*, quoted and analysed by Pirenne-Delforge (1998, 140–141), who also notes that observations of this form are rare.
2 Using a more subtly varied approach S. Alcock (1996, 251–256) studies the role of the Persian Wars in order to shape a "landscape of memory" in the sequence of references to ex-votos following battles: in her view these references to other times would be a way of resisting Rome.
3 As D. Musti (1996, 9–14) has shown, the wording echoes Herodotus 1.5, who announces "I shall proceed as my account progresses, covering without distinction the great cities of men and the little ones." This obviously refers both to descriptions of landscapes and accounts of events, which suggests reading the text of Pausanias in the same way.
4 See Jost (in press).
5 After Elsner, M. Dillon takes up the words 'pilgrims' and 'pilgrimage' in a sense which is very general but somewhat different: they apply to travel outside the territory of one's own city to go to *a* sacred place whose prestige surpasses that of the local sanctuaries (Dillon 1997, XV).
6 Cf. already Jacob 1980, 85, who writes of "cultural travels".

Bibliography

Alcock, S. E. (1993) *Graecia capta. The landscapes of Roman Greece* (Cambridge).

Alcock, S. E. (1995) 'Pausanias and the *Polis*: use and abuse', in M. H. Hansen (ed.) *Sources for the ancient Greek city-state (CPCActs 2)*, 326–44 (Copenhagen).

Alcock, S. E. (1996) "Landscape memory and the authority of Pausanias", in J. Bingen (ed.) *Pausanias historien. Entretiens sur l'Antiquité classique* 4, 241–76 (Geneva).

Alcock, S. E. (1999) 'The Roman territory of Greek cities', in M. Brunet (ed.) *Territoires des cités grecques*, *BCH* Suppl. 34, 326–44 (Paris-Athens).

André, J.-M. and Baslez, M.-F. (1993) *Voyager dans l'antiquité* (Paris).

Arafat, K. W. (1996) *Pausanias' Greece: ancient artists and Roman rulers* (Cambridge).

Arapoyanni, X. (2001) 'Ανασκαφές στη Φιγάλεια', in V. Mitsopoulos-Leon (ed.) *Forschungen in der Peloponnes. Akten des Symposions anlässlich der Feier '100 Jahre Österreichisches Archäologisches Institut in Athen'*, 299–305 (Athens).

Bearzot, C. (2001) 'La nozione di κοινόν in Pausania', in D. Knoepfler and M. Piérart (eds) *Editer, traduire, commenter Pausanias en l'an 2000*, 93–108 (Geneva).

Bowie, E. (2001) 'Inspiration and aspiration. Date, genre, and readership', in S. E. Alcock, J. F. Cherry, and J. Elsner (eds.) *Pausanias. Travel and memory in Roman Greece*, 21–32 (Oxford).

Casson, L. (1994) *Travel in the ancient world* (Baltimore and London).

Dillon, M. (1997) *Pilgrims and pilgrimage in ancient Greece* (New York and London).

Dubois, L. (1986) *Recherches sur le dialecte arcadien* II, *Corpus dialectal* (Louvain-la-Neuve).

Elsner, J. R. (1992) 'Pausanias: a Greek pilgrim in a Roman world', *Past and Present* 135, 3–29.

Elsner, J. R. (1994) 'From the Pyramids to Pausanias and Piglet: monuments, travel, and writing', in S. Goldhill and R. Osborne (eds.) *Art and text in ancient Greek culture*, 224–54 (Cambridge).
Elsner, J. R. (1995) *Art and the Roman viewer: the transformation of art of the Roman Empire AD 100–450* (Cambridge).
Elsner, J. R. (2001) 'Structuring 'Greece': Pausanias' *Periegesis* as a literary construct' in S. E. Alcock, J. F. Cherry, and J. Elsner (eds.) *Pausanias: Travel and memory in Roman Greece*, 3–20 (Oxford).
Habicht, C. (1985) *Pausanias' Guide to Ancient Greece* (Berkeley-Los Angeles-London).
Heberdey, R. (1984) *Die Reisen des Pausanias in Griechenland* (Prague).
Hiller von Gaertringen, F., and H. Lattermann (1911) *Arkadische Forschungen* (Berlin).
Hunt, E. D. (1984) 'Travel, tourism, and piety in the Roman Empire: A context for the beginnings of Christian pilgrimage', *EMC* 28, 391–417.
Jacob, C. (1980) 'The Greek traveller's areas of knowledge: Myth and other discourses in Pausanias' *Description of Greece*', *Yale French Studies* 59, 65–85.
Jacquemin, A. (1991) 'Les curiosités naturelles chez Pausanias', *Ktèma* 16, 123–30.
Jost, M. (1973) 'Pausanias en Mégalopolitide', *REA* 75, 241–67.
Jost, M. (1986) [1990] 'Villages de l'Arcadie antique', *Ktèma* 11, 145–58.
Jost, M. (1996) 'Le vocabulaire de la description des paysages dans les Arkadika de Pausanias', *CRAI*, 719–38.
Jost, M. (1998a) 'Versions locales et versions 'panhelléniques' des myths arcadiens chez Pausanias', in V. Pirenne-Delforge (ed.) *Les panthéons des cités, des origins à la Périégèse de Pausanias* Kernos Suppl. 8, 227–40 (Liège).
Jost, M. (1998b) 'Notice', in Pausanias, *Description de la Grèce*, Tome 8, Livre VIII, text by M. Casevitz, translation and commentary by M. Jost, with participation by J. Marcadé, Collection des Universités de France, Belles-Lettres (Paris).
Jost, M. (2002a) 'Mystery cults in Arcadia', in M. Cosmopoulos (ed.) *Greek mysteries: The archaeology and ritual of ancient Greek secret cults*, 143–68 (London-New York).
Jost, M. (2002b) 'L'identité arcadienne dans les *Arkadika* de Pausanias', in C. Muller and F. Prost (eds.) *Identités et cultures dans le monde méditerranéen antique*, 367–84 (Paris).
Jost, M. (2005) 'Quelques epiclèses divines en Arcadie: typologie et cas particuliers', in L. Pernod and F. Prost (eds.) *Nommer les dieux: Onomastique et religion en Grèce ancienne, Actes des Colloques de Rennes et Strasbourg 2001–2*, 367–84 (Turnhout).
Jost, M. (in press) 'Unité et diversité: la Grèce de Pausanias' (to appear in *REG* 120, 2007).
Leake, W. M. (1846) *Peloponnesiaka* (London).
Musti, D. (1996) 'La struttura nel discorso storico in Pausania', in J. Bingen (ed.) *Pausanias historien: Entretiens sur l'Antiquité classique* 41, 9–34 (Vandoeuvres-Geneva).
Nielsen, T. (2002) *Arkadia and its poleis in the archaic and classical periods, Hypomnemata* 140 (Göttingen).
Pirenne-Delforge, V. (1998) 'La notion de 'panthéon' chez Pausanias', in V. Pirenne-Delforge (ed.) *Les panthéons des cités, des origines à la Périégèse de Pausanias* Kernos Suppl. 8, 129–48 (Liège).
Pirenne-Delforge, V. (2001) 'Les rites sacrificiels dans la *Périégèse* de Pausanias', in D. Knoepfler and M. Piérart (eds.) *Editer, traduire, commenter Pausanias en l'an 2000*, 109–34 (Geneva).
Pirenne-Delforge, V. (in press) 'La portée du témoignage de Pausanias sur les cultes locaux.'
Porter, J. I. (2001) 'Ideals and ruins: Pausanias, Longinus, and the Second Sophistic', in S. E. Alcock, J. F. Cherry, and J. Elsner (eds.) *Pausanias: Travel and memory in Roman Greece*, 21–32 (Oxford).
Pritchett, W. K. (1982) *Studies in ancient Greek topography* I (Amsterdam).
Pritchett, W. K. (1999) *Pausanias Periegetes* II (Amsterdam).
Puillon Boblaye, M. E. (1836) *Expédition scientifique de Morée: Recherches géographiques sur les ruines de la Morée* (Paris).
Rhomaios, K. (1957) 'Τεγεατικὸν ἱερὸν Ἀρτεμιδος κνακεάτιδος', *Arch. Eph.* 114–163.

Rutherford, I. (2001) 'Tourism and the sacred: Pausanias and the traditions of Greek pilgrimage', in S. E. Alcock, J. F. Cherry, and J. Elsner (eds.) *Pausanias: Travel and memory in Roman Greece*, 21–32 (Oxford).
Siebert, G. (1974) 'Réflexions sur la notion de pélérinage dans la Grèce antique', *Pélérinages. Etudes d'histoire des religions* I de l'Université des Sciences humaines de Strasbourg (Paris).
Veyne, P. (1983) *Les Grecs ont-ils cru à leurs mythes ?* (Paris).

Greek Intellectuals on the Move: Travel and *Paideia* in the Roman Empire

Maria Pretzler

The elite of the Roman empire could take travelling for granted. Texts of the Roman imperial period often mention journeys, and some literary works specifically focus on travelling, be it Pausanias' *Periegesis* with its detailed descriptions of cities and sites in Greece, Aristides' *Sacred Tales* which trace his many trips inspired by Asclepius, or the novels that usually focus on fateful journeys. I explore the cultural context of these texts to explain what made travelling so important to these authors and their audience. Peace and prosperity in the Roman empire made travelling easier for everyone, not just for the elites, and there is good evidence for large numbers of people on the move for various reasons (Casson 1994, 115–37). Most ancient literary sources, however, document the viewpoint of a very small elite, and I shall focus on this particularly vocal group.

The literary output of the second century AD in particular is dominated by works connected to the Second Sophistic. Philostratus coined this term in his *Lives of the Sophists* (*VS* 507; Anderson 1986, 11–21), focusing on some of the most vocal authors of the period who were indeed professional sophists, teachers of rhetoric and rhetorical performers. Other Greek authors of the period and some Latin writers as well, most notably Apuleius, share in the same elite culture that had a crucial influence on their writings. The elites in many cities of the Roman empire saw Greek *paideia* – education or culture – as their ideal. The Greek intellectuals mentioned in my title would have called themselves *pepaideumenoi* – men who are educated and who have achieved *paideia* (Anderson 1993, 8–11). As we shall see, travelling was closely connected to acquiring an education, and once this goal was achieved, there were many reasons that kept a member of the cultured elite on the move. Indeed, travel experiences and expertise were an important part of the self-representation of the wealthy, educated upper-class (Anderson 1993, 28–30).

Greek texts of the classical period focus on the world of the Greek city, which one leaves on campaign or political business, or, if one is very unlucky or criminal, as an exile. Being forced to be away from one's city is a misfortune: the *zoon politikon* is bound to his *polis* and not a whole being outside it (Aristotle, *Ath. Pol.* 1253a1–4; Whitmarsh 2001, 271). In the Roman imperial period the Greek East of the empire was still a world of cities with their own cultural identities, histories and 'national' (rather than merely civic) pride. This was the main arena for elite activities, and local patriotism was seen as the correct behaviour for a man of truly Hellenic culture (Swain 1996, 69–70). Thus, writers of the Second Sophistic period always hark back to the ideal of the *polis*, and many texts of the time focus on historical themes set before Alexander's conquests (Bowie 1974, esp. 170–4; Anderson 1993, 103–5; Swain 1996, 93–96).

Nevertheless, there was no denying the fact that the role of the Greek city had changed fundamentally ever since the beginning of the Hellenistic period. Greeks may have lamented the fact that their *poleis* were no longer independent states but the elite adapted to the new circumstances, especially under the Roman empire which offered the local ruling classes in the provinces increasing opportunities to gain a share in the power. Elite activities on a local, civic level were now carried out alongside duties on a supraregional level, often on behalf of the empire and its administration. The late first century saw the first Roman senators from the Greek East, and by the time of Trajan Greeks could also reach higher senatorial offices, including the consulship. There were also prestigious provincial positions which gave local elites a stake in the empire, for example priesthoods of the imperial cult.

At the same time Greek cities' survival depended on their prominent citizens. Where members of the elite reaped the benefits of the large and peaceful empire it was increasingly possible that the fortune of a few individuals matched or surpassed the wealth of a whole city. Pausanias remarks quite matter-of-factly that there were cities that lacked the means of even a moderately wealthy man (Paus. 8.33.2). In all except the very largest cities private benefactors would belong to just a handful of families at most, and smaller cities may not have had a single family that could compete even on a provincial level. The most obvious aspect of elite activities in support of their city were their financial contributions to the daily expenses of a city, and, more crucially, they paid for special events, buildings and improvements to the civic infrastructure.

A Greek city also had to ensure its success and survival among its neighbours and within the wider context of the empire, and for this it had to rely on the supraregional contacts of its elite families. Close links between inter-city diplomacy and family relations had a long tradition, as far back as Archaic Greece where aristocratic family ties dominated the foreign activities of many *poleis*. Although Greek cities in the Roman empire no longer acted as independent states, diplomatic activities were still crucial. The survival of a city as a viable community depended on the integrity of its territory, on good relations with neighbours who might otherwise dispute boundaries or rights, and on good relations with the emperor (Alcock 1993, 201–2). Cities competed for attention from the central administration, in particular the emperor, who could grant them significant privileges.

The reputation of a city was the main capital in this struggle for recognition, and elite individuals could do much to help. An illustrious past was especially important in this context, and patriotic *pepaideumenoi* could enhance the effect by keeping local history alive, or by embellishing it with reference to prestigious literature such as the Homeric epics or to the widely known mythical tradition (Pretzler 2005a; Robert 1977, 120–129; *SEG* 2.549: Argos honouring a scholar for historical 'research'). The city then relied on rhetorically skilled elite members to spread the word among neighbouring cities, or, more rarely, in front of the emperor. Professional sophists in particular could be expected to argue their city's case with officials and influential Romans: apart from the necessary education personal acquaintances in Rome and around the empire were therefore especially useful and prestigious (Bowersock 1969, 43–58, 76–88). Some outstanding individuals could assist their city by their international prestige alone: according to Philostratus, Polemo's ostentatious style contributed to the glory of Smyrna (Philostr. *VS* 532) and he managed to procure privileges for his city even from beyond the grave when just after his death a speech he had prepared for the occasion was read out to the emperor (Philostr. *VS* 539–40). It should not come as a surprise, therefore, that Greek cities saw their famous intellectuals as a great asset, as we can see in Strabo's *Geography* (esp. books 13 and 14) where descriptions of cities of the Greek East often include lists of resident philosophers and scholars (Salmeri 2000, 65–77; Desideri 2000; Brunt 1994, 24–5, 34–5).

An acquaintance with the wider world was crucial for wealthy Greeks and their activities on behalf of their city. In fact, for members of the elite the narrow ancient *polis* world was a convenient and conventional cultural vehicle, while in reality their lives were no longer restricted to just one city. Notables of the Eastern empire often had widespread family ties, and many held citizenships in several cities. Polemo, for example, was actually from Laodicea in Caria, but he had also become a citizen of Smyrna. Some cities were especially attractive to such distinguished intellectuals and sophists, especially those that could offer the company of many *pepaideumenoi* and a good infrastructure for learned activities (Bowersock 1969, 17–21). Smyrna was, in fact, one such city, as was Pergamon where many members of the provincial elite assembled in the sanctuary of Asclepius (Behr 1968, 42–3). Many distinguished men were keen on becoming Athenians, for example Arrian of Nicomedia who, after a Roman career, settled down in Athens and even became archon there (Stadter 1980, 5–18; cf. Dio Chrysostom: Dio 13.31, 38.1, 41.1–2, 42.3–5, 44.6, Salmeri 2000, 77–92).

Small cities were lucky if their eminent men did not turn their backs on them, or if they continued to pay attention to them while enjoying the advantages of living in one of the great intellectual centres. Plutarch was probably an exception when he decided to stay in his small town of Chaeronea in Boeotia because he did not want it to become even smaller. Even Plutarch, however, points out what an advantage it is to live in a large, famous city which offers access to a large number of books, and, presumably, stimulating intellectual company (Plut., *Dem.* 2). Some exceptionally wealthy men could turn their attention to several places, for example Herodes Atticus, whose generosity benefited many places in Greece and beyond

(Ameling 1983, 84–94; Philostr., *VS* 551). Elite intellectuals may have been ready to express their local patriotism when it was expedient to do so, but in practice many could not be seen as belonging to one city only. No wonder, perhaps, that Favorinus criticises people who restrict themselves to their own small patch: he thinks that one should regard the whole world as one's home (Favorinus, *De ex.* 10.4; Whitmarsh 2001, 301, cf. Philostr. *VA* 134).

By the second century AD most members of the elite enjoyed Roman citizenship. The most distinguished provincials also gained access to a Roman career, and even if they did not choose this path they were expected to take on prestigious positions in their province (Bowersock 1969, 34–42; Brunt 1994, 34–5; Salmeri 2000, 58–63). Only a very small number actually reached the highest offices of the empire, but nevertheless the lifestyle connected to the Roman *cursus honorum* may well have had an impact on attitudes to travelling. As the Roman empire grew, climbing the career ladder increasingly meant going abroad at regular intervals. In the West being a successful politician had long involved long periods abroad, and few would have tried to avoid these absences from Rome, especially because provincial postings could mean considerable financial gain. In the imperial period a series of positions in various provinces was standard not only in the traditional *cursus honorum* which led to the consulship, but also for less distinguished equestrian and senatorial administrative careers, let alone military ones. Provincials would perhaps first move to Rome and then serve in various functions in Rome or anywhere around the empire. Once stationed in a province a governor and his staff, but also provincial priests and officials who functioned on a more local level, would find themselves travelling from city to city to fulfil their public duties. The emperors themselves often had travelled widely when they came to the throne, and some continued to travel during their reign. Hadrian in particular spent most of his life on the move, visiting virtually all provinces of the empire (Halfman 1986, esp. 188–210; Birley 1997, 1). Roman administrative habits meant that power and influence were directly connected with extended travelling and this was bound to have an impact on elite attitudes and lifestyles.

The Roman empire did not only require distinguished individuals to travel, it also provided circumstances that made travelling much easier than it had been ever before. This was in Rome's own interest, since the wealth of Rome and Italy depended on safe transport of goods and people to and from the provinces, but the whole empire profited from increased connectivity around the Mediterranean. For about 200 years the empire could guarantee internal peace and stability which made travelling comparatively safe. The Romans even ensured relative security from robbers and pirates, even if these provide crucial and ubiquitous plot devices in the novels of the period (Braund 1993, 204–10; Anderson 1984, 77; Hägg 1983, 114). It seems that at least in the densely populated areas one could happily ride along on one's own at any time of day or night, although travelling in style usually meant travelling with numerous attendants (Aristides, *ST* 5.15–18).

There was dense traffic on the Mediterranean Sea and beyond, and on land most areas were provided with good roads and the infrastructure necessary for travellers. Wherever one went one could use the same currency, one could rely on similar legal standards and one language, or two at most, would suffice to make oneself understood. Even more importantly, perhaps, in most parts of the empire the elite had a similar lifestyle and standard of education so that a distinguished traveller's status would be easily recognised wherever he went. In fact, elite networks could probably ensure that in most parts of the empire a visitor could make contact with his peers and find a host who would offer him hospitality more appropriate to his status than what most inns would provide (Apuleius, *Metamorphoses* 1.21–2; Casson 1994, 87–90, 197–209; Pretzler 2004, 204–5).

It is, therefore, not surprising that many Second Sophistic authors mention travelling in passing, as a normal aspect of life. Most of them, even those who are known as relatively settled such as Plutarch, were probably expert travellers with an intimate knowledge of the practicalities involved (cf. Aristides *ST* 5.13–18) and some even found ways of passing the time spent on the road, for example by reading and writing in a carriage (Pliny, *Ep.* 3.5.14–16 on the elder Pliny; Aristides *ST* 4.4). Travelling became so common, it seems, that Pliny could complain that people knew foreign lands better than the sights of their own home (Pliny, *Ep.* 8.20.1–2). Given the important role of travel for the elite of the Roman empire it should come as no surprise that the ideal of Greek culture and education was intimately connected with mobility. In fact, acquiring a respectable level of *paideia* usually meant going abroad. Basic education for children would be available locally, but some young men would have to move to the next large city for quality education at some point during their teens, for example Apuleius of Madaurus who was educated in Carthage, some 200 km from his home town (today M'daurouch in Algeria. Ap., *Florida* 20.9–10; Harrison 2000, 1–5; Sandy 1997, 18).

A man who aspired to become a true *pepaideumenos* needed to study rhetoric with one of the distinguished sophists. The best locations for such studies were Athens and a number of cities in Asia Minor, especially Smyrna or Ephesos. Philostratus stresses that the most prominent of the sophists had pupils from the whole Greek world (e.g. Philostr., *VS* 518, cf. 516, 530, 591; Bowersock 1969, 17–18; Anderson 1993, 22–4). Aspiring sophists could also travel around to hear different teachers, or they had the opportunity to hear famous sophists on their lecture tours. As a consequence, people in the business would know each other and their rhetorical styles, so much so that parodies of different sophists were a possible mode of learned entertainment (Philostr., *VS* 586).

Young men from outside the (classical) Greek world also aspired to joining this exclusive circle of *pepaideumenoi*, for example Lucian of Samosata on the upper Euphrates, Apuleius from North Africa or Favorinus of Arelate (Arles) in Gaul, which means that Greek sophists did accept pupils who were not Greek native speakers. Some of these outsiders did become successful sophists, Lucian and

Favorinus using Greek, while Apuleius returned to writing in Latin. Members of western elites had started to achieve proficiency in Greek as early as in the second century BC, but higher education in a Greek centre of learning meant more than acquiring perfect language skills. For the outsiders travelling to study with a sophist meant to aspire to the ideal of *paideia*. The most successful among these aspiring sophists from the margins of the Greek world became Greek, or rather they learned how to assume a Greek persona (Swain 1996, 33–51). Lucian, for example, represents his younger self as a barely civilised Syrian with a thick accent who is taken to Ionia where he gets the opportunity to become a Greek sophist (Luc., *Bis accusatus* 27, cf. *somnium* 15; Jones 1986, 6–14).

Since a Greek education acquired in the cultural centres of Greece conferred prestige, an intellectual journey to the east of the Roman empire also became a status symbol. In his *Apology* Apuleius explains how he spent his inherited money, and he proudly lists a stay in Athens together with some travelling among other respectable causes such as giving various kinds of support to friends (Ap., *Apology* 23; Harrison 2000, 5–6; Sandy 1997, 4, 8). Like Apuleius, young men of the elite would not just stay with their sophist teacher, but they would also travel to see important cities and interesting historical sites. The great sanctuaries and sites of Greece and Asia Minor, for example Olympia, Delphi, Athens and Troy would have a high priority on such a Grand Tour, centres of learning and culture such as Pergamon or Alexandria were also worth a visit, and many would travel to Egypt to see the ancient pharaonic monuments (Casson 1994, 229–37, 253–62). The experience gained on such trips could later be put to good use in speeches and learned works, and, in the case of Aristides, they recur even in dreams (Behr 1968: 16–20; e.g. Aristid., *ST* 1.24, 26, 61, 3.3–4, 38). While a knowledge of the Greek world and all things Greek was crucial for all educated men in the empire, Rome and the Latin speaking West rarely interested the authors of the Second Sophistic period (with the notable exception of Plutarch). A trip to Rome was nevertheless considered a crucial part of an aspiring sophist's career because a good knowledge of the city and, more importantly, contacts to important people in the imperial capital were likely to be useful for any member of the elite.

Once a young man had reached sufficient levels of *paideia* he could aspire to become a professional sophist. In this capacity he would teach rhetoric himself, usually in a school based in a particular place. Some stars of the profession could command impressive fees for lecturing and rhetorical performances even in the centres of Greek learning. Good sophists who were less fortunate found that far beyond the Greek world there were many who were willing to pay good money for high standard Greek rhetoric. Lucian, for example, mentions that he practiced in Gaul where he earned fees as high as any distinguished sophist elsewhere (Lucian, *Apology* 15). As a Syrian Lucian may have been an outsider in Greece, but the niche market in the West offered him good opportunities.

Distinguished sophists and all who aspired to that title had to keep moving to remain competitive in the supraregional community of their peers. They had to go on tour to perform as public speakers in order to keep up a reputation beyond their own cities which would attract pupils and gain them respect from fellow-sophists (e.g. Aristides, *ST* 5.56). Rhetorical performances on such speaking tours could focus on standard classical themes, for example an argument concerning a political situation known from classical authors such as Thucydides or Demosthenes. It was also possible to get away with praising a city by using general commonplaces and the general impression gained on a short visit (e.g. Aristid., 26, *Praise of Rome*). At times, however, visiting sophists chose to address specific local issues, and in this case the speaker would actually have to know a good deal about the city he was visiting (e.g. Dio 31 on Rhodes; 33, 34 on Tarsus; 35 on Apameia in Phrygia). One might expect that the visiting sophist would stay in a city for a while to give some lectures and rhetorical performances. At the same time he could make the acquaintance of the local elite and (if it was worthwhile) do some sightseeing. If used in an appropriate way both the knowledge and the personal contacts gained in this way could enhance a sophist's standing.

Well known orators would also be invited to speak at festivals and special occasions such as the opening of new buildings or the visit of a notable Roman (e.g. Philostr., *VS* 533). Other sophists would attend even if they were not explicitly invited because the mass gatherings at festivals in particular offered good opportunities for anyone seeking publicity. This could be a sophist who would want to become known in the area by declaiming in front of a large audience (Lucian *Herodotus* 7), but some individuals opted for more extravagant actions. The most extreme example is perhaps that of Peregrinus who committed public suicide at the Olympic games of AD 167 which attracted worldwide attention and scathing criticism from Lucian (Lucian, *Peregrinus*, cf. Philostr., *VS* 563; Casson 1994, 136–7).

Travel, therefore, was crucial to maintain sophists' careers, and the experience and contacts gained in the process gave them an advantage in supraregional politics which distinguished and exposed them among local elites. Cities expected their resident professor of rhetoric to use his skills and contacts in negotiations with other cities, governors and the emperor (Bowersock 1969, 26–9). Such activities involved great expense and, yet again, extensive travelling. Negotiations with the authorities could bring great honour, but at times they were conducted at great personal risk because eloquent ambassadors could attract the anger of an emperor or governor just as well as his goodwill. Some prominent sophists, therefore, found themselves sent into exile.

Just as ideas about a man's dependence on his city had changed, so the image of the exile could also be interpreted in new ways. As a citizen of the whole *oikoumene* an exiled sophist could take on the guise of the wandering philosopher. Dio Chrysostom suffered this fate and once the political situation had changed to allow him a return to the centres of Greek culture his time in exile served him well in his speeches. With a new regime in place he could boast of his resistance to Domitian, and his stories of lone wandering without dependence on worldly means allowed him to adopt the persona of a wise and simple philosopher, a useful rhetorical device because this image provided a conscious contrast to the sophisticated culture of the Greek elite (Whitmarsh 2001; Dio 1.50, 7.1–7, 12.17–20, 13.2–11, 36.1–6).

Given that travelling was such a crucial aspect of life for most Greek writers of the Roman imperial period, we can expect it to play an important role in their texts as well. I shall now proceed to exploring ways in which travel is represented and used in literary texts, and how such references could reflect upon the (often carefully constructed) persona of an author.

Personal experience was important to enhance an author's credibility. This has a long tradition in Greek literature: the classical historians were already backing up their claims in this way, and from Herodotus and Thucydides onwards a knowledge of important places and perhaps even historical figures gave a writer special authority. Personal experience influences the meaning of a text because it gives the author a stake in the argument. The closer the author shows himself to the content of his text the more he defines his persona in relation to the events or places described, and the more the reader will have to think about the connections between the author's agenda and the information he is offering. At times too close a relationship could therefore be a disadvantage, and an author may choose to conceal just how involved he is with his story, for example when Xenophon never explicitly says that he, the 'anonymous' author of the *Anabasis*, is in fact the same person as the Xenophon who features so prominently in the narrative.

Most authors, however, took advantage of a claim of personal involvement and experience, and in the Roman empire in particular this often involved knowledge gained through extensive travelling. Polybius, the first Greek whose work deals with a Greek world under Roman influence, points out that Greeks were now no longer in the position to pursue military or political careers, which meant they had time to explore a world where, thanks to the Romans, travelling had become much easier (Polyb. 3.59). All this seems somewhat ironic coming from a man who was forced to go to Italy as a hostage, but these statements seem to be quite sincere. Polybius had a sense that the Roman empire made it necessary for the Greek elite to redefine their position, and he suggests that intellectual pursuits were the best way of doing so (Bowie 1974, 175–78; Nicolet 1988, 79; Henderson 2001). He himself felt that his involvement in important events was a crucial incentive to write his *Histories* (Polyb. 3.4), and once he was allowed to do so he himself made extensive use of the opportunity to travel in order to enhance the credibility of his historical accounts (e.g. Polyb. 3.48, 3.59, 12.25, 27; cf. Ephorus, *FGrHist* 70 F 110).

Autopsy played an especially crucial role for scholarly arguments concerning geography and 'global' history, and, due to the Romans, better access to scarcely known areas allowed new research into these areas. One could, in fact, take the tradition of exploration by travelling all the way back to the *Odyssey* (and to an extent also to the *Iliad*) which still defined the way in which Greeks thought about

Geography and history of the regions around the Mediterranean (Strabo 1.1.2, 8. 3. 3). Some Hellenistic scholars were even ready to criticise Homer by contrasting their own topographical research with information given in the Homeric epics (Engels 1999, 115–20). By the time Strabo composed his *Geography* it was necessary to state one's travelling experience (Strabo 2.5.11). Strabo boasts that he has travelled far, although most modern commentators agree that much of Strabo's work is, in fact, not based on autopsy. Strabo's claim and his attack on Eratosthenes on the grounds that his work was not sufficiently based on autopsy therefore seems like a commonplace of scholarly writing (Strabo 1.2.2; Engels 1999, 28–32, 109–10; Dueck 2000, 15–30).

Second Sophistic writers were well aware of this scholarly tradition, and they turned (more or less justified) claims to autopsy into a forceful literary device. At times the mere setting of an account could influence its meaning and authority. Dio often made use of this, using his wanderings as a philosopher in exile as a backdrop for (probably partly imaginary) travel experiences. For example, he discusses the life of the poor by telling a story about a poor Euboean family he claims to have stayed with, and some of his ideas on kingship allegedly come from a prophetess he met in a rural Arcadian sanctuary (Dio 1.50–56, 7.1–7). These stories allow him to give his ideas an independent external source while reminding his audience of his own experience with hardship and the consequences of exile. In a speech delivered in his home-town of Prusa Dio claims to recapitulate a discussion he had in Borysthenes, a scarcely Greek city on the River Hypanis (Bug) north of the Black Sea. The discourse starts with a realistic description of the city, followed by an exploration of some essentially Greek problems from a carefully constructed 'Barbarian' viewpoint (Dio 36). In all three cases most of the argument does not have much to do with the actual knowledge of the region in which the story is set, but the setting itself allows Dio to give his argument a particular twist, while at the same time enhancing his credentials as a philosopher who has seen the world.

Claims to personal experience are often used in a more traditional, scholarly way, for example when Aristides refers to his trips to Egypt while discussing traditional theories on the floods of the Nile (Aristid. 36). In fact, these personal observations do not actually add anything to the scientific argument, but presumably they were still a good device to give Aristides' opinion on the matter more weight (Behr 1968, 16–20). At times sophists liked to present themselves as serious scholars by referring to their own original research. Aristides, for example, says that he took measurements of Egyptian monuments, and when Dio speaks of a trip to the Getai on the lower Danube he stresses that the sole purpose of his journey was scholarly interest (Aristides 36.1: Dio 12.17–20). In Lucian's work we find this principle subverted into parody: his hero Menippus is dissatisfied with the philosophers' teachings on the heavens and on ethics and he decides to fly to sun, moon and stars and to visit the underworld in order to find hard evidence to answer problematic questions. Even parody acknowledges the connection between travel and scholarly authority (Luc., *Menippus*, esp. 6 ; *Icaromenippus*, esp. 10).

This attitude is the context for Pausanias' *Periegesis* which is based on years of painstakingly detailed research in hundreds of cities and sites in Greece. For Pausanias autopsy is crucial (Paus. 2.22.3; see Arafat 1996, 17–18), and much of his work is built around the authority and originality that one can achieve by original research on site. Habicht thought of Pausanias as an eccentric loner who followed his esoteric interests without managing to attract an audience (Habicht 1985, 26–7). The cultural context of his work, however, would suggest a very different picture. Pausanias' tireless research activities may well have brought him admiration among his educated peers, and it is likely that the knowledgeable and interested visitor from Asia Minor was a welcome guest in many of the places he passed through (Pretzler 2004, 205–7; Pretzler 2005b, 237–9, Hutton 2005, 47–53).

There were certainly travel books that offered detailed descriptions of specific ancient sites, for example four books on the Athenian Acropolis by Polemo of Troy (Strabo 9. 1. 16). Pausanias offers a guide to a large part of mainland Greece, and, given the experience of travellers who still used his book as a guide in the early nineteenth century (Dodwell 1819, 403–4; Leake 1830, viii), his *Periegesis* could be useful as a guidebook, especially in a time when local people could complement its learned commentary with information concerning the exact location of particular monuments (Pretzler 2004, 201–4, Hutton 2005, 242–7).

A description of mainland Greece in particular would be useful to anyone who had a claim to Greek *paideia*. After all, most of the texts that were part of a standard higher education were set in Greece and consequently rhetorical exercises, contemporary literary works and learned conversation would often require a good knowledge of Greek historical topography. Since many in an audience of *pepaideumenoi* probably knew Athens, if not some of the other famous sites of Greece, it was important to have exact information about historical locations and significant monuments in the best known sites. Pausanias' *Periegesis* could provide such details even for readers who could not go and see Greece for themselves.

Even when it was not necessary to claim personal knowledge of particular sites or places there were still many aspects of education that were related to an acquaintance with different parts of the (Greek) world. Athenaios' *Deipnosophistae* illustrates and exaggerates the setting for a veritable trivia competition among a group of *pepaideumenoi* who try to surpass each other by presenting out-of the way facts and quotations about all aspects of dinner (Too 2000). In this context a list of where the best wheat or honey can be found is just as useful as a story about a strange local custom somewhere inside or beyond the Greek world. Second Sophistic writers liked to show off this sort of information, from Plutarch and his collection of local peculiarities in his collections of *Greek* and *Roman Questions* to Aelian's *Varia Historia*. Pausanias' *Periegesis* also provides many such details, often supported by a credible claim of autopsy, and some of this information is even offered in easily remembered lists, for example when Pausanias presents springs or rivers with special properties (Paus. 4.35.8–12, 8.17.3–4, 8.28.2–3). Details about cities in particular were not only useful when *pepaideumenoi* showed off their knowledge, but they also supplied comparative material, for example for occasions where an orator praised or criticised a city in a speech (e.g. Dio 32.52, on Alexandria; cf. Dio 31.33). In a world where cities were in constant competition such comparisons made for forceful arguments, and an orator may well have been inclined to supplement his own travel experience with information from books such as Pausanias' *Periegesis*. Some fields of knowledge were less easily learned from books than lists of natural curiosities or local monuments. The best example for such expertise is art connoisseurship, which ranked highly as an elite pursuit, especially in the Roman imperial period which regarded the 'old masters' of the Classical period some 500 years earlier with special esteem. It is quite striking what expertise some ancients reached in this field, an expertise which can only be acquired by comparing and analysing many examples (Arafat 1996, 45–75; Snodgrass 2001).

Educated men were quite able to assess the style of a statue or painting and to compare it to a canon of numerous famous artworks. They could also expect that their peers would be able to understand such connections because they would know what the works cited as reference looked like. For example, Arrian describes a statue he saw on his trip on the Black Sea by comparing it to Phidias' Meter in Athens (Arrian, *Periplous* 9.1). Pausanias expects his readers to understand how one recognises the styles of individual artists, and to be familiar with the style of sculptors such as Phidias or Polycleitus and painters such as Polygnotus (Paus. 2.4.5, 3.19. 2, 5.17.2–3, 5.25.5, 7.26.6, 9.11.4). He even uses sophisticated comparisons of style, technique and material to interpret artworks and to determine relative dates (Arafat 1996, 45–75). Lucian confirms that Pausanias was not alone in expecting such expertise from his audience. As so often, the sophist from Samosata finds a creative way to exploit his contemporaries' interests: in his *Eikones* he describes a woman by assembling pieces of famous statues and paintings, and he clearly expects his readers to draw on their knowledge of these artworks in order to create the image in their minds (Lucian, *Eikones* 6–7).

Given the surviving examples of ancient sculpture, copies of classical statues were relatively common, certainly in private collections in Italy, and probably there were also copies of the most celebrated paintings by the Old Masters (Lucian, *Zeuxis* 3). Nevertheless, for anyone who did not live in the few centres with large numbers of accessible originals or copies, some travelling would be necessary to acquire the level of expertise that Pausanias and Lucian seem to expect. Especially celebrated originals apparently attracted visitors who came specifically to see the one artwork, for example the Aphrodite of Knidos or the Zeus of Olympia (Lucian, *Amores* 11; Dio 12, esp. 12.25; Casson 1994, 229–37).

Members of the elite in the Roman empire were, however, not just passive admirers of art. They also had an active stake in it because as benefactors they could, to a certain extent, commission new monuments, buildings and artworks. This active contribution to the memorial landscape of a site was not always restricted to a man's own city.

For example, on a trip made as governor of Cappadocia Arrian found some statues and buildings in Trapezous unsatisfactory and promptly started on improving them; he even asked Hadrian to send a better statue of Hermes to complete his efforts by giving the temple a new image worth of its setting (Arrian, *Periplous* 2.1). In this case nothing is known of the reaction on the part of the locals, but such actions were at times controversial, as Dio found out when he initiated a building programme in his city, Prusa (Dio 47, cf. 40.1–15, 45.12–14). In any case, individuals who acted as private benefactors themselves were likely to have a keen eye for the impact of art and architecture when they visited elsewhere. They also had an interest in seeing monuments preserved for posterity, since this was a main incentive for spending money on monuments in the first place (Dio 31, Favorinus *Corinthian oration* = Dio 34; Quaß 1993, 30–39). Like Arrian on his governor's tour of the Black Sea wealthy visitors might be inclined to add something of their own to the memorial landscape of a site, be it a small votive offering or, in exceptional cases such as Herodes Atticus, a whole temple, a water supply system, a stadion or a few statues (Ameling 1983, 84–94; Philostr., *VS* 551, cf. Paus. 8.9.7–8, 10.1: Hadrian in Mantinea).

Many trips on the quest for a Greek education or in search of noteworthy sights and monuments led to the great sanctuaries of the Greek world. Many visitors to such sites would not come as mere tourists, but they would also be attracted by the spiritual aspect of ancient sacred places. Most ancient authors of the period were in some way involved in religious practice, not least because religious activities were an important part in the life of a model citizen, but some were also devout believers, or they found it expedient to present themselves in this way (Apuleius, *Metamorphoses* 11.12–30; possibly Lucian, *Dea Syria*, see Lightfoot 2003, 177–82).

Aristides provides some of the most striking examples for travelling that is best described as pilgrimage. His sacred tales illustrate the goings on at one sanctuary, the Asclepieum of Pergamon, where a number of long time elite visitors spent their time with intellectual pursuits and activities connected to the cult of Asclepius (Behr 1968, 42–3). In his search for healing and a spiritual closeness to Asclepius, Aristides felt compelled by his god to travel intensively for many years, and in the process he also acquired a good knowledge of the whole region (Rutherford 2001, 51–2). Devotion and travelling was closely connected for many people of all walks of life; many sanctuaries attracted large numbers of visitors. Such trips to sanctuaries could be made for a variety of reasons: some discovered unfamiliar and exotic rites, some wanted to return to their roots and identity or to discover age old traditions, some came for the attractions offered by festivals (e.g. Paus. 8.8.3, 8.42, 9.39.4–14; Arrian, *Periplous* 2.3; Lucian, *Peregrinus* 35, *Dea Syria* with Lightfoot 2003, 177–183 and Elsner 2001; Elsner 1992; Rutherford 2001).

Wealthy visitors could also take part in local cults; for example, prominent individuals, most notably emperors, were keen on initiation in the Eleusinian mysteries at Athens. It is quite possible that in a small town or sanctuary such a visit would offer a rare opportunity for a costly sacrifice which would benefit a large number of people. For Pausanias sacrificing at sanctuaries he visited was apparently standard, so much so that he finds it worth noting when he did *not* sacrifice an animal at a sanctuary where blood sacrifices were not allowed (Paus. 8.42.11).

In many sanctuaries wealthy travellers could, in fact, expect to be welcomed by a member of the local elite, someone who had perhaps travelled abroad himself and who was likely to share some of the visitor's interests. After all, the most distinguished men in a city would usually have close links to local sanctuaries, often both as priests and as benefactors, and in this capacity they would also interact with high ranking guests. Thus in many places an educated traveller would be able to find a fellow *pepaideumenos* to introduce him to monuments, religious traditions and local history. Pausanias apparently drew on this resource, and he certainly was not satisfied with the services of common commercial tourist guides. (Paus. 5.20.4–5, 6.23.6, 26.6 (distinguished guides), 2.23.5–6, cf. 1.34.4, 2.30.5 (critique of local guides); Habicht 1985, 144–7; Jones 2001; Pretzler 2004, 204–7). Plutarch provides an insight into the perspective of the local expert dealing with educated travellers. He was a priest at Delphi, and one of his Delphic dialogues uses a visitor's tour to the famous site as its setting. In fact, the topics discussed on this fictitious tour around the sanctuary and the interests documented in Pausanias' *Periegesis* seem to illustrate a perfect (if historically impossible) match between learned visitor and local expert. (Plut., *De Pythiae Oraculis* = *Mor.* 394D–409D ; Jones 2001).

Many of the meanings of travel explored in this article are closely connected with Greek cultural identity. No ancient author takes the connection between travelling and understanding Greek culture quite as literally as Pausanias who painstakingly assembles his own image of Greece and its past from countless small details and experiences gained on many long trips. There are, however, many ways of approaching Greekness through travelling.

As we have seen with non-Greek sophists such as Favorinus, Lucian and (to some extent) Apuleius, one could travel to Greece or Ionia and acquire Greekness. One could also travel to the sites of important events and to the ancient sanctuaries and explore what Greece once was. In their school exercises, speeches and texts, even in their dreams, educated Greeks encountered ancient Greece on a day-by-day basis. No wonder that they went to see many of the places they had read, written and talked about so often, taking the opportunity to place themselves into the scenery of the texts they knew so well.

Greekness could therefore be enhanced by getting closer to Greece, but the opposite was also possible. After all, Greeks had originally defined themselves to a large extent through contrast to the barbarian other (Hall 1989, 3–13). In the Roman world, where Greeks had to acknowledge the existence of 'civilised barbarians' who had become their rulers (Woolf 1994, 128–30; Swain 1996, 66–71), such contrasts should have lost their meaning, but following a long tradition of literary *topoi* Greeks could still discuss Greek culture by references to the edges of the civilised world. Arrian's *Periplous* offers a particularly interesting example of this phenomenon. The work is composed as a letter of Arrian, the governor of Cappadocia, to the emperor Hadrian, but this Roman official who hails from Nicomedia on the edges of the Greek world prefers a thoroughly Greek genre, the *Periplous*, to more conventional forms of published governor's reports (cf. Caesar's *Commentarii* or Pliny's letters). This allows him to show his trip as the encounter between himself as a Greek and a 'barbarian' world. In the first sentence Arrian juxtaposes his own experience with that of Hadrian and Xenophon: three great travellers close to the edges of the known world (Arrian, *Periplous* 1.1). The trip along the coast of his province becomes a trip within different worlds, Greek, Roman and Barbarian, past and present, familiar and unfamiliar, but the perspective is firmly Greek (Stadter 1980, 32–41).

The ancient genre of the *periplous* is a poignant reminder of the fact that from the Dark Ages onwards the Greek world was shaped by people who were willing to be mobile. This development did not just affect historical geography, it also determined how Greeks thought about themselves and their history. Few Greek regions had a (myth-) history of continuous settlement, and those who did had claims to colonies abroad. By the Roman imperial period the (myth-) histories of most cities in the empire started with a colonising founder who had come from Greece or Asia Minor.

Greek literary tradition played an important part in making travel a particularly Greek activity. It is no coincidence that ancient *pepaideumenoi* (e.g. Dio 1.50, 13.4, 45.11, Aristid. *ST* 2.60) liked to compare themselves to Odysseus, the hero whom the Odyssey (1.3) introduces as one 'who saw many cities and became acquainted with the customs of many peoples'. Odysseus encounters the 'other' and learns through travelling just what it means to be Greek and to come home to Greece. Herodotus also influenced attitudes to travelling, and again his accounts are concerned with defining Greek and 'other' by drawing on experiences from his own journeys beyond the Greek world (Elsner & Rubiés 1999, 8–15; Whitmarch 2001, 292).

The Romans, in contrast, could be seen as a people who preferred staying at home and who certainly were not very comfortable at sea. They retained this image in spite of their long lasting extensive far flung military and naval operations, and in spite of all the travelling Roman officials had to do in order to keep the empire together. While the Greek mythical past was dominated by colonisation, naval expeditions and adventures at sea Romans preferred to see their forefathers as farmers who were mainly interested in preserving and expanding their own city. A history of spectacular naval plunders of the Romans in their first overseas wars (e.g. Polyb. 1.39, 51) just seems to fit this picture. Even Roman sophists could be more sedentary than their Greek counterparts: Philostratus (*VS* 625) relates that Aelian was praised for never having travelled outside Italy because the Romans thought that in this way he honoured their traditional lifestyle. Aelian was proficient in Attic Greek, the most important aspect of Greek culture, but by staying in Italy he chose to remain a Roman.

If a far travelled Greek *pepaideumenos* therefore used the experience of his journeys to embellish his speeches and texts he could think of himself as following a time honoured Greek tradition that would set him apart from the (by definition, if not in reality) more sedentary Romans. An activity that was common to members of the elites throughout the empire, east and west, could in this way be interpreted as specifically Greek. In fact, the travelling *pepaideumenos* could take his culture wherever he went. As Philostratus (*VA* 1.34) puts it: to the wise man everywhere is Greece.

Bibliography

Alcock, S. E. (1993) *Graecia Capta: The Landscapes of Roman Greece* (Cambridge).

Ameling, W. (1983) *Herodes Atticus* (Hildesheim and New York).

Anderson, G. (1984) *Ancient Fiction: The Novel in the Graeco-Roman World* (London).

Anderson, G. (1986) *Philostratus. Biography and Belles Lettres in the Third Century AD* (London).

Anderson, G. (1993) *The Second Sophistic* (London).

Arafat, K. W. (1996) *Pausanias' Greece. Ancient Artists and Roman Rulers* (Cambridge).

Behr, C .A. (1968) *Aelius Aristides and the Sacred Tales* (Amsterdam).

Birley, A. R. (1997) *Hadrian the restless Emperor* (London and New York).

Bowersock G. W. (1969) *Greek Sophists in the Roman Empire* (Oxford).

Bowie E. L. (1974) 'Greeks and their Past in the Second Sophistic', in M. I. Finley (ed.) *Studies in Ancient Society*, 166–209 (London and Boston).

Braund, D. (1993) 'Piracy under the Principate and the Ideology of Imperial Eradication', in J. Rich, G. Shipley (eds.) *War and Society in the Roman World*, 195–212 (London and New York).

Brunt, P. (1994) 'The Bubble of the Second Sophistic', *BICS* 38 (1994), 25–52.

Casson, L. (1994, 2nd edition) *Travel in the Ancient World* (Baltimore and London).

Desideri, P. (2000) 'Strabone e la cultura asiana', in A. M. Biraschi and G. Salmeri (eds) *Strabone e l'Asia Minore*, 25–44 (Perugia).

Dodwell, E. (1819) *A Classical and Topographical Tour Through Greece, During the Years 1801, 1805 and 1806*, vol. II (London).

Dueck, D. (2000) *Strabo of Amasia: A Greek Man of Letters in Augustan Rome* (London).

Elsner, J. (1992) 'Pausanias: a Greek Pilgrim in the Roman World', *Past and Present* 135 (1992), 5–29.

Elsner, J. (2001) 'Describing Self in the Language of the Other: Pseudo (?) Lucian at the temple of Hierapolis', in S. Goldhill (ed.) *Being Greek under Rome* 123–53 (Cambridge).

Elsner, J. and J. Rubiés (1999) 'Introduction', in J. Elsner and J. Rubiés (eds.) *Voyages and Visions: Towards a Cultural History of Travel*, 1–56 (London).

Engels, J. (1999) *Augusteische Oikumenegeographie und Universalhistorie im Werk Strabons von Amaseia* (Stuttgart).

Habicht, C. (1985) *Pausanias' Guide to Ancient Greece* (Berkeley, Los Angeles and London).

Hägg, T. (1983) *The Novel in Antiquity* (Oxford).

Halfmann, H. (1986) *Itinera Principum: Geschichte und Typologie der kaiserreisen im Römischen Reich* (Stuttgart).

Hall, E. (1989) *Inventing the Barbarian: Greek Self-definition through Tragedy* (Oxford).

Harrison, S. J. (2000) *Apuleius: a Latin Sophist* (Oxford).

Henderson, J. (2001) 'From Megalopolis to Cosmopolis: Polybius, or there and back again', in S. Goldhill (ed.) *Being Greek under Rome: Cultural Identity, the Second Sophistic and the Development of the Empire*, 29–49 (Cambridge).

Hutton, W. (2005) *Describing Greece: Landscape and Literature in the* Periegesis *of Pausanias* (Cambridge).

Jones, C. P. (1986) *Culture and Society in Lucian* (Cambridge MA and London).

Jones, C. P. (2001) 'Pausanias and His Guides', in S. E. Alcock, J. F. Cherry and J. Elsner (eds.) *Pausanias: Travel and Memory in Ancient Greece*, 33–39 (Oxford).

Leake, W. M. (1830) *Travels in the Morea* (London).

Lightfoot, J. L. (2003) *Lucian on the Syrian Goddess* (Oxford).

Nicolet, C. (1988) *L'inventaire du monde : Géographie et politique aux origines de l'Empire romain* (Paris).

Pretzler, M. (2004) ''Turning Travel into Text. Pausanias at Work', *Greece and Rome* 51 (2004), 199–216.

Pretzler, M. (2005a) 'Pausanias at Mantinea: Invention and Manipulation of Local History', *PCPhS* 51, 21–34.

Pretzler, M. (2005b) 'Pausanias and Oral Tradition', *CQ* 55.1, 235–49.

Quaß, F. (1993) *Die Honoratiorenschicht in den Städten des griechischen Ostens* (Stuttgart).

Robert, L. (1977) 'Documents d'Asie Mineure', *BCH* 101, 43–132.

Rutherford, I. (2001) 'Tourism and the Sacred: Pausanias and the Traditions of Greek Pilgrimage', in S. E. Alcock, J. Cherry and J. Elsner (eds.), *Pausanias: Travel and Imagination in Roman Greece*, 40–52 (Oxford).

Salmeri, G. (2000) 'Dio, Rome and the Civic Life of Asia Minor', in S. Swain (ed.) *Dio Chrysostom: Politics, Letters, and Philosophy*, 53–92 (Oxford).

Sandy, G. (1997) *The Greek World of Apuleius: Apuleius and the Second Sophistic* (Leiden, New York and Cologne).

Snodgrass, A. M. (2001) 'Pausanias and the Chest of Kypselos', in S. E. Alcock, J. Cherry and J. Elsner (eds.), *Pausanias: Travel and Imagination in Roman Greece*, 127–41 (Oxford).

Stadter, P. A. (1980) *Arrian of Nicomedia* (Chapel Hill).

Swain, S. (1996) *Hellenism and Empire* (Oxford).

Too, Y. L. (2000) 'The Walking Library: The Performance of Cultural Memories', in D. Braund and J. Wilkins (eds.) *Athenaios and his World: Reading Greek Culture in the Roman Empire* (Exeter).

Whitmarch, T. (2001) ' "Greece is the World": exile and identity in the Second Sophistic', in S. Goldhill (ed.) *Being Greek under Rome*, 269–305 (Cambridge).

Woolf, G. (1994) 'Becoming Roman, Staying Greek: Culture, Identity and the Civilising Process in the Roman East', *PCPhS* 40, 116–43.

Travel in the Greek Novels: Function and Interpretation

John Morgan

This paper is not a Greek novel, so I shall give the ending away on the first page. My study of travel and its functions in the novels has led me to two modestly revisionist positions, which it will be helpful at the beginning to set in a wider context.

The five extant Greek novels[1] present an obviously tightly knit generic corpus: to put it at its most basic, they all tell the story of a beautiful young girl and a handsome young man, who fall in love, and then pass through a number of adventures including separation and travel, before reaching a stereotypical happy ending and living (implicitly) happily ever after. My first conclusion concerns what we might call the 'master-history' of this genre.

Scholars of the novels have always felt impelled to reach beyond the reading of individual texts towards some sort of formulation to explain the emergence, the agenda, and the trajectory of the corpus as a whole. For many years the dominant view was that of Erwin Rohde, who read the novel in evolutionary terms as the product of a hybridisation of narrative Hellenistic love poetry and what he termed *Reisefabulistik*, travellers' tales whether true, embroidered or wholly fictitious, a tradition he traced from the *Odyssey*, through such stages as the poem of Aristeas of Prokonnesos, the travel narratives of Pytheas of Massilia, Ktesias and Megasthenes, with various oriental accretions, to the fictitious Utopian narratives of Theopompos, Euemeros and Iamboulos, and eventually to the strange travel novel of Antonius Diogenes, which he took to be a point of transition to the canonical romances (Rohde 1876). The discovery of papyrus fragments necessitated a radical rewriting of the chronology of the genre that rendered Rohde's developmental schema untenable, but his fundamental idea that the novels are compounded of two basic ingredients – narrative of love on the one hand and of travel and adventure on the other – still continues to exert great influence. In particular the formal connection of the novels to travel-literature proper leads to an assumption that the novels work to the agenda of travel-literature: that they take the reader to foreign parts in the imagination, either to purvey encyclopaedic knowledge or to allow him a different perspective on the world.

In the 1960s and 1970s a new 'master narrative' emerged, which read the novels as the product of the social dislocation of the Greek world in the Hellenistic period. On the one hand, the emphasis on love was read as symptomatic of a reconfiguration of the Self, moving from the politically constituted identity of the classical period to a concern with the individual and his or her emotional concerns; on the other, the travel and adventure elements were taken to inscribe a sense of deracination and powerlessness felt by individuals in the Hellenistic super-states.[2]

Now a new orthodoxy seems to be emerging, which takes as its starting point the reassertion of Hellenism in the Imperial period. On the one hand, the love story, with its culmination in marriage, now assumes a social and political point, highlighting the continuation of the elite within the polis structure from the classical period in which the plots are set through to the first readers' own times, whether this is taken to be directed at the threats to Hellenic identity posed by Roman domination or at the threats to social continuity posed by radical antisocial asceticism of the kind that early Christianity rode to such success. On the other hand, the travel plot maps Hellenic identity in a more literal sense, staging a series of cultural confrontations between the Greek protagonists and people of other (generally eastern) races, much as Herodotos had to go abroad to discover the essentials of his Greek-ness; the classical setting of the novel plots allows the overriding cultural negotiation with Rome to be conducted in a displaced and disguised fashion.[3]

This paper will seek to qualify and nuance this view. It appears that in the earliest novels travel is not thematised – in other words there is little interest in travel as such –, that there is a marked lack of local colour and geographical specificity to distinguish other places from the Greek centre, and that social and cultural differences between Greeks and other nations are not emphasised as we might have expected had matters of ethnic and cultural identity been central to these writers' agendas. Such concerns undoubtedly do surface in later novelists, but their absence from the earlier representatives leads me to think that they were not a factor in the formation of the genre as a whole but were stirred into the mix later by sophisticated writers who sensed the potentialities and needs of an already existing recipe and began at a relatively late stage to use the novel form as a means of exploring Greek and other cultures by imaginatively mapping the world.

Even in the earliest novels travel certainly occurs, of course. Classicists may think back to the *Odyssey* as the model for travel narrative, but the Journey is a fundamental structural basis for narration in all cultures at all periods.

> *The initial situation of a traditional fairy tale shows a state of harmony: everything and everybody is in his proper place … The disturbance of the initial harmony not only sets the plot in motion … the mobile heroes leave their original spheres of activity and go 'out of bounds' … These phenomena reveal essential semiotic properties of literary space and its significant articulation … 'It is precisely because the impossibility of penetrating the boundary is part of the structure of any model of culture, that the most typical construction of the plot is movement across the spatial boundary. The scheme of the plot appears as a struggle against the structure of the world.*[4]

A number of basic plot-types are simply tropes of travel: the Journey, the Wandering, the Odyssey (exile and return), the Going-forth (such as plots of escape or the hero's call to adventure), the Quest. The last of these generates a set of recurrent subtypes: religious Quests (such as the Grail stories and the Pilgrimage type), Quests of war and adventure, Utopias, Quests to satisfy curiosity and find explanations, Quests for wealth and fortune, or Quests for a person (Adams 1983, 148–60, with some odd misreadings of Longus and Heliodorus at 156–7). In formalist terms it is not difficult to place the plots of the ancient novel in one or more of these shifting categories. Large sections of most of them can accurately be classed as stories of exile and return, or as quests for a person, generally for the beloved after the generic separation. My argument is not that travel was not important from the inception of the genre, but that to begin with its function was less ideological than essentially narratological, providing opening and closure, on micro and macro levels, and articulating a characteristically episodic structure. Travel, we might say, provides form rather than content.

My second conclusion concerns the 'master structure' of the novels. There has always been a tendency to dwell on the similarities between the novels, sometimes to the point of reading them as no more than cosmetic recyclings of the same story. This tendency is, if anything, exacerbated by our interest in the novels as documents of gender history: the shared romantic ideology has clearly resulted in erotic plots of essentially similar types. However, if one changes focus and concentrates instead on the travel plots of these texts, major structural differences begin to emerge. These innovations have been too little noted, but lead at least to a qualification of the lazy view of the genre's monolithic uniformity.

The earliest of the complete novels is generally agreed to be that of Chariton of Aphrodisias, entitled *Kallirhoe* after its heroine (c. mid 1st century CE). The story begins and has its centre in Syracuse. After the protagonists Chaireas and Kallirhoe fall in love and marry, an intrigue by Kallirhoe's rejected suitors causes Chaireas to attack her in a fit of jealousy: she collapses, is presumed dead and entombed, only to revive in the tomb. The travel sections begin when tomb-robbers break into the vault, find her alive and steal her along with the treasure. They sail with a favourable wind past islands and towns until they reach Attica; this voyage is not narrated in any detail, the narrative time between departure and arrival being filled almost entirely by the heroine's lamentations (1.11.1–4). After deciding not to sell her in Athens, the robbers sail straight on to Miletos, which they reach without incident after two days (1.11.8): again the voyage is simply elided in the narrative. The second book is devoted to events in Miletos, where Kallirhoe is sold to the local magnate, Dionysios, who duly falls in love with her, and secures her consent to marry him after she finds that she is pregnant by her first husband.

In the third book Chaireas leaves Syracuse in search of Kallirhoe (3.3), and promptly runs into the ship of Theron, leader of the tomb-robbers, which had sailed for Crete after leaving Miletos and then got caught in storm. Chaireas takes Theron back to Syracuse in a journey that again is not narrated (3.3.18). Having extracted from him the truth about Kallirhoe, Chaireas decides to go to Miletos in quest of her. There is a poignant scene of farewell with his parents, and a pathetic apostrophe to the sea (3.5.9), but once again the voyage to Ionia is not narrated. Thanks to a convenient wind, Chaireas simply arrives there, without incident, in the next sentence (3.6.1). On arrival he is ambushed by the local Persian garrison, and sold into slavery, ending up in Karia. His journey thither is not even mentioned in the text, but is simply covered by the phrase 'sold them into Karia' (3.7.3). There ensues a stationary intrigue: the Persian satrap Mithridates falls in love with Kallirhoe at a ceremony held to honour the supposedly dead Chaireas, discovers Chaireas among his slaves and gets him to write to Kallirhoe in the hope of separating her from Dionysios. The letter, however, is intercepted and falls into the hands of another satrap, Pharnakes, who is also in love with Kallirhoe. He writes to Great King, and all the interested parties are summoned to Babylon for a formal hearing.

The journey of Dionysios and Kallirhoe from Miletos to Babylon is narrated at 4.7.5: whole towns turn out to see her, which distresses him, while she is upset at being parted from her first husband's tomb and from the sea. There is a significant marker when they reach the Euphrates:

> *As far as Syria and Kilikia, then, Kallirhoe found her journey easy to bear: she heard Greek spoken; she could see the sea that led to Syracuse. But when she reached the Euphrates, beyond which there is a vast stretch of unending land – it is the threshold of the King's great empire – then longing for her country and family welled up in her and she despaired of ever returning' (5.1.3).*

The importance of this river crossing is further marked by a lengthy lament that Kallirhoe addresses to Fortune (5.1.4–7): she sees it as a final geographical severance from her home, but appears not to register the river as a cultural frontier between Greece and Persia, a dividing line between freedom and autocracy. Once across the river, Dionysios and Kallirhoe continue to be escorted from community to community.

Meanwhile Mithridates is coming through Armenia, but there are no details of his journey, and he simply arrives in Babylon in a participial phrase (ἀφικόηενος οὖν εἰς Βαβυλῶνα, 5.2.2). The last stage of Kallirhoe's journey is occluded by the narration of Mithridates' reception by the King's eunuch and lamentations by Chaireas. The focus returns to her only as they enter the suburbs of Babylon, and it is only at this point that Chariton mentions that she is travelling in a covered carriage, and implicitly has been doing so since leaving Miletos (5.2.9).[5]

For two books or so the story remains static in Babylon, during which time the King himself falls in love with Kallirhoe, until news comes of a revolt in Egypt. Five days later the King marches out from Babylon, taking Kallirhoe with him: there is some implicit geographical sense of distance here, in that he is grateful that he does not have to march all the way from Baktria or Ekbatana (6.8.6). Chaireas decides to join the rebels, and tags on to the back of the king's army until they reach Syria, where he deserts. With the sole mention of the Euphrates this journey passes unnarrated (7.2.2).[6] The ensuing military activity brings Chaireas to Tyre, but Chariton gives us no detail or explanation about how he gets there. At 7.4.11 the narrative reverts to the Persian king, who decides to leave his women on the island of Arados for safety; again we are given no details about how he gets them there. In the battle that now follows the Egyptian land forces are defeated but their navy, under Chaireas' command, is victorious, and captures Arados, where after some suspense and irony the protagonists are reunited. Some loose ends are tied, and Chaireas and Kallirhoe sail home to Syracuse. The way that the voyage is handled is typical of Chariton's procedure throughout this text: the voyage begins at 8.5.1 with the words 'So they were off on their journey across the sea'; the voyage itself is occluded by a scene where the Persian king is reunited with his wife and Dionysius is informed of his loss; the next we hear of the voyage is at 8.6.1:

> *This then was the situation in Asia. Meanwhile, Chaireas completed the journey to Syracuse successfully; he had a following wind all the time*

An analeptic aside (8.6.9) reveals that they have come via Cyprus, only when this item of information is needed to explain something else. At the very end of the novel Dionysios prepares to return to Miletos (8.5.15), but the journey itself remains no more than an implication so far as this novel is concerned.

I have summarised Chariton's novel in a way that privileges the travel over the erotic. There are a number of observations that one can make about this material. Firstly, the movements of both protagonists constitute a pattern of excursion and return, and it is easy enough to rephrase this formulation as a journey from the centre to the periphery and back. Since the centre is constituted by Syracuse, a fully developed democratic Greek polis, and the ultimate margins by the Persian empire, with its institutions of absolute autocracy, the romantic mapping of the world can easily be read as a culturally Hellenocentric one, with centre and periphery defined as respectively Greek and non-Greek. Polemically, even Athens is located on the way to the edge. Miletos is a liminal location where Greek and barbarian meet. The grand political geography is articulated by two boundaries: first the sea which separates Syracuse from Miletos (and Athens), and second the river Euphrates which marks the decisive boundary on the road between civilised Greek-speaking and barbarian territory, the latter characterised by the institution of despotic monarchy.[7] However, the fact that Chariton's geography in the abstract invites this kind of reading is not quite to say that its potentialities are actuated in the novel text itself.

As well as a geographical and, perhaps, a politico-cultural journey, the story also traces an erotic trajectory. At each of the story's nodes Kallirhoe encounters a powerful man. She ascends the socio political scale from commoner (Chaireas), to local magnate (Dionysios), to satrap (Mithridates and Pharnakes), to Great King, and the final happy-ending return to Chaireas romantically endorses true love as a higher value than the pinnacle of worldly power. It would enhance our estimation of Chariton's artistry if Kallirhoe's ascent of the social ladder on her journey eastwards were counter-pointed by a descent of its erotic equivalent, from ideal love to its antithesis, and to a degree this is what happens. Her love with Chaireas is consensual and passionate, though clouded by the attack of insane jealousy that leaves the novel's heroine apparently dead on its fourth page. In structural terms Dionysios plays the generic role of 'rival', but Chariton paints him in sympathetic colours. Although he purchases Kallirhoe as a slave from the tomb-robbers, his over-riding wish is that she should love him for himself, and, despite urging from various of his minions, he refuses to use the compulsion which lies within his legal rights. He is in short a gentleman and a scholar (*pepaideumenos*, 3.2.6). We must assume that Kallirhoe allowed him to consummate the marriage, since he believes the child she is carrying is in fact his, and at the end of the novel she uses him with affection and respect, if not quite love. The two satraps are stereotypically wily orientals, who use dishonesty and duplicity in their attempts to win Kallirhoe for themselves. At no point do they concern themselves with her feelings towards them. The Great King breaks the sequence, however. He is not at all the Grand Guignol villain we might have expected. As an almighty despot he cuts a very bourgeois figure, agonises over his passion, and conspicuously does not use his absolute authority to satisfy his desires, any more than Dionysios pressed his rights of ownership. Instead Chariton treats us to scenes of sleepless nights (6.1.8 ff., 6.7.1 ff.), in which he behaves like any romantic lover, and a magnificent hunt that the King stages to try to take his mind off the beautiful Greek woman (6.4.1 ff.). After Kallirhoe's departure there is a touching domestic scene where he is reunited, through Chaireas' chivalry, with his own beloved wife Stateira, who had been captured on Arados (8.5.5 ff.). Nevertheless, the plot derives some residual tension from the potential erotic threat that the King's absolute political authority might pose, and that threat is never fully defused until Kallirhoe is physically out of his reach.

These parallel social and erotic plot-structures are inscribed in Chariton's geography. Syracuse, Ionia and Babylon each host a distinct and distinctive section of the plot. The boundaries of sea and river that divide Chariton's map of the world also divide his narrative into its major episodes. In this sense the geographical structure of the novel corresponds to its literary structure: geographical movement articulates the plot and makes its form and internal mechanisms readily apprehensible to the reader. But we will do better to think of the geography on which the action is projected as a diagram of the novel's structure, dressed up with suitable names and décor from reality, than as an exploration of the real geo-cultural world through the medium of fiction.

I am not suggesting that Chariton is geographically unaware. It is perfectly possible to plot his plot on a map, though the very exercise somehow traduces it and begs the question of the nature and function of his geography.[8] He has a sense of distance, particularly the distance separating the protagonists when Kallirhoe in Miletos thinks of her husband in Syracuse (as she believes), or the distance separating Babylon from the sea, though we should note that these distances are affective as much as physical, and that the author makes no attempt to quantify them. He also, in a deeply self-referential moment, refers to Chaireas' wanderings as the epitome of his story so far, and identifies them with the adverse experiences he has undergone. 'Chaireas ... had wandered the world from west to east and gone through untold suffering' (8.1.3). But here we should note that the Greek vocabulary equates Chaireas' journey from west to east (ἀπο δύσεως εἰς ἀνατολὰς) with a journey from sinking to rising, from depression to exaltation: the metaphorical nature of the geographical movement as concretisation of plot structure could hardly be clearer. Although the plot requires him to move his characters from one significant location to another, he shows virtually no interest in the process of how they get from place to place. The majority of Chariton's journeys take place out of view, as it were, and nothing of much note happens in the course of them. The romantic heroes, of course, have by the very nature of the genre various difficulties and ordeals to confront and overcome, but in this text none of them is travel-related. The terrain traversed is not in itself perilous, and such dangers as arise are encountered at one of the static sites around which the plot is suspended. Even the pirates, who are a staple of romance plotting, and who reflect dangers of the real world, strike at Syracuse and not while the characters are en route. This is what I meant when I said that travel is not thematised in this book. It is rather the almost invisible thread on which the pearls of action are strung. If one were to gather together all the sentences narrating travel and edit out everything else, the novel could be compressed into a page or so of text.

It is also the case that Chariton's geography has very little specificity or sense of place, either physically or culturally. There is no description of landscape, other than a short aside to explain the nature of Arados (7.5.1), a narratological necessity since although plausibly placed for the needs of the plot the island was perhaps not an item of general knowledge in the repertoire of every reader. Places passed through on the various journeys make no impact on the characters. The islands and cities between Syracuse and Athens are anonymous; the landscape of the Asian mainland does not impinge on Kallirhoe in her covered carriage. Even the foci of the story are essentially undifferentiated. Syracuse has a theatre where the assembly gathers, to discuss a love affair; Miletos could be any Greek port city. Apart from the fact that it has a big palace with a throne room, Babylon is not registered as being any different from a familiar Greek polis. Its architecture, scale, climate, language – all go unremarked; everyone in Chariton's world speaks Greek, just as everyone in *Star Trek* speaks English. When Chariton wants to give an idea of the excitement in the streets created by Kallirhoe's arrival, he simply assimilates Babylon to Olympia or Eleusis.[9] It is easy to contrast this to travel-literature proper – from Herodotos onwards – whose interest is precisely in the myriad otherness of the places visited. The want of foreign-ness at Chariton's 'periphery' and the author's failure to activate the semiotic charges of cultural difference already carried by each of the three primary locations are disturbing for those who want to find in the novel a formative generic agenda of staking out Hellenism in contrast to other ethnicities. Instead of contrast one finds a fictional homogeneity: Chariton's world certainly is Hellenocentric, but in the uninteresting sense that he unreflectively extends Greek 'normality' to all other nations.[10] There is a sense in which this romance could be rewritten without the geography at all. Of course setting, in the form of space or place, is a formal necessity for narrative, but the love intrigue, which is the plot's real essence, would work perfectly well if the *mise en scène* were completely unitary. Dionysios would not be out of place in Syracuse – he is no one's moral inferior. Satraps and Great Kings are convenient and exciting threats and allow the extension of the power hierarchy upwards beyond the highest level to which any private citizen in Syracuse could have aspired; but despite the colourful but intermittent appurtenances of oriental magnificence and toadying eunuchs, they are either dead stereotypes or just Greeks in costume. There is no consistent sense of measuring Hellenism against other cultures, no sense of allowing the reader to try on in his imagination an alternative perspective on the world. Ultimately what matters about Chariton's Great King is that he is powerful, not that he is Persian; and in fact he is Persian only in those aspects where it would have required a conscious and deliberate effort to make him otherwise.

Almost reluctantly I am driven back to the conclusion that the distribution of *Kallirhoe*'s plot over three main geographical locations is primarily a narratological device to make clearer the significances that were intrinsic to the plot all along. The spatial structure of excursion and return, for instance, makes concrete a love plot of estrangement and reunion that is not location dependent; geographical separation of the episodes underlines the formal transitions between them and facilitates their distinctive ethical colouring. Let us say that this novel is less about using the story to map the world than about using the world to map the story. The story gives the author an opportunity to explore the cultural map that he conspicuously fails to take. In many ways it misrepresents this particular text to talk at all of its representation of the world in such evaluative and hierarchical terms as centre and periphery, except in terms of its erotics. Travel as such is almost an embarrassing formal consequence of dividing the action, a nugatory entr'acte while the characters migrate from one backdrop to another.

A rather different picture emerges from the other 'pre-sophistic' novel, the *Ephesiaka* of Xenophon of Ephesos. Before the analysis begins, we must enter a by now generically obligatory caveat that the text we have may be a not wholly satisfactory epitome of something larger and better, and consequently that one may be doing the original author a grave injustice in the remarks that follow.[11] If, in Nick Lowe's memorable phrasing, 'Xenophon's characters seem to pin-ball wildly around the Mediterranean for reasons at times known only to God and the author' (Lowe 2000, 230), it may not always have been thus. In fact, although the erotic furniture of the novel is very close to that of Chariton's, leading to a generally held view – if not articulated in quite these terms – that Xenophon is Chariton's idiot brother, if we concentrate our attention on the travel element, it seems that the author of the *Ephesiaka* was attempting something radically different. It is difficult to summarise the vertiginous movement and frenzied narrative of this text – which already reads like a summary in many places. Nevertheless it will be useful to run through, as briefly as possible, the movements of the main characters. It is important to note that in addition to the romantic protagonists, we must also include an important secondary character, in order to savour the full succulence of Xenophon's invention.

The protagonists, Habrokomes and Anthia, are natives of Ephesos. They fall in love and are married within a couple of pages. In response to an oracle warning of dangers at sea, their parents oddly decide to send them on a trip abroad. After an emotional farewell, they sail to Rhodes, via Samos, Kos and Knidos (1.11.2, 6). When they set sail again, for an unnamed destination, they are ambushed by pirates, who take them to Tyre (1.14.6), where two pirates fall in love with them, and then the daughter of the pirate chief takes a fancy to Habrokomes. This intrigue leads eventually to the hero being imprisoned and the heroine being packed off to Antioch (2.9.1) and given to a goatherd, who instead of killing her sells her to some Kilikian merchants (2.11.9). Their ship is wrecked on the way to Kilikia and the survivors, including Anthia, are captured by a band of robbers headed by the third main character Hippothoos. Habrokomes is released and sets off in pursuit of his beloved, riding to Kilikia (2.12.3). However, Hippothoos' robbers are attacked and killed by the eirenarch Perilaos, who takes Anthia to Tarsos (2.13.5) and falls in love with her. On his way to Kilikia Habrokomes encounters Hippothoos, and goes with him to Mazakos in Kappadokia to start a new bandit group (3.1.1), a journey of ten days and a completely redundant expedition, since as soon as they arrive Hippothoos tells Habrokomes about the beautiful girl he had captured and, recognising Anthia in the description, Habrokomes plans to head straight back to Kilikia (3.3.5). Anthia evades Perilaos' advances by committing suicide, except that the kindly old doctor who supplied the poison had substituted a sleeping draught, so that she is entombed alive, only to be rescued by tomb-robbers who take her to Alexandreia (3.8.5). Habrokomes is now back in Tarsos (his journey there is not mentioned), and after being told about the tomb robbery, he takes a chance ship to Alexandreia, in the 'forlorn hope' (3.10.4), of catching the pirates who have stolen his beloved; our text gives no foundation for a belief that she is in Alexandreia. Hippothoos, meanwhile, moves to Syria and Phoenicia (3.10.5). In Alexandreia Anthia is sold to an Indian prince called Psammis. Habrokomes' ship is wrecked at the mouth of the Nile, and he is taken to Pelousion and sold to a retired soldier whose hideous wife promptly falls in love with him, and murders her husband. Habrokomes is taken to Alexandreia for punishment (3.12.6). Hippothoos and his men leave Tarsos, and make their way through Syria, stopping at Laodikeia, to Egypt and eventually, via Pelousion, Hermoupolis, Schedia, Memphis, Mendes, Taua and Leontopolis, and other towns of little note, to Koptos on the borders of Ethiopia (4.1.4), where he is just in time to ambush Psammis taking Anthia to India, but he fails to recognise his captive. Habrokomes is cleared and sails to Italy, hoping, for no apparent reason, to find news of Anthia there (4.4.2), but he is blown off-course to Sicily (5.1.1) where he takes lodgings with an elderly fisherman who keeps the embalmed corpse of his wife in his bedroom. Anthia kills a rapist, and is left in a pit with huge starving dogs, only to be rescued by another infatuated man who takes her to Koptos (5.2.6). Hippothoos and his men head north, sacking villages such as Areia and Schedia as they go (5.2.7). They are attacked by the prefect near Pelousion, but Hippothoos gets away to Alexandreia and sails off to Sicily in the hope of rich pickings there (5.3.3). In the course of a nationwide search for Hippothoos, Anthia falls into the hands of the prefect and is taken to Alexandreia, but is then sold to an Italian brothel-keeper by the prefect's jealous wife, and ends up in Taras (5.5.7). Hippothoos is now in Tauromenion, where he marries a rich widow who promptly dies, but Habrokomes has left for Italy, and takes a job working in the stone quarries at Nuceria (5.8.1). Hippothoos sails over to Italy with his new boyfriend and meets Anthia in Tarentum where she has preserved her chastity by pretending to be epileptic. This time they do recognise each other; Anthia explains about Habrokomes, who turns out to be Hippothoos' friend. Habrokomes gives in his cards at the quarry, and heads home to Ephesos via Sicily, Crete, Cyprus and Rhodes, a roundabout route which is not explained but does not seem to be by chance (5.10.2). On Rhodes he at last meets up with Anthia and Hippothoos who are also on their way to Ephesos; and they sail home together and live happily ever after.

In places Xenophon's narrative is so spare that it is virtually impossible to abbreviate it, and the rapid alternation of storylines hardly aids clarity. But even this breathless summary reveals a number of salient points. In the first place it is obvious that the number of separate locations is much greater than in Chariton. Not all of them provide the formally required setting for narrative episodes, though some do; others are mentioned simply as places through which the characters pass, out of pure geographical verisimilitude. Sometimes the shift of location seems to have no function other than to demarcate a particular episode. The trip to Mazakos, for instance, seems to have no function other than to introduce an exchange of stories between Habrokomes and Hippothoos, leading to the realisation that the latter's captive was none other than the former's wife. But Hippothoos has also told a story of his own past which is of paradigmatic importance in the novel's erotic system; its displacement in chronology is mirrored in the redundant spatial excursion that frames it (on Hippothoos' story and its importance, see Konstan 1994, 26–30). Where a relatively extended stationary episode is appended to the thread of travel, it is hard to see that there is consistently any semiotic charge colouring that segment of the story. Why for instance does the necrophiliac fisherman have to be in Sicily, why are parallel encounters between the hero and lustful women set in Tyre and Pelousion, or what specifically Egyptian or Kilikian overtones attach to the episodes of banditry in each of those countries, particularly when the same person, a Greek, is responsible in both cases?

Secondly, although the basic story patterns of exile and return and of loss and recovery are still plainly discernible, the movement in Xenophon's novel cannot, even wishfully, be described as one to the periphery and back to the centre. With the exception of the episodes in Koptos and Anthia's embroilment with her Indian rajah, and the strangely abortive diversion to Kappadokia, the scenarios play out entirely in the Greek world, and although Ephesos is clearly home, and thus represents narratological closure, it is not contrasted with or implicitly evaluated against other zones of the world. Psammis' behaviour is indistinguishable from that of all the other important men with whom Anthia is involved at various stages; there is no ethnic differentiation, and in fact he behaves in a more acceptably 'civilised' way than the Greek eirenarch or the prefect of Egypt. The world represented is again Hellenocentric, but by dint of simply ignoring everything which is not Greek, not by building significant antitheses. The crucial border is that between civilisation and outlawry, into which both protagonists fall repeatedly, and this is not a simple geographical line. Oddly, if there is a periphery to Habrokomes' and Anthia's world, it seems to be sited in the Italian west. Both protagonists reach their nadir in Italy, in the mines of Nuceria and in the brothel of Tarentum; but they do not reach their lowest point *because* they are in Italy. Even here the ambience is Greek and their experiences are not unrelievedly negative: Habrokomes at least achieves one of his most positive moments when he is lodging with the Sicilian fisherman and realises that true love is forever (5.1.12). So the ethics and affect of the story are not mapped on to the fictional geography with any degree of consistency: unlike Chariton's world that of Xenophon is not ethically constructed.

Thirdly, if the world is not mapped in the same way as it is by Chariton – that is to say ethically and erotically, with geography used to articulate meaning – Xenophon's geography is nonetheless highly detailed and precise, and apparently well-informed (Henne 1936). Much more than Chariton he is interested in routes: despite his paucity of elaboration in other regards, he tells us exactly how the protagonists get from Ephesos to Rhodes, how Hippothoos goes from Kilikia to Egypt, and his exact route back to the north, including the names of villages sacked. Place names proliferate in this text, and Xenophon seems almost to invite us to map his plot in real geography. When we do, we see that all the main characters move, more or less, clockwise around the Mediterranean (Lowe 2000, 231).

This brings us to the most fourth and most important point, which is Xenophon's innovation. By separating his hero and heroine at a relatively early stage, and keeping them separated, he was able to double his plot line, using the figure of Hippothoos to correlate and synchronise the two strands.[12] Superimposed on the conventional structure of excursion and return is thus a new one of pursuit (Lowe 2000, 230-1 for a more detailed analysis). Although Xenophon seems little more interested than Chariton in the practicalities and the actual process of travelling[13]and there is still a tendency for characters to set off somewhere and then simply arrive at their destination or elsewhere, with an ellipse of narrated time covering the actual journey, nevertheless Xenophon's pursuit plot is powered by the physical movements of his characters, and in one sense at least the plot *is* the travel that takes place within it. This novel could not be rewritten so as to observe any sort of unity of space. The whole point lies in the near misses in time and space. For instance, Habrokomes returns to Tarsos to find that Anthia has just been stolen from her tomb; by coincidence he chooses to sail to Alexandreia, which is where Anthia happens to be, and the reader expects that a reunion is imminent, only to have his expectation thwarted. The hero's arbitrary excursion to Italy is followed by the heroine's despatch to a Tarentine brothel, and again the impression is that somehow a meeting is being engineered – not very skilfully perhaps but with the added ironic frisson that Habrokomes has at this point overtaken Anthia and she is now unwittingly pursuing him. But the plot remains a thing of moving the pieces around the board: there is still no sense of place or local specificity (unless that too has been epitomised out of existence), no encyclopaedic curiosity about the places the characters visit, no landscape (except for a mountain in Ethiopia and some forests that appear when the bandits need somewhere to lurk), no sense of cultural difference.[14] Travel is newly important here, but its importance is still purely narratological, the product of a different and interesting type of plot. It is not used positively for its own intrinsic interest or to enable any imaginative engagement with or mapping of the world outside the fiction, such as a deliberate exploration of Hellenism might entail.

It is conventional to divide the five fully extant novels into two groups. Those we have so far examined are termed pre-sophistic. The remaining three – by Achilleus Tatius, Longus, and Heliodoros – show the influence and concerns of the Second Sophistic, whatever that may be. These are works of greater literary accomplishment, narratological complexity, and conceptual and emotional depth. They retain, however, the canonical plot structure of love, separation or difficulty, and reunion or success. Longus' is a maverick text that eliminates the element of travel almost entirely: the action of *Daphnis and Chloe* never leaves the shores of Lesbos, except for a parody of the conventional shipwreck episode, when pirates abduct the hero who is promptly rescued by the antics of a herd of performing cows. Such travel as there is takes place along the axis between country and city, and I have argued at length elsewhere that this road is the road leading from childhood to maturity, from ignorance and sterile, if charming, innocence to responsibility and marital fecundity (Morgan 1994, and more fully Morgan 2004).

In the final section of this paper, then, I want to sketch out two new aspects of the treatment of the theme of travel in one of the sophistic novels. The first is that which I have just adumbrated in the case of the static Longus: that the journey informing the story at the mechanical level becomes a metaphor for some inner affective or spiritual development. The second is that there appears to be a growing accommodation, on the part of some writers at least, with real travel literature, resulting in a new interest in the physical settings of the story, an enhanced concreteness and specificity, and at last a sense of important and functioning cultural difference being explored and defined. It is perhaps at this later stage that the cross-fertilisation with travel literature, which Rohde saw as germinal for the genre, really occurs. I do not want to argue that these novels' representations of the world suggest that the novelists had themselves travelled and researched their locations; it is easy to pick holes in their settings and even easier to find the literary sources for much of their furniture. We are dealing here with cultural and imaginative representations, but even on that level it is striking that these authors are no longer content to leave their stories to float free in undifferentiated albeit named geographical space.

This second point is the easier to argue and illustrate. The *Ethiopian Story* of Heliodoros begins *in medias res* at the mouth of the Nile. Immediately the scenery comes into play as a band of robbers peer over the crest of a hill at a wrecked ship below them. A second gang derives them off, plunders the ship's cargo and incidentally takes prisoner a young man and woman, who will turn out to be the hero and heroine of the novel. They take their captives to their hideaway in a reed marsh, which Heliodoros describes in precise and evocative detail.[15] These bandits are authentically Egyptian *Boukoloi*, whose inability to speak Greek is an important detail in building the enigmatic suspense of the first book.[16] There is no need to summarise the whole story here; but the point is that the narrator repeatedly evinces an almost Herodotean interest in the places and cultures the plot visits. The protagonists' journey up the Nile shows them a crocodile (6.1.2) and a flamingo (6.3.2), and eventually the lovers find their way to Memphis, whose imposing and barbaric architecture affects the characters emotionally and provides an atmospheric backdrop to the action (7.12.3). And thence they travel to the border-town of Syene, which is put under siege by the Ethiopian king, Hydaspes, with a stratagem involving the diversion of the Nile into an artificial lake; thus the city's real-life proximity to the river is indispensably functional within the fiction. Furthermore the succeeding events are precipitated by the arrival of the annual inundation (9.8.2 ff.), so that the characteristic behaviour of the real Nile is also part of the fictional economy: the plot would not work with just any old river. The novelist adds local colour by describing a characteristically Egyptian festival to celebrate the onset of the flood (9.9, the festivities also have their function in the story), adding information about Egyptian religion in a digression that smells of Herodotean mannerisms (9.9.3ff; Herodotean 'religious silence' at 9.10.1). Later he has the victorious Ethiopian king visit the sights for which Syene was in reality famous (9.22). The final sequences of the novel are set in the Ethiopian capital of Meroe, where people speak Ethiopian, and Heliodoros goes out of his way to explain why Greek is understood there and how the dialogues he reports happen to be in Greek; there is a climactic moment when Sisimithres switches to the local language to maximise comprehension of the story's resolution (10.39.1). Heliodoros devotes a chapter to describing the geography of Meroe, a continent-sized island in the Nile, surrounded by branches of the river authentically called Astaborrhas and Asasobas, producing extraordinarily large plant and animal life (10.5). The population of Meroe crosses the river in minutely described dugout canoes to meet their king returning in triumph (10.4.6). The various subject nations of Ethiopia are each separately characterised. The scenery of this last episode again involves local architecture, as the king and queen of Ethiopia sit in state in a pavilion constructed of bamboo (10.6.2 ff.).

The action of the novel is also culturally linked to the locations visited. So the scenes set in Egypt involve an episode of necromancy (6.14–15), and the climax of the story a rite of human sacrifice in Ethiopia. It is immaterial to ask after the accuracy in historical terms of these depictions. The point is that the plot, as it carries the reader into foreign parts, also confronts him with episodes that are fundamentally foreign in their ethos, and differentiated appropriately from each other: the reader's experience is thus very much concerned with the otherness of the places the plot visits. The travel, in other words, the space in which the story is set, has become directly operative in defining the nature of elements of the story.

As with Chariton and Xenophon, the structure of Heliodoros' plot is articulated by movement through space. Here is the barest outline of it. Although the text opens in Egypt, the meeting of the lovers, Theagenes and Charikleia, took place at Delphi, where Theagenes was leading a *theoria* from Thessaly; Charikleia was living there as the daughter of the Delphic priest, but, as is revealed by detective work recounted in retrospective inset narrative nearly halfway through the text, she is in fact the daughter of the Ethiopian king and queen, exposed at birth because of a freak accident that resulted in her being born white. The detective and narrator is an enigmatic wandering Egyptian priest called Kalasiris, who may or may not have been commissioned by the Ethiopian queen to track down and bring home her long-lost child. He reveals Charikleia's identity to her and facilitates the lovers' elopement from Delphi, to head for the land of her birth, Ethiopia. They are, however, shipwrecked at the Nile delta, which is where the text begins. In Egypt they undergo a series of adventures, involving short-term separation and reunion, and an encounter with the nymphomaniac wife of the Persian satrap. After the death of their guardian and mentor, Kalasiris, they are being taken under guard to the satrap himself, who is fighting the Ethiopians and who has discovered his wife's misdemeanours, when they are captured by Ethiopian troops, and become, as the first captives of the war, victims for the thanksgiving human sacrifice to mark the king's return home. So they are taken to Meroe under guard, but before they can be sacrificed Charikleia is recognised, Theagenes is reprieved, and the barbarous rite is abolished in perpetuity.

The complex action is thus distributed between three distinct geographical zones: Greece, Egypt, and Ethiopia. In broad terms the narrative's movement through these zones constructs a moral and spiritual hierarchy. Although Delphi is an exalted location, classical Athens is characterised within an inset New Comedy style sub-narrative as the home of the antitype of true love. Ethiopia has utopian elements, as always in classical thought (though Heliodoros piquantly plays this off against an alternative contemporary Christian semiotics linking black with evil and Ethiopians with Satan and sin (treated more fully in Morgan 2005)). The Ethiopian king, for example, behaves towards defeated enemies with chivalry and generosity, and renounces any ambitions for territorial expansion as a result of his victories over the aggression of Persia. His people love him as a father, and the state is run on principles of piety. Such faults as it possesses, such as the readiness to expose embarrassing babies, or to sacrifice human beings to the gods, derive from an excess of moral scruple and religious devotion. Morally and spiritually as well as geographically Egypt stands between the two. In each of the three zones Charikleia has a separate priestly father figure: in Delphi she lives as the adopted daughter of Charikles, well meaning and kindly but intellectually challenged and irredeemably worldly. She is escorted from Greece and through Egypt as far as Memphis by Kalasiris, a figure as ambiguous and ambivalent as his native land. At one level he is the embodiment of the higher wisdom, and is the first character to discern the gods' governance of the story in which he finds himself. At another level he is a charlatan and showman, ready to employ mystifying hocus-pocus to achieve his ends and to act the part of a common or garden magician. And in Ethiopia Charikleia has two fathers: her natural father the king with whom she is reunited at the end, and a priestly father, the gymnosophist Sisimithres, fount of god-given ascetic wisdom who saved her life on religious principle when she was an exposed baby, reared her for the first seven years of her life, and then saves her life again when she is threatened with human sacrifice on her return to her family. The journey from Greece to Ethiopia is thus framed to invite a metaphorical or allegorical reading of spiritual improvement or ascent, however exactly the individual critic might choose to phrase that. This is well-travelled ground in the scholarship on Heliodoros.[17]

Thus far, Heliodoros' *modus operandi* is generally similar to that Chariton, who also, as we have seen, distributes his action over three geographically separated and at least potentially ethically coloured locations. That is to say that the geographical movement within the story articulates and embodies the issues that the story raises, though Heliodoros has succeeded, where Chariton seems barely to have tried, in making organic connections between his locations and the ethos of the action. But we must now note a raft of important differences and advances.

First, and most obviously, Heliodoros' travel is hugely more graded and detailed. It is no longer appropriate to think of the travel simply as the thread on which the episodic beads are strung. To pursue the metaphor: there are now more beads, they are each less monolithic and the thread is thicker and more interesting in itself. Within the Greek zone for instance, Theagenes has come to Delphi from Thessaly, and this movement is used to characterise him as a reincarnation of Achilleus. After eloping from Delphi the lovers visit Zakynthos, where there is a star turn from a comically deaf fisherman, with whom they take lodgings, and Crete. These staging posts mark the transition from civilisation and polis-culture to piracy and lawlessness. Within Egypt, they travel from the opening scene at the mouth of the Nile, to the bandit encampment in the swamp, to the village of Chemmis (the scene of the retrospective narration by Kalasiris that fills in the section of the plot before the novel's opening scene), to the town of Bessa (close to which is enacted the scene of necromancy), to the city of Memphis (where they have their encounter with the nymphomaniac princess, and Kalasiris dies), and thence to Syene, which is the frontier and transition to the theocratic Utopia of Ethiopia. To quote Nick Lowe:

> *there is thus a clear, even hyperschematic path to be traversed from wilderness to utopia, anarchy to divine monarchy, individualism to ever greater community, poverty to fabulous wealth, the known world to the fabled. That does not mean it is an easy path to traverse; on the contrary, the scale of danger increases from the crude animal thuggery of the bandits through the more deadly urban intrigues of Memphis, to the epic warfare at the disputed border between nations, and finally to a grade of peril known only to fabled barbarians*
>
> Lowe 2000, 236–7

Furthermore travel between the various locations does not simply occur out of narration. The sea crossing from Greece to Egypt is itself an adventure and the pirates that infest it are a necessary plot-element, both narratologically and ethically. Within Egypt, the movement from one narrative locus to another is not elided, and provides the venue for significant encounters and revisions of direction. The expansive scale of the novel allows a new concern with the practicalities of travel: we are shown how to hitch a lift on a ship (4.16 ff.), how to find lodgings in a strange port (5.18), the problems of a woman travelling alone with a man or of being a foreigner with no sponsor in a big Egyptian city (5.4 ff., 7.12 ff.). Frontiers exist between the zones: the sea (again a structural device) and the cataract at Syene (not the desert, interestingly), but the areas they demarcate are no longer smooth narrative monoliths.

Secondly, it is something of a commonplace in discussion of this novel to point to its linear rather than circular movement. Long ago Mikhail Bakhtin described the typical Greek novel in terms of a chronotope of adventure time and space apparently sealed off from the urban chronotope of romance and marriage that begins and ends the novel (Bakhtin 1981, 84–258 (written in 1937–8)). If the basic narrative shape is one of excursion and return, closure is provided by simple resumption of the status quo ante. In looping back to its starting point the plot writes itself off as an abandoned meander in the heroes' lives. Experiences in adventure time leave no discernible trace on the protagonists, so that Chaireas and Kallirhoe, Anthia and Habrokomes pick up pretty much where they left off, having learned nothing from their experiential *katabaseis* into the hells of stone quarry or quayside brothel.

In Heliodoros it is not like that. The plot does not move from the centre to the periphery and back; in fact it calls into question the very hierarchical conception of the world that those terms imply, since the heroine's story at least starts and ends in Ethiopia. But even this circularity is strategically distanced: all movement *from* Ethiopia is quarantined in the form of inset narratives: all the movement in the primary narration is southwards. There is no return ticket from Ethiopia, and no one would want one: to be in Ethiopia is to be in an altered state. For Theagenes and Charikleia arrival in Ethiopia represents first the opportunity to consummate their love under all the proper sanctions; second, elevation to a royal status that is the one's by birthright, but that she has never previously enjoyed; third, exaltation to a new spiritual level as priest and priestess of the sun and moon. So the closure of the story brings with it the most profound and fundamental changes. It is not quite that the journey through physical space is paralleled by one of spiritual development and moral improvement, since Theagenes and Charikleia are victims of congenital perfection. It is rather that their journey certifies their inherent worth and qualifies them to reap its just deserts.

Moreover, the *Aithiopika* is full of people travelling. Whereas in Chariton or Xenophon of Ephesos the protagonists are mobile but the people they encounter are static and can be left behind as the journey continues, in Heliodoros virtually the entire cast is on the move, each plying his or her significant journey. The theme of journey structures the stories of all the main characters in subtly but significantly different ways. Only for Charikleia is the pattern the generic one of exile and return. Exposed as a child and passed from Ethiopian to Greek priest in Egypt, her story is a *nostos*, with all the predictable intertextual engagement with the *Odyssey*. At one level this journey reverses the Hellenocentric world-view of the genre: at the end of the novel the centre of Charikleia's world is in Meroe, on the cartographic limits of the Greek cosmos, and sure enough in the final pages the Ethiopian king talks of Greece as the ends of the earth (10.16.6). But this geographic re-centring of the journey is more an act of cultural colonialism than an adoption of an alternative perspective. Charikleia has been to finishing school in Greece and in the end goes home with all the cultural values of the land where she grew up. The Ethiopian court is already Greek speaking, and once it is cured of its regrettably barbarian tendency to immolate its captives, Ethiopia becomes an idealised Hellenic community, symbolised by Theagenes' victory over an Ethiopian giant in a wrestling competition, Greek skill triumphing over barbarian brutishness.[18]

Charikleia's *nostos* is not of course shared by Theagenes. For him the journey to Ethiopia has a different shape and a different meaning: his journey is only one-way, ever. This differentiation has a profound literary effect: from the deepest structural level upward, Heliodoros' two protagonists are separated and individualised. Charikleia makes the journey because she has to; Theagenes makes it because he loves Charikleia, and it is a sign of his devotion that he is prepared to reassign his ethnic, cultural and social identities to be with her for always. The equation of absolute reciprocity between romantic lovers is destabilised, introducing a new and interesting brittleness into the central relationship. It is not that the novel primarily writes the story of the heroine, reducing the hero to an accessory, more that it writes importantly different stories for the two of them, the differences crystallising out around the theme of the journey.[19]

The priests Kalasiris and Charikles both travel in pursuit of wisdom. In each case the journey is undertaken for consolation following a personal crisis: the death of Charikles' daughter and wife, the threat posed to Kalasiris' chastity by the arrival in Memphis of a Greek courtesan. But although travel characterises both as 'wise man' – the encyclopaedism of the novel resides largely in the persona of Kalasiris – the differences in their travel embody the differences in their wisdom.[20] Charikles' first voyages have their limit at the cataract at Katadoupa, well to the north of the Ethiopian border. It is here that he encounters Sisimithres and is entrusted with the infant heroine, whereupon he promptly returns to Greece (2.33.2). It is clear that Ethiopia allegorically represents an ideal that he is not yet worthy to attain. Kalasiris, on the other hand, travels to Ethiopia itself specifically in pursuit of wisdom, and attains particular honour there for deifying the wisdom of Egypt by the addition of that of Ethiopia (4.12). At the very end of the novel, when all the loose ends are being tied, Charikles suddenly turns up at Meroe, whither he has followed the trail of his 'daughter' and her abductor. His journey to the heart of Ethiopia is the one un-narrated major piece of travel in the novel, a silence that generates the effect of surprise. As the protagonists are ordained into the Ethiopian priesthood, the scene is presented through the perceptions of Charikles as he suddenly perceives the unity and integrity of the plot (its divine governance), in a way reminiscent of a similarly epiphany experienced by Kalasiris when he discovered Charikleia's identity and perceived the coherence of events (10.41.2; Kalarsiris' epiphany at 4.9.1 ff). This heavily focalised revelation, through a character not hitherto noted for his darting intellect, inscribes the reader's ultimate comprehension of the plot, a wisdom that can only be attained by visiting Ethiopia. Sisimithres the Ethiopian priest has this insight all along.

For another character, the Athenian Knemon who for a while acts the cameo role of hero's friend, travel is again an important indicator of status and character within the plot. Knemon's story is a *nostos* in reverse. He swims against the southward tide of the plot's movement to return to the carnality and moral compromise of Athens, having contracted a highly lucrative marriage with a rich merchant's daughter. Again it seems clear that Knemon can only progress so far towards the spiritual salvation that Ethiopia represents. Heliodoros' use of travel, then, not only drives the plot in the mechanical sense but also coheres with the entire system of ethical metaphor that underlies it.

In this paper I have sketched out the function of travel in three of the Greek novels. Much of what I have said is not new, or else will have been obvious to anyone who knows these texts. Nevertheless, the exercise has been an eye-opener to me at least, in several respects, adumbrated at the start of this paper and here restated by way of conclusion. First there is the sense that in all three novels, travel is used to articulate and shape the plot, that the map of the geography of the fictional world, with its barriers such as seas and rivers, is also a map of the structure of the plot with its divisions and transitions between episodes, that the journey described in the novel is thus somehow analogous to the journey of reading the book, that plot is journey. These travels are all profoundly self-referential. Second, it is easy to overstate the sameness of the novels. There is clearly a motif repertoire for these things, but if travel stands for the structure of the plot, then there is more and more radical difference, even at the structural level, between these authors than critics usually see or allow: these three apparently similar love stories turn out, when viewed from the perspective of their travel plots, to be respectively a circular plot of excursion and return, a pursuit plot, and a unidirectional ascent superimposed on an Odyssean *nostos*. Third, although it is dangerous to talk in such terms, especially when dealing with a selection from an already statistically small sample, there does appear to be a development going on within the genre of romance, from a purely narratological use of travel towards a more sophisticated employment which is simultaneously more concrete and more symbolic in itself. Far from travel narrative with all its attendant agendas being, as it were, an ingredient of the original recipe of the Greek romance, it looks as if it was just another item in the intertextual wardrobe that the genre acquired in the hands of its more skilful exponents.

I am very aware of having presented a partial picture. In particular, a more complete treatment of travel in the novels would have paid more attention to two extraordinary works known to us primarily from summaries in the *Bibliotheke* of Photios. The *Babyloniaka* of Iamblichos was another pursuit novel, but was the only novel we know of set entirely outside the Greek world, and with a wholly non-Greek cast-list. Photios' summary hints tantalisingly at vivid local colouring, but fails to deliver as much as a single place-name. *The Wonders beyond Thoule* of Antonius Diogenes seems to have been an amazing amalgam of travel-text and love-novel. Parts of it were cast in the form of reported first-person narrations in which various characters recounted their wanderings, echoing the form of the authentic traveller's narrative. Between them these narrators appear to have covered the entire known world, and the extreme length of the work (24 books) suggests that there was a large quantity of ethnographic and paradoxographical material included. Photios even tells us that the author listed sources at the beginning of each book. The only one of these he names, however, is Antiphanes of Berge, whose name was synonymous in the ancient world with lying tales. In pushing his narrative to the edges of the world and beyond, Antonius seems to have been playing with the border areas of travel fact and travel fiction, and there are indications that this was connected at a deeper level with a Pythagorean or neo-Pythagorean subtext. Further I have omitted any mention of the picaresque Latin novels of Petronius and Apuleius, each in its different way dominated by themes of journey. These things must await another occasion.

Notes

1 Those of Chariton, Xenophon of Ephesos, Achilleus Tatius, Longus and Heliodorus. They are translated, along with related fragments, etc. in Reardon 1989. All quotations from the novels in this paper are taken from this collection.

2 The *locus classicus* for this reading of the genre is Perry 1967; see also Reardon 1969, Holzberg 1986 (significantly modified in the second edition of 2001).

3 For example see Perkins 1995, Swain 1996, Lowe 2000, Whitmarsh 2001. On Herodotos see especially Redfield 1985.

4 Van Baak 1983, 47-8 (quoting Lotman 1975); compare van Baak 77: 'The road or journey offers the most archaic and fundamental type of plot … it is a succession of difficulties, dangers and obstacles which become increasingly threatening and hard to surpass for the hero whose heroism consists in the conquest of these difficulties and often in the attainment of the end of the road which usually represents some cultural or sacral value'.

5 The narrator refers to 'the carriage' as if his reader already knew about it.

6 'They caught up with the army at the river, attached themselves to the rearguard, and followed along; but when they reached Syria they deserted to the Egyptian side'. Note that this time even the crossing of the Euphrates, a significant boundary marking the geographical limit of the King's power is merely implied, not directly narrated.

7 For this kind of geo-politic-cultural reading see e.g. Lowe 2000, 229-30; Daude 2001.

8 There are maps of the action of all the novels by J. Alvares in Schmeling 1996, 803-14. The problem, of course, is that accurate cartography is just another system for representing the world, and one that is alien to the representation of ancient fiction. Maps enforce a connection between the fictional action and 'real' geography that distorts their subjective maps of distances and relativities of position and importance.

9 5.4.4, '*Everyone found the appointed interval too long, including the King himself. What Olympic Games, what Eleusinian nights ever promised such passionate interest?*'; 6.2.1, '*All Babylon was in commotion. Just as you can see the competitors at Olympia arriving at the stadium escorted by a procession, so you could see these contestants*'

10 In this he is close to the earliest known Greek novel, the fragmentary *Ninos Romance* (translated in Reardon 1989, 803-8). In this text the Ninos and his beloved Semiramis are transformed from figures of awesome barbarity to two tongue-tied little cousins, constrained by very Hellenistic notions of respectability. Chariton is thus not untypical of the earliest *tranche* of Greek fiction.

11 The most influential statement of the epitome theory was Bürger 1892. For attacks on it see Hägg 1966, O'Sullivan 1995. I shall not enter into this complex issue here, other than to say that I am not wholly convinced by either side. My current guess is that our text is one manifestation of a very fluid tradition, possibly intended for use as the basis of oral performance to be elaborated impromptu.

12 For full analysis of Xenophon's techniques of parallelism and alternation, see Hägg 1971, 154-78.

13 This *may* be a consequence of abridgement. There are notably one or two places where, for example, the mode of transport is specified (like Habrokomes *riding* to Kilikia) without any narratological necessity to do so. And, contrary to Chariton's practice, some of Xenophon's adventures (piracy and shipwreck) occur in the course of travel itself.

14 Though there are signs of an intermittent awareness that language differences are a problem in real-world travel: so Hippothoos' journey to Mazakos is assisted by the fact that he can speak Kappadokian like a native (3.1.2).

15 1.6, although many of the details that generate the *effet du réel* are drawn from Herodotos' account of the lake-dwelling Paionians (5.16).

16 It does not matter for the present argument that the *Boukoloi* are a fascinating site of interaction between fact and fiction. The account of their revolt in 171-2 CE given by Cassius Dio (72.4) is clearly related to their fictional activities in the novels of Achilleus Tatius, Heliodoros and perhaps Lollianus. All these writers seem to be drawing on a sensational mythology of 'the other' rather than on dull fact. For discussion see Sandy 1979, Winkler 1980, Alston 1999.

17 For the zoning of Heliodoros' world see Szepessy 1957, and, with a more modern emphasis, Selden 1998, Whitmarsh 1999; on the Athenian episode Morgan 1989; on Kalasiris Sandy 1982, Winkler 1982; on 'serious' meanings Dowden 1996.

18 This simplifies a passage of profound and complex negotiation, which I have discussed more fully in Morgan 1998, 72 -8. At the same time as Ethiopia becomes fully ideal, Theagenes and Charikleia become fully Ethiopian. It is clear that Ethiopia, whose sovereigns trace their descent to the Sun, is a displaced version of Syrian Emesa, centre of the sun cult and home of Heliodoros, who is also a descendant of the Sun (10.41.4). The issue of Hellenism and Hellenocentrism is a live and personal one for this author. But he resolves it not by replacing one hierarchical view of the world with another, but by assimilation and identification.

19 The best treatment of this theme is in an unpublished dissertation: Pletcher 1997, 12 ff.

20 For travel as source and certification of wisdom compare Elsner 1997, on Philostratos' novelistic biography of Apollonios of Tyana, a text commissioned by the Emesan empress Julia Domna, and clearly an intertextual target for Heliodoros.

Bibliography

Adams, P.G. (1983) *Travel literature and the evolution of the novel* (Lexington).

Alston, R. (1999) 'The revolt of the Boukoloi: geography, history and myth', in Hopwood, K. (ed.) *Organised crime in antiquity*, 129–53 (London).

Baak, J. J. van (1983) *The place of space in narration: A semiotic approach to the problem of literary space* (Amsterdam).

Bakhtin, M. M. (1981) *The dialogic imagination*, trans. Emerson, C. and Holquist, M. (Austin and London).

Bürger, K. (1892) 'Zu Xenophon von Ephesus', *Hermes* 27, 36–67.

Daude, C. (2001) 'Le personage d'Artaxerxès dans le roman de Chariton, *Chairéas et Callirhoé*: fiction et histoire', in Pouderon, B. (ed.) *Les personages du roman grec*, 137–48 (Lyons).

Dowden, K. (1996) 'Heliodorus: serious intentions', *CQ* 46, 267–85.

Elsner, J. (1997) 'Hagiographical geography: travel and allegory in the Life of Apollonius of Tyana', *JHS* 117, 22–37.

Hägg, T. (1966) 'Die Ephesiaka des Xenophon Ephesius. Original oder Epitome?', *Classica et Medievalia* 27, 118–61, translated as 'The *Ephesiaca* of Xenophon Ephesius – Original or Epitome' in T. Hägg (2004) *Parthenope: Selecteds Studies in ancient Greek fiction* (1969–2004), 159–98 (Copenhagen).

Hägg, T. (1971) *Narrative technique in ancient Greek romances: Studies of Chariton, Xenophon Ephesius, and Achilles Tatius* (Stockholm).

Henne, H. (1936) 'La géographie de l'Égypte dans Xénophon d'Ephèse', *Revue d'Histoire de la Philosophie et d'Histoire Générale de la Civilisation* 4, 97–106

Holzberg, N. (1986) *Der antike Roman. Eine Einführung* (Munich and Zurich).

Hunter, R. L. (1998) *Studies in Heliodorus* (Cambridge).

Lotman, J. M. (1975) 'On the metalanguage of a typolgical description of culture', *Semiotica* 14, 97–123.

Konstan, D. (1994) *Sexual symmetry: Love in the ancient novel and related genres* (Princeton).

Lowe, N. J. (2000) *The Classical plot and the invention of western narrative* (Cambridge).

Morgan, J. R. (1989) ' The story of Knemon in Heliodoros' *Aithiopika*', *JHS* 109, 99–113; reprinted in Swain 1999, 259–85.

Morgan, J. R. (1994) '*Daphnis and Chloe*: Love's own sweet story' in J. R. Morgan and R. Stoneman (eds.) *Greek fiction: the Greek novel in context* (London and New York).

Morgan, J. R. (1998) 'Narrative doublets in Heliodoros' *Aithiopika*', in Hunter 1998, 60–78.

Morgan, J. R. (2004) *Longus: Daphnis and Chloe. Edited with introduction, translation and commentary* (Warminster).

Morgan, J. R. (2005) 'Le blanc et le noir: perspectives païennes et perspectives chrétiennes sur l'Éthiopie d'Héliodore', in B. Pouderon (ed.) *Lieux, décors et paysages de l'ancien roman des origines à Byzance*, 309–18 (Lyons).

Perkins, J. (1995) *The suffering self: Pain and narrative representation in the early Christian era* (London and New York).

O'Sullivan, J. N. (1995) *Xenophon of Ephesus: his compositional technique and the birth of the novel* (Berlin and New York).

Perry, B. E. (1967) *The ancient romances: A literary-historical account of their origins* (Berkeley, CA).

Pletcher, J. A. (1997) *Narrative structure and narrative texture in the Aithiopika of Heliodoros* PhD dissertation, St Andrews.

Reardon, B. P. (1969) 'The Greek novel', *Phoenix* 23, 291–309

Reardon, B. P. (1989) *Collected ancient Greek novels* (Berkeley, CA).

Redfield, J. (1985) "Herodotus the tourist", *CPh* 80, 97–118, republished in T. Harrison (ed.) *Greeks and Barbarians*, 24–49 (Edinburgh).

Rohde, E. (1876) *Der griechische Roman und seine Vorläufer* (3rd edition revised by W. Schmid, Leipzig 1914).

Sandy, G. N. (1979) 'Notes on Lollianus' *Phoenicica*', *AJP* 100, 367–76.

Sandy, G. N. (1982) 'Characterization and philosophical décor in Heliodorus' *Aethiopica*', *TAPA* 112, 141–67.

Schmeling, G. L. (1996) *The novel in the ancient world* (Leiden).

Selden, D. L. (1998) '*Aithiopika* and Ethiopianism', in Hunter 1998, 182–217.

Swain, S. (1996) *Hellenism and empire: Language, classicism, and power in the Greek world AD50–250* (Oxford).

Swain, S. (1999) *Oxford Readings in the Greek Novel* (Oxford).

Szepessy, T. (1957) 'Die Aithiopika des Heliodoros und der griechische sophistische Liebesroman', *AntHung* 5, 241–59, reprinted in H. Gärtner (1984) *Beiträge zum griechischen Liebesroman*, 432–50 (Hildesheim).

Whitmarsh, T. (1999) 'The writes of passage: Cultural initiation in Heliodorus' *Aethiopica*', in R. Miles (ed.) *Constructing identities in late antiquity*, 16–40 (London and New York).

Whitmarsh, T. (2001) *Greek Literature and the Roman Empire: The politics of imitation* (Oxford).

Winkler, J. J. (1980) 'Lollianus and the desperadoes', *JHS* 100, 155–81.

Winkler, J. J. (1982) 'The mendacity of Kalasiris and the narrative strategy of Heliodoros' *Aithiopika*', *YCS* 27, 93–158, reprinted in Swain 1999, 286–350.

'Travel Narrows the Mind': Cultural Tourism in Graeco-Roman Egypt

Colin Adams

Cultural tourism, or travel with the purpose of learning about and experiencing cultures other than one's own, is often claimed to be a purpose of travel by individuals. A deeper purpose, or even result, is that such travel and experiences allow one better to understand his or her own culture or to reinforce its values – certainly a feature, for example, of the Grand Tour undertaken by affluent British citizens in Europe, where arguably the company one kept or who one met along the way was as important as visiting cultural sites. Beyond this, it is sometimes the rigors of the physical act of traveling that allows for an appreciation of home. For some religion is an important stimulus to travel, and there are those who can claim a spiritual experience. Indeed it is sometimes impossible to separate these aspects of travel.

The purpose of this paper is explore some of the features of what we might call cultural tourism in the Graeco-Roman period in Egypt, a region perhaps most associated with such a phenomenon, and to present the evidence for the various attractions visited. It will also explore the links between tourism and pilgrimage and assess the importance of each site to one or the other. Recent work has tried to place pilgrimage in the Graeco-Roman period into a wider Egyptian context, but my focus here is broader (Frankfurter 1998; Rutherford 1998 and 2003). The central question is what the purpose of travel was – why visitors were interested in the various sites visited, and what this can tell us about the travellers themselves. But, at the outset, we should note that the phenomenon of cultural tourism seems only to have been a feature beginning in the Graeco-Roman period. Elsewhere in this volume, John Baines and Alan Lloyd have shown that there is nothing in our evidence from Egypt in earlier periods to show any interest on the part of Egyptians for such travel. A notion of cultural superiority to their neighbours militated against any interest in their cultures, buildings or material culture beyond showing domination over it. There is a good deal of evidence for tourism in Egypt in the Graeco-Roman periods, not only in the literary evidence, but perhaps most interestingly in the epigraphic record. Cultural superiority is a feature of Graeco-Roman attitudes too, but displayed in a different way. There is certainly a desire to experience different cultures, perhaps as a way of confirming that superiority.

We should begin by noting some general perceptions of travel in our literary sources. A full survey is not possible, but a number of examples will serve to frame

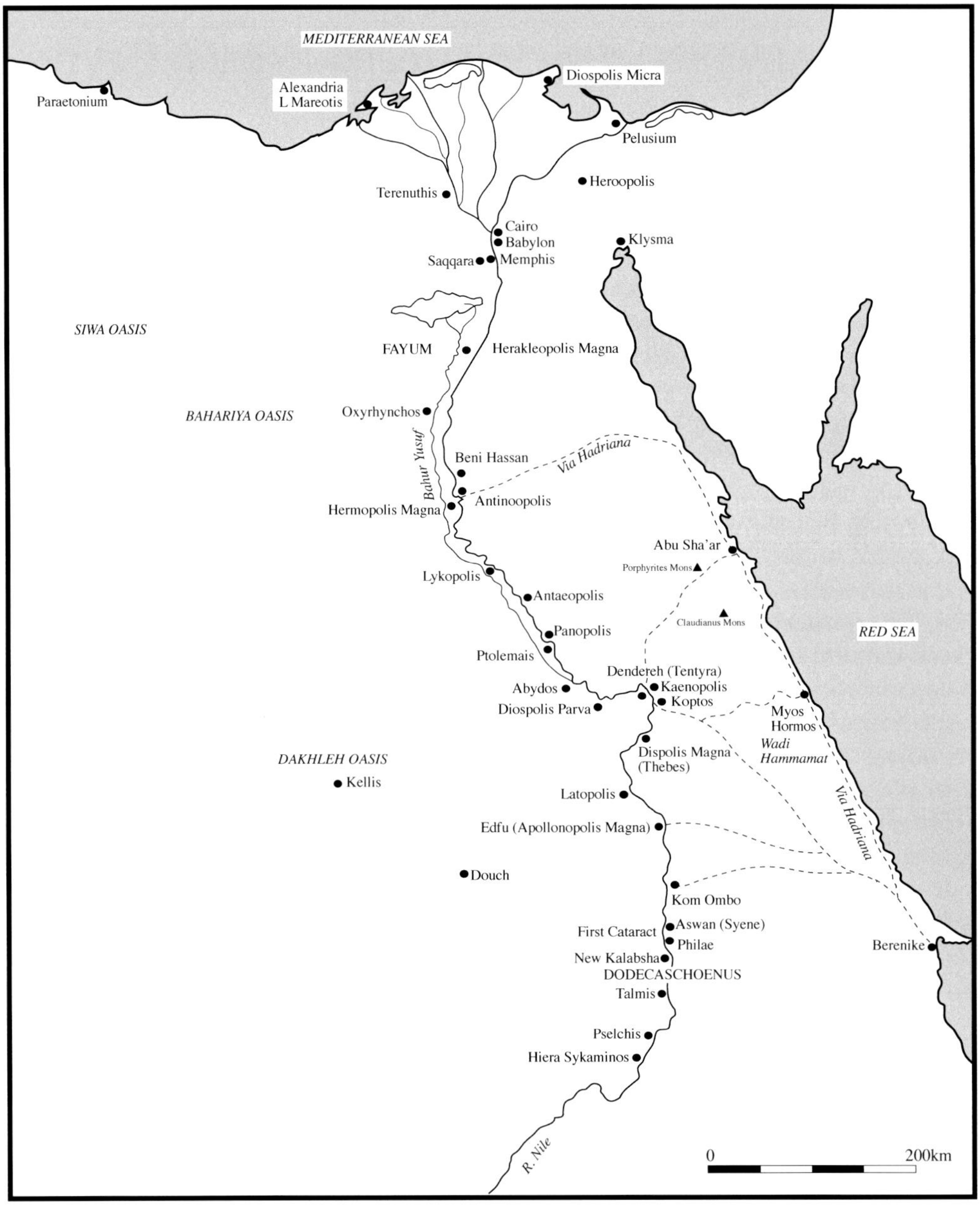

Fig. 22 Map of Graeco-Roman Egypt.

a question. In a particularly illuminating letter, Seneca conceded that travelling does one good in some ways, but not in others:

> *What travel will give is familiarity with other nations: it will reveal to you mountains of strange shape, or unfamiliar tracts of plain, or valleys that are watered by ever-flowing springs, or the characteristic of some river that comes to our attention. We discern how the Nile rises and swells in summer, or how the Tigris disappears, runs underground through hidden spaces, and then appears with unabated sweep; or how the Maeander, that oft-rehearsed theme and plaything of the poets turns in frequent levelings, and often in winding comes close to its own channel before resuming its course. But this sort on information will not make better or sounder men of us.*
>
> Seneca, Epistulae 104.15 (trans. Gummere)

Seneca here conveniently identifies some of the main benefits and results of recreational travel: historical interest (not necessarily the equivalent of the Greek 'enquiry' – *historîe*), natural history and wonders, to which we could add art, although this is less important.[1] Lucian, in a fictional work about a voyage and a parody of other travel narratives and ethnographic literature, explains his purpose: 'my voyage was prompted by an active intellect and a passionate interest in anything new' (*A True Story* 1.5 (trans. Reardon)). The story then related is certainly parody and pure fancy, even if the original sentiment or purpose does reflect one of the real purposes of travel. The popularity of Egypt and other regions of the Roman empire in both terms of intellectual interest and travel is confirmed in an uncomplimentary letter of Pliny the Younger:

> *We are always ready to make a journey and cross the sea in search of things we fail to notice in front of our eyes, whether it is that we are naturally indifferent to anything close at hand while pursuing distant objects, or that every desire fades when it can easily be granted, or that we postpone a visit with the idea that we shall often be seeing what is there to be seen whenever we feel inclined. Whatever the reason, there are a great many things in Rome and nearby which we have never seen nor even heard of, though if they were to be found in Greece, Egypt or Asia, or any other country which advertises its wealth of marvels, we should have heard and read about them and seen them for ourselves.*
>
> Pliny, Epistulae 8.20

This passage raises three points. First, the interest in the exotic; second, the link between discussion of travel and other countries between Pliny and his peers, literature concerning them, and the decision to experience them personally; and third, it points towards an ancient discourse on the nature and purpose of travel, which, given the modern interest in travel writing, provides an interesting counter-balance to modern debate.

But purely recreational travel represents only part of the picture, for many individuals visit sites of religious importance in pilgrimage, and others in the course of their professional duties, and it is, as noted before, difficult to separate these, and it may not even be appropriate to do so. But the spirit of enquiry was strong, and often appears as a motive for visiting certain locations. Naturally the examples we have in our literary sources are of important figures: Germanicus' discovery of the antiquities of Egypt or Septimius Severus' investigations in Egypt, which left no stone unturned.[2] Interestingly, though, the same motives and vocabulary turn up in our documentary evidence from Egypt, as we shall see.

But travel has a deeper meaning and purpose. Travel is a partner of geographical knowledge, for the urge to travel as a tourist arises out of learning of a region and then wanting to visit it to see for oneself. If travel is a partner of knowledge, then knowledge is a partner of empire, for establishing knowledge of a region or mapping it is never innocent. Our evidence for tourism in Graeco-Roman Egypt shows clear signs of imperialism and cultural appropriation. The Egyptian past was appropriated and fitted into a Homeric landscape, which allowed Greeks and then Romans to distance themselves from Egyptian culture, to understand better their own past, and to signify their Greekness and superiority. To this extent, then, is it possible to suggest that travel, rather than broadening the minds of Greek and Roman tourists, actually narrowed their cultural perceptions? Simon Gikandi, writing about the experience of English travellers in the West Indies suggests that travel allowed 'imperial travellers to reflect on, question, demonize, and sometimes assimilate, monuments of other times and places' (Gikandi 1996, 89). Visitors to Egypt were integrated and connected by their experiences (and this is clear from what they wrote as graffiti), and this served also to underline the integrity of Greek culture. Egypt was constructed according to the values and cultural system of it visitors, and the Homeric landscape and Greekness was the basic comparison or point of reference. There is an important purpose of Graeco-Roman geographical literature and accounts of travel to create a view of other cultures against which Greek culture (the norm) can be measured. It is an important feature of the Egyptian epigraphic evidence for Graeco-Roman travel, that this imperial/cultural phenomenon can be traced in graffiti.

It is now appropriate to set the context for travel and tourism in Egypt.

Greek and Roman visitors to Egypt

Egypt was a land that held a particular fascination for Greeks and Romans on many levels. There was its great antiquity and impressive monuments, its timeless feel, very different from the 'Romanized' provinces of the West. Its natural wonders – principally the Nile – were the subject of much interest, so too were its flora and fauna, which inspired the Roman imagination to fuel the production of mosaics and wall-paintings depicting Nilotic scenes (Versluys 2002). The Palestrina mosaic is the best-known, but good examples of mosaic and wall painting can be found in Praeneste and commonly in Pompeii and Herculaneum (Meyboom 1995 and Versluys 2002). Egyptian architecture and sculpture was imitated: the villa of Hadrian at Tivoli is the obvious example, and it is no surprise that a Canopus was included, after the notorious city in the Delta; Severus' villa apparently included a labyrinth and a part called Memphis (HA, *Had.* 26.5; Epiphanius, *De Mens et Pond.* 14). Indeed, according to his biographer, Severus was fascinated by Egypt, and he records of his visit there:

> *This visit was pleasant for him – as Severus himself afterwards often stated – because of his devotion to the god Serapis, as he came to be acquainted with the antiquities and saw wild rare animals and strange places. For he diligently inspected Memphis and Memnon, the pyramids and the labyrinth.*
>
> HA, *Sev.* 17

Ancient novels often included tales of Egypt, usually of a fantastic nature, and these were of perennial interest and are instructive of the Roman image of Egypt.[3] While certainly a focus of fascination, not least because of animal worship, Egypt was also a focus of much dislike and criticism. Juvenal's vitriolic satirical attack on the barbaric practices of Egyptians can only have been effective, or funny, if relevant to widely-held views (Juvenal, *Satires* 15). Perhaps one reason behind this was the discomfort invoked by memories of Cleopatra, and the consequent reluctance of emperors to allow the Roman aristocracy to visit Egypt, famously explained by Tacitus (Smelik and Hemelrijk 1984, 1955; Tacitus, *Histories* 1.11; *Annals* 2.68). But there is perhaps something else here – the Greek definition of barbarian is not just one who speaks in a foreign language, but also one ignorant of city life and used to the rule of kings.[4] Tacitus' disapproval of the Egyptians has its roots in politics as much as culture, and he can use Augustus' control of Egypt to highlight his autocratic position. Pliny the Elder writes negatively about Egypt, and recommends his readers forget their interest in its history and culture (Versluys 2002, 431, citing Pliny *NH* 36.103). What seems clear in nearly all Roman literature, from poets to historians, is that the authors did not try to understand or engage with Egyptian culture, but rather, as Maehler has pointed out, they refer to Egypt in pursuit of their own agendas, which might reflect Augustan propaganda against Cleopatra or a view of Egyptians similar to that of Tacitus as a naturally hot-tempered and volatile lot (Maehler 2003). But this is a view prevalent among the Roman intellectual elite. How far does it represent what others thought? As we shall see, one of the benefits of the Egyptian evidence is that it allows us to get closer to the views of individuals outside this group.

In earlier periods, many Greeks visited Egypt – Herodotos the most famous of them. Diodorus Siculus followed in both his footsteps and those of Hecataeus of Abdera. The tradition of philosophical journeys to Egypt is also well established. The Egypt of the Ptolemies, and its great city of Alexandria, with its library and museum, was a mecca for writers, thinkers, and scholars of all kinds – some of them Roman (Meyboom 1995, 164–6). Beyond an interest in scholarship and learning, we have evidence on a papyrus of the so-called Zenon archive that records the visit of *theoroi* ('visitors') from Argos in Greece to the Fayum, coming to 'see the sights' (*P. Lond.* VII 1973). A better-known papyrus from Tebtunis in the Fayum, preserves a contemporary account of a visit by Lucius Memmius, a Roman senator in 112 BC:

> *Hermias to Horus, greeting. Below is a copy of the letter to Asclepiades. Take care then that its instructions are followed. Goodbye. Year 5, Xandicus 17, Mecheir 17.*
>
> *To Asclepiades. Lucius Memmius, a Roman senator, who occupies a position of great dignity and honour, is sailing up from Alexandria to the Arsinoite nome to see the sights. Let him be received with special magnificence, and take care that at the proper spots the guest-chambers be prepared and the landing places to them be completed, and that the gifts mentioned below be presented to him at the landing place, and that the furniture of the guest-chamber, the tit-bits for Petesouchos and the crocodiles, the conveniences for viewing the Labryinth, and the offerings and sacrifices be provided; in general take the greatest pains in everything to see that the visitor is satisfied, and display the utmost zeal …*[5]

It is not unreasonable to connect Lucius Memmius to diplomatic visits to the Ptolemaic court, and his taking the opportunity to tour the country was not unusual.[6] Roman visitors in the Ptolemaic period also left their names inscribed in the walls of the temple of Isis at Philae.[7] A pattern emerges indicating that most Roman visitors in the Ptolemaic period visited Egyptian sites in the course of professional duties. This is true also of the Roman period, as we shall see, but this pattern may be influenced by the restrictions on travel to Egypt placed on senators and equites.

The Egyptian Evidence

There is no doubt that there is a rich and diverse range of evidence for travel in the Graeco-Roman period, but it is loaded with difficulties of interpretation – the class and gender bias peculiar to our evidence, propaganda, prejudice, or dictates of literary form (satire for example). But evidence from Egypt preserved in the papyrological and epigraphic record allows for a different picture. There is much evidence for travel preserved on papyri (Kotsifou 2000; Adams 2001), but the focus of this paper is the evidence of graffiti left by visitors at sites of cultural or historic importance. By their nature these graffiti are informal writings, and are thus unofficial, separate in character from other forms of inscription such as edicts, temple inscriptions and so on. In large part they are spontaneous writings, but an important feature of graffiti is that they encourage repetition and response, and thus create a dialogue linking the writers (Adams forthcoming) – something clearly demonstrated, for example, by the graffiti subculture present today in modern cities. This means that graffiti encourages response and therefore has an audience; it is a form of written *communication*. Who this audience is, in the case of our Egyptian graffiti, is an important indicator of its purpose and cultural importance. For it is written in Greek and Latin (sometimes both) for Greeks and Romans, and thus provided a cultural link between the visitors and established a cultural dialogue serving to repeat and strengthen the link between the various sites visited and their connection to a Hellenic past as represented in Greek literature (especially Homer). But their interpretation is a little more complicated than suggesting that they are merely informal. In a major study of graffiti in the Pharaonic period, Peden suggested that graffiti was 'a form of written communication that is invariably free of social restraints' (Peden 2001, xxi), and highlights the unpretentious nature of the texts. Graeco-Roman graffiti largely follow this pattern, but do depart from it dramatically in some instances, especially on the Colossos of Memnon. Most graffiti simply record a name or an act of adoration to a god (*proskynema*), but some provide much more information, and importantly for our purposes here, sometimes observations about the places visited. Also, in quite a number of inscriptions, what we might call Homeric language and allusion are present, and some show considerable linguistic flair. It is arguable, therefore, that even graffiti in this case are the preserve of the intellectual elite, and are thus not free from social constraint. They are thus an important source of evidence for cultural tourism.

Pilgrimage and tourism

It is difficult to separate pilgrimage from tourism, and indeed, to do so might create a false distinction. Compounding this problem is the nature of our evidence, largely graffiti, which does not provide all the information that we might want. Pilgrimage and religious curiosity lay behind a significant proportion of travel in the ancient world.[8] There were certainly religious reasons for travel to temples and shrines, but there was significant passing-trade, for example at Paneia or local shrines, and temples often held other attractions which would have been of interest to visitors – the crocodiles in the Fayum are a good example.[9] Other examples of additional attractions certainly exist outside Egypt – sculpture and works of art, curiosities both savory and unsavory, artifacts of men and heroes, some authentic others not, beautiful gardens, and of course the information provided by guides or priests (see Friedländer 1908–13, 268–78). A visit to the healing shrine at the Serapeum of Canopus might be combined with several days of hedonism at its famous hostelries (Strabo 17.1.17). The conjuntion of recreational and religious purpose behind journeys can clearly be seen in a letter preserved on papyrus, dating to the early second century AD:

> *Nearchus [to Heliodorus greeting]. Since many [these days go on voyages?] and even set forth upon the sea to Egypt to visit the artistic creations of man, I made a voyage (?).*
>
> *Starting upon the journey upstream, I came to (or passed by?) Syene from*

> *whence the Nile flows, and to Libya, where Ammon gives oracles to all men, and I visited (or examined) the cuttings (?), and for my friends, by name, I engraved there in the holy places an eternal record of their homage.*
>
> *Address: To Heliodorus.* (*P. Lond.* III 835 = *P. Sarap.* 101 (early second century)).

On the surface, the papyrus preserves details of a journey made by Nearchos, which he relates to his friend. But is this really the case? Another interpretation is possible (*P. Sarap.* 101 intro). The geographic order of Nearchos' visit makes no sense if he is recounting an actual journey and opens many questions. Why visit Syene, then the Oasis of Siwa, and the Valley of the Kings ('the cuttings') in that order? What route did he take to Siwa, why indeed did he go there? It might be that he alludes to literary accounts of journeys in Egypt – perhaps Herodotos, which might also be betrayed by the flowery language of the letter. Perhaps the literary pretensions of Nearchos shine through, and here we should be mindful of the connection between travel and literature shown by the letters of Seneca and Pliny discussed above and of Lucian's fictional journey in his *True Story*. Whatever the authenticity of the journey was, it is clear that several factors stimulated the journey or Nearchos' imagination: interest in natural wonders, in visiting oracles, the repetition, perhaps, of the journey of Alexander to Siwa, and historical enquiry at the Valley of the Kings. Such features are also clear in Strabo's account of Egypt in Book Seventeen of his *Geography*. His progression through Egypt lists temples, shrines and 'tourist attractions' in equal measure – his description of Abydos for example (17.1.42) begins not with the temples, but with a brief discussion of the architecture of the Memnonion, a fountain, and an acanthus grove sacred to Apollo. Cultural appropriation is striking here, for this ancient cult centre was that of Osiris, who the Greeks later called Dionysius. There is little doubt that aspects of a Homeric world-view, especially its concern with the divine and its inherent connection to history, heavily influenced Strabo's account of Egypt, as it influenced many travellers.

Although pilgrimage, as distinct from festivals, seems not to have been an essential component of Egyptian religion, indeed Herodotos mentions only one instance, during the Ptolemaic and Roman periods it becomes more common.[10] There certainly came to be temples which were the focus of pilgrimage: principally at Abydos, Deir el-Bahri and Philae.[11] Temples sometimes assumed a more specific importance, especially as healing shrines: the Serapea at Alexandria and Canopus, the temple of Dendara, which housed a sanatorium. Particular gods also came to be associated with healing and became the focus of pilgrimage – Bes at Abydos and Dendara (Frankfurter 1998, 47–9 on Dendara, and Rutherford 2003 on Abydos). Other temples, such as the Serapeum at Memphis, or Ammon at Siwa, housed oracles, consulted through incubation.

Principal tourist attractions

The tourist itinerary in Egypt is exemplified by the tour of Germanicus Caesar in AD 19, reported by Tacitus (*Annals* 2.59–61). Like many visitors to Egypt, he began his journey at Canopus in the Delta, as tradition had it, founded by the Spartans in honour of the helmsman of Menelaus, and a haven for revellers. Tacitus continues (and reflects Pliny with the literary topos of the conspicuous display of wealth):

> *Germanicus was interested in seeing other wonders too, in particular the stone statue of Memnon, giving out when struck by the sun's rays the sound of a voice; the pyramids, mountainous monuments to the pride and wealth of their kings, built on drifting and pathless sands; the artificial lake to receive the Nile's overflow; and elsewhere gorges and depths unknown. He then came to Elephantine and Syene, formerly frontiers of the Roman empire, which now extends to the Red Sea.*
>
> *Annals* 2.61 (trans. Grant).

It is clear that a number of monuments were not connected to any particular deity, but were visited due to their architectural or historical interest. Arguably the most striking and famous monuments of Egypt, the pyramids at Giza, were certainly a source of wonder to the Greeks and Romans, even if some could not resist the temptation to appropriate them to Greek culture, for Strabo accepts that the smallest pyramid, that of Mycinerus, actually belonged to the Greek courtesan Rhodopis (Strabo 17.1.33; even Herodotos rejects this notion, 2.134). Where Herodotos, Diodorus and Strabo agreed that these were impressive achievements, and the pyramids of Cheops and Chephren were among the Seven Wonders of the ancient world, Romans were typically less impressed. Pliny the Elder wrote of them, again picking up the theme of the evils of kingship and perhaps thinking of Nero:

> *We will mention also cursorily the Pyramids, which are in the same country as Egypt, that idle and foolish exhibition of royal wealth. For the cause by most assigned for their construction is an intention on the part of those kings to exhaust their treasures, rather than leave them to successors or plotting rivals, or to keep the people from idleness. Great was the vanity of those individuals on this point.*
>
> *NH* 36.12

Although it is clear that many visitors left graffiti as a record of their visit on the pyramids, the stripping of the marble outer casing since the Roman period has removed nearly all. The three that we know of were recorded in later sources, and in common show that the visitors were interested in viewing the pyramids as objects of admiration (*I. Metr.* 128). Curiously, the Sphinx is not mentioned by any Greek or Roman source before Pliny the Elder (*NH* 36.17). An inscription, dating to the reign of Tiberius, was set up in honour of a *strategos*, Pompeius Sabinus, which suggests that the Sphinx was at least known locally at this time (*SB* V 7738 = *SEG* VIII 527). But, an inscription from Nero's reign may provide the answer to this conundrum. In it, the prefect of Egypt, T. Claudius Balbillus, is thanked by the inhabitants of the nearby village of Bursiris for petitioning the emperor, probably for the clearing of sand from the monument (*IGRR* I 1110 = *OGIS* 666 = *SB* V 8303). Two similar inscriptions demonstrate a continued interest in the maintenance of the monument: during the reign of Marcus Aurelius in AD 166, repairs were made to the enclosure wall, and in the reign of Septimius Severus, Caracalla and Geta, pavements were restored (*SB* V 8305 = *IGRR* I 1112 (AD 166); *SB* V 8561 = *IGRR* I 1113 (AD 199/200)). It is interesting that Septimius was involved in this matter. It follows from his interest in Egypt, already mentioned, but also because he ordered repairs to made to the colossus of Memnon, as we shall see.

The damage to the outer casing of the Sphinx is profound, and while it is probable that there was a large number of graffiti, only a handful has been preserved. There are a number of *proskynemata* (including an inscription of footprints *ex-voto* (*SB* V 8560)), but this does not necessarily mean that the sphinx was an object of pilgrimage rather than tourism. Others are descriptive, and in one the Sphinx is described as '… a sacred countenance, animated by the breath of god, but it has the limbs and stature of a lion, the king of animals' (*SB* V 8550 = *I. Metr*. 130; on the Sphinx, see Bernand 1983). There are simply not enough inscriptions to make a sound appraisal of visit patterns. Bernand, on the strength of what survives, states that the nature of the visitors to the Sphinx was different to that of the Colossi of Memnon – less distinguished visitors frequented the Sphinx, no important functionaries, or soldiers, who left their names on the Memnon colossus (Bernand 1983, 189). There is not enough evidence to make such a claim, the proximity of the Sphinx to the Pyramids and to Memphis place it square on the tourist's intinerary (an argument *ex silentio*, but none-the-less, they must have passed it), and the level of imperial interest shown by repair made suggests rather more importance. If it was not of interest to Graeco-Romans in terms of cult, there is the possibility that the Sphinx was of some importance to local pilgrims, as it may have come to represent the image of the god Harmakhis (*I. Metr.* 127; Volokhine 1998, 80). We can be fairly sure that it was an attraction of some importance, but perhaps less so than others, as it could not so easily be set in a Homeric landscape.

To the south west of Giza lies the Fayum. The attractions of this area for Germanicus Caesar lay not only in the famous Labyrinth, but also in its landscape, for he wanted to inspect the irrigation channels of the Fayum. The interest of tourists in natural history is clear in this example, but there is also little doubt that Germanicus had other reasons for inspecting the channels, both administrative and economic, for the Fayum was an important producer of grain. The sacred crocodiles, as we have seen, were an attraction, but it is clear that they were not so from a religious point of view, but were merely curiosities. Strabo provides a graphic account of the spectacle of the crocodile Souchos at the city of Arsinoe: 'and there is a sacred one there, which is kept and fed by itself in a lake, and is tame to the priests. It is called Souchos; and it is fed on grain and pieces of meat and on wine, which are always being fed to it by the foreigners who go to see it' (17.1.38). No doubt Romans were amused by the animal-worshipping Egyptians (Smelik and Hemelrijk 1984).

More widely known, and more important to Greeks, was the Labyrinth, thought to be the temple of Amenemhet III at Hawara. Herodotos' description is long and glowing – more impressive than the Pyramids, he claims (2.148). Strabo follows suit: 'In addition to the things mentioned, this nome has the Labyrinth, which is a work comparable to the pyramids, and near it, the tomb of the king who built the Labyrinth' (17.1.38; see also Pliny the Elder *NH* 36.19). For Diodorus Siculus, the builder of the Labyrinth was an otherwise unknown king, Mendes (1.66.3). For Strabo, however, the king was Imandes. But for both, there is an oblique connection to Greece and Greek mythology. Diodorus notes that the Labyrinth in Egypt was used as a model for the building of the same name constructed for Minos, the king of Crete, to house the Minotaur (1.61.3–4). With Strabo a complication arises, and this connects the Labyrinth to the Memnonia at Abydos and Thebes, a point to which we will return.

Perhaps the most important tourist attraction in Egypt of the Graeco-Roman period was Thebes, although, oddly, Herodotos does not describe it in detail.[12] Diodorus offers more information; he begins by quoting Homer's famous lines on Thebes with her hundred gates, and then to justify the tradition that 20,000 chariots once issued from her gates.[13] He goes on to give the most detailed account of the Theban temples that we have preserved, especially of Karnak, with its colossal statues and obelisks. Strabo's account is rather more brief, merely acknowledging the scale of the temples, and continuing the probably fictitious account of their looting by Cambyses, providing a further connection to Herodotos and connection to the past.[14] It is striking that Strabo moves quickly onto his description of the West Bank of the Nile, an area he calls the Memnonia. The central attraction here was the Colossus of Memnon, one of two statues of Amenophis III set at the entrance to his mortuary temple. Little remains of this today, and probably even in Roman times the remains were not remarkable – it was the colossi, and the northernmost of the two in particular, which commanded attention (Fig. 23):

> *Here are two colossi, which are near one another and are each made of a single stone; one of them is preserved, but the upper parts of the other, from the seat up, fell when an earthquake took place, so it is said. It is believed that once each day a noise, as of a slight blow, emanates from a part of the latter that remains on its throne and its base; and I too, when I was present at the places with Aelius Gallus and his crowd of associates heard the noise at about the first hour, but whether it came from the base or the colossus, or whether the noise was made on purpose by one of the men who were standing all round and near to the base, I am unable positively to assert …*
>
> 17.1.46 (trans. Jones)

Diodorus does not mention the colossi, but rather focuses on the Ramesseum, with its great statue of Ramses II, identified with Shelley's Ozymandias.[15] It is difficult to explain why Strabo and Diodorus select one particular attraction and not another.

Fig. 23 The Colossos of Memnon.

Diodorus' whole account of Egypt, although he too relies heavily of Herodotos construction of Egypt, seems more sympathetic to Egyptian culture and history than that of Strabo, who seems often to contextualize the cultural topography of Egypt within an almost Homeric landscape. Strabo avoids the obviously important temples – the Ramasseum, the temple of Ramses III at Medinet Habu, and the mortuary temple of Seti I – in favour of the colossi, for these were interesting on two levels. First, they could be appropriated into a Greek past and literary tradition, and second, the noise that emanated from the northernmost statue satisfied the Graeco-Roman interest in wonders.[16]

No Ptolemaic visitor to the area mentions the noise emanating from the statue, so it is the most likely hypothesis that the damage cause by the earthquake of 26 BC was the origin of the damage resulting in the emanation of sound. From then until some time in the third century, the statue was a great attraction. The nature and origin of the noise was disputed, but is seems clear that a low humming noise came from the lower part of the statue when the sun's rays were cast upon it at dawn.[17] The statue attracted many visitors, who have left inscribed on its flanks a large amount of graffiti in both Greek and Latin, some professionally carved.[18] The earliest datable inscription is from AD 65, although there is little doubt that many previous visits had been made. There are clusters of inscriptions dating to the Flavian period, when the tradition of recording one's visit in a graffito had become well established, the Hadrianic period, the best attested, and into the early third century. At some point in the third century, the statue was repaired, and was from that point silent. The traditional view, that repairs were ordered by Septimius Severus, was based on the observation that no graffiti could be dated after AD 199, and has now been discredited with the subsequent dating of a graffito to AD 205.[19] Bowerstock has suggested an alternative solution, that the statue was repaired during a programme of restoration ordered by the Palmyrenes Zenobia and Vabalathus after their seizure of Egypt in AD 272.

Fig. 24 I. Memnon *40 (AD 134), graffito of M. Petronius Mamertinus, prefect of Egypt.*

Many different individuals left their names, from soldiers to prefects of Egypt (in these cases, no doubt passing in the course of their professional duties). In all, nine prefects visited the colossus and left an inscription, no doubt in the course of their *conventus* (Fig. 24); another senior equestian official, the *epistrategos* Statilius

Fig. 25 I. Memnon *23 (AD 123), graffito of Keler.*

Maximus, visited in AD 156. Numerous soldiers inscribed their names, and it is likely that most accompanied these officials or imperial entourages. Others might have been based in the area of Thebes, likely for example in the case of one Lucius Tanicius, a centurion of *Legio III Cyrenaica*, who, over the course of eight months, visited the Colossos of Memnon thirteen times (*I. Memnon* 7 (AD 80–1)). As with this case, officials who visited were not always from further afield and passing through, but could be local. This is clearly the case with Lucius Funisulanus Charisius, who left a memorial of his visit and an epigram (*I. Memnon* 18 and 19 (AD 122)), and who was *strategos* of the nearby Hermonthite-Latopolite nome. Some years later, one Chaeremon (whose alias is lost in lacuna), *strategos* of the same nomes, visited and heard 'the most divine Memnon' (*I. Memnon* 43 (AD 134)). Finally, a visit was made by Artemidoros, son of Ptolemy, who was the Royal Scribe of the Hermonthite and Letopolite nomes (*I. Memnon* 34 (AD 130)). But the difficulty is assessing the prime motive for visiting the region (and the difficulty of distinguishing between tourism and pilgrimage) is to be seen most clearly in the example of the *strategos* Keler (Fig. 25), who visited Memnon on his way to visit the oracle at Deir el-Bahri, but only heard Memnon's voice upon his return for second visit after consulting the oracle (*I. Memnon* 23; *Insc. Deir el-Bahri* 124).

But scholars and cultural tourists also left their mark, such as Arius, the Homeric poet and muse (*I. Memnon* 37). The best-known visitors were the Emperor Hadrian, his wife Sabina, and his entourage, which included Julia Balbilla, who left a fitting tribute to Hadrian's visit:

> *(Poem of) Julia Balbilla, when Augustus Hadrian heard Memnon.*
> *I was told that the Egyptian Memnon, warmed by the rays*
> *Of the sun, spoke from Theban rock.*
> *When he saw Hadrian, ruler of all, before the rays of the sun,*
> *he greeted him as much as he could.*
> *But when Titan, driving forth with his white horses through the air,*
> *Was casting a shadow on the second measure of the hours,*
> *As if a brazen vessel had been struck, Memnon cast forth his noise again,*
> *Deep-toned, and in greeting, he even omitted a sound for the third time.*
> *Lord Hadrian then greeted Memnon in return and*
> *He left behind for posterity some lines cut in stone to reveal*
> *what things he had seen and what he had heard.*
> *It was clear to all that the gods love him.*
>
> *I. Memnon* 28 (trans. Rowlandson)

Literary skill is clear in this case, as is the Homeric allusion. This is certainly not the only graffito to contain such allusion. Some examples will serve to illustrate: a graffito of Mettius Rufus, prefect of Egypt, alludes to the despoiling of the statue in Homeric language (*I. Memnon* 11 (AD 89–91); and an inscription of T. Petronius Secundus, a prefect of Egypt, is bi-lingual (Latin and Greek), the Greek epigram containing a phrase found the Oddessy (*I. Memnon* 13 (AD 92), and refers to the damage to the statue. The damage to the statue is referred to in a number of other inscriptions specifically linking it to Cambyses, which also established a link to Greek literature (*I. Memnon* 29, 72, and 94). An interesting and important feature of graffiti can be seen here; it is certain that visitors have read the graffiti of others and respond to it, clear, for example, in the example of a graffito of Pardalas of Sardis, which copies the verse of Mettius Rufus' inscription (*I. Memnon* 22 (AD 122/3?)). Such intertextuality is common in graffiti, for, as noted above, graffiti have an audience and are not simply personal memorials. They were read by visitors, and in some cases copied; this shows that there was a culture of inscribing one's name and that this formed a common link between visitors. This is explicit in one case where Quintus Apuleianus wrote that he heard Memnon along with the others who inscribed their names (*I. Memnon* 35, who visited the statue in the company of Artemidorus son of Ptolemy (*I. Memnon* 34)). The graffiti themselves confirmed and perpetuated the link between the colossus and Memnon, and repeated the Homeric allusion. But graffiti also represent a statement about the writers themselves. Not only does it contextualize Egypt in a Greek historical and literary narrative, it also served as a statement of identity for the writer. It was a token of participation in the pursuit of cultural tourism and allowed the writer to engage in a conversation; it confirmed the writer's ability to participate in such a conversation in the language of Rome's educated, Hellenizing elite. It shows that Roman visitors and others were choosing to express themselves in the language of contemporary intellectual culture.

It is pertinent to the argument that Pharaonic history was not relevant to the Greek and Roman visitors to the statue that in only one of the 108 inscriptions is there any sign knowledge of or allusion to Egyptian history. In this inscription, a man named Achilles wrote that he had made an act of adoration to the divine Memnon, who he calls the divine son of Ammon of No, and that he had left words for all time that the rock would preserve (*I. Memnon* 99 (AD 75/6)). It is possible, as Bernand suggests, that this connects Achilles' Memnon to Amenophis III and to Thebes. At any rate, it is the only inscription that nods to any link with an Egyptian past.

But the colossus was not the only attraction in the region. Nearchos, as we have seen, was keen to visit 'the cuttings', probably the Valley of the Kings. They were more commonly known as the *Syringes* after the Greek word *syrinx* meaning 'pipe'.[20] Of the forty or so tombs known by the Greeks and Romans, ten, based on the remaining Greek graffiti, seem to have been of interest in this period. Some 2105 Greek inscriptions have been found, and these date, where it is possible to date them, between the early third century BC the fourth century AD.[21] By far the most popular tomb was that of Ramses VI. Here some 995 or 47% of the inscriptions are located – for this was held to be the tomb of Memnon. The majority of the graffiti merely record a visit, and only a name is left. The names themselves can provide important evidence for the places of origin of the visitors. Most Egyptian and Graeco-Egyptian names can be placed with some accuracy, and they show that there were many visitors from the Theban area, but many from further, sometimes much further afield. Other inscriptions are more revealing: some are specific about the origins of the writer, many make a record of their impressions, but the common thread is that there is no overt religious purpose. In two graffiti, Phalastrios of Alexandria records his visit, first to the tomb of Ramses VI, and second to Ramses IV, where he notes that he has come to Thebes to see with his own eyes the rocks and depths of the Syringes (Baillet, *Syringes* nos. 1139 and 245 = *I. Metr.* 145 and 140). Uranius the Cynic recorded in the tomb of Ramses VI that he had come to admire the venerable Memnon and the Theban Syringes (Baillet, *Syringes* 562 = *I. Metr.* 141). Iasios of Neo-Caesarea, again in the tomb of Ramses VI, recorded that he had come to hear the voice of Memnon and marvel at the Syringes – 'one was without voice, but the artistry of the other was marvelous' (Baillet, *Syringes* 777 = *I. Metr.* 142). Finally, graffiti in the tomb prove the association with Memnon, for example, one Besas claims that he has come to admire the Syringes, but that it is the tomb of Memnon that is the most impressive (Baillet, *Syringes* 1277 = I. *Metr.* 147), and Hermogenes of Amasia stated that he had visited other tombs in the valley and admired them, but the tomb of Memnon in which he left his name surpassed them all (Baillet, *Syringes* 1283, Fig. 26 and 27)

Fig. 26 Graffiti in the tomb of Ramses VI, including the graffito of Hermogenes of Amasia (after Baillet).

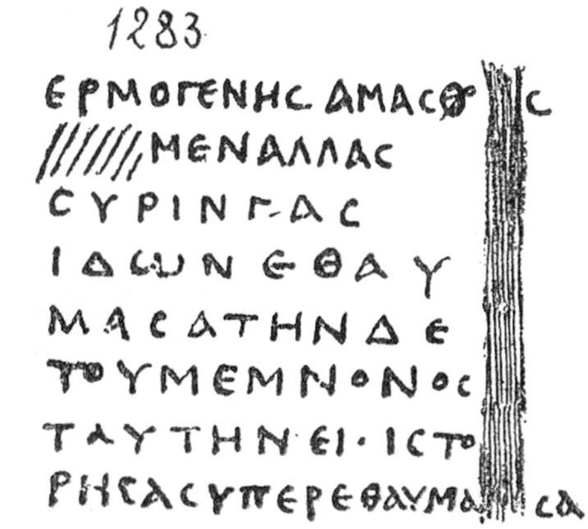

Fig. 27 Transcription of Hermogenes' graffito (after Baillet).

But what was the connection between Amenophis III, Ramses VI and the mythical hero Memnon? Memnon was a king of Ethiopia, son of Eos and Tithonus. The Egyptian connection is therefore understandable, given the proximity of Ethiopia to Egypt. But the identification of Egyptian Pharaohs with the hero seems to be based on Greek interpretation of Pharaonic throne names, and is rather complex. It is possible that the throne name of Amenophis (Nebmaatre) may have converted to something like Memnon. Strabo's Ismandes, the builder of the Memnonion at Abydos, is close to the throne name of Ramses III (Usermaatre Meyamun), and most pharaohs after Ramses II took the name Tatene, which may be close to Tithonus. Perhaps the most plausible explanation is that Ramses VI (Nebmaatre mrj-Jmn Meamun) is to be connected to Memnon, rather than his father Ramses III, and that Ramses II is Tithonus.

Whatever the case, the attraction of the region is clear. The connection of these Pharaohs and their monuments and tombs to a Homeric past, and the wondrous nature of the spectacle of Memnon's voice were what interested Greek and Roman visitors. They were in no way interested in an Egyptian past. Even when they mention it, or the achievements of kings such as Ramses II, it is only passing and usually to make a point about vanity and eastern despotism.

Our final example of a tourist attraction falls similarly into this pattern. Nearchos,

Fig. 28 Relief from the Gateway of Hadrian at Philae.

our fictional traveler, was keen to view the source of the Nile, commonly held to be at Syene. The debate among ancient scholars on the source of the Nile is well known, and not really relevant here, except that it must have generated great interest among those who read and heard these scholars. So it came to be on the tourist itinerary because it was widely discussed in Greek literature. Hadrian dedicated a gateway at the nearby temple of Philae on which a relief depicts the source of the Nile (Fig. 28). The source of the Nile was an attraction is its own right for it was a natural wonder, which we have seen were often central to a desire to travel, but it was also renowned for its white water rafting, which Aelius Aristeides notes, and could not resist trying himself, taking the spirit of inquiry to its limits (Strabo 17. 1. 49; Aelius Aristeides *Or.* 36. 50). But, many officials visited Syene in the course of their duties, and soldiers were garrisoned in this frontier region. It was an important visit on the calendar of the prefect of Egypt, for a ceremony celebrating the rise of the Nile had to be attended. We should note that all of the *proskynemata* left by prefects on the Colossi of Memnon date between the 12 February and the 20th March, leaving time to reach Syene to perform the necessary sacrifices, as there was a tradition which forbade kings and prefects to travel on the Nile when it is rising (Pliny the Elder, *NH* 5. 51). But Syene was also close the great temple of Isis at Philae; it lay near the boundaries of the Roman empire, and was also close to the temple of Mandoulis at Kalabsha, which attracted many pilgrims from Nubia in the south, so it was possible to combine pilgrimage with taking in a tourist attraction. It is to pilgrimage that we must finally turn.[22]

Principal sites of pilgrimage

No doubt many temples, shrines and tombs attracted pilgrimage at a local level, and may have benefited also from 'passing trade'; indeed we even have some graffiti left in the course of journeys between sites, for example, some has been found on the routes linking the Valley of the Kings to the Nile Valley (Bataille 1939a and b). Much of this is concerned with writers seeking the protection of gods for their journey, often on treacherous paths (Adams, forthcoming). Good examples of temples close to tourist sites are the temple of Hatshepsut at Deir el-Bahri and the small Ptolemaic temple to Hathor at Deir el-Medina on the west bank at Thebes. Both were foci of local pilgrimage, but also lay on the tourist trail between the colossi of Memnon and the Valley of the Kings. Even into the fourth century, Deir el-Bahri was the point of pilgrimage for a guild of ironworkers from the city of Hermonthis, some 20 km distant. They have left *proskynemata*, or testimonial devotions inscribed on the walls of the temple, which they visited to celebrate the New Year festival commemorating the defeat of the god Seth (Lajtar 1991). The temple was also associated with the healing cults of Imouthes, Asclepius and Hygeia, and again here we should note the moulding of the sacred landscape to suit different cultural backgrounds – Egyptian and Greek. Sites of religious importance remain in the same place on the landscape, but take on a relevance and associated god according to the interests and needs of the visitor.

But there were more important centres of pilgrimage. Abydos, the cult centre of Osiris, was perhaps the most important. It had been one of the few foci of pilgrimage, both real and imagined, in the Pharaonic period (Rutherford 2003). But it was burial there that ancient Egyptians sought, or at least to establish a cenotaph or stela to their memory. From the Middle Kingdom onward, wealthy Egyptians had representations of journeys to Abydos on the walls of their tombs, which probably represent symbolic journeys rather than real. The practice of erecting stelae continued into the Graeco-Roman period, for the necropolis at Abydos houses a large number in Greek and demotic, and even foreigners left epitaphs.[23]

In the Graeco-Roman period, the principal focus of pilgrimage at Abydos was the Memnonion, the mortuary temple of Seti I.[24] Originally sacred to Osiris, in our period it became associated with Sarapis and then an oracle of the dwarf god Bes. However, a festival of Osisris was still held in the month of Choiak (27th November – 26th December), and a survey of the graffiti shows that this was a popular month in which to visit.[25] Numerous graffiti have been left in a number of different languages – Carian, Aramaic, Phoenician, Greek – showing that over the period from the 6th century BC to the 4th century AD, the temple attracted Egyptians as well as foreigners. *Proskynemata* begin to appear in our period, dedicated to Sarapis, and often appeal for the healing of ailments. No doubt the inscribing of *proskynemata* was part of the incubatory process, and served to leave a memorial to an individual's visit. In his excellent discussion of Abydos, Rutherford has noted two main points central to our discussion, first the re-interpretation of the Memnonion at Abydos as a building linked to a Greek past, and secondly the phenomenon of 'pilgrimage in passing' (Rutherford 2003). But there is no sign of tourism here, and little sign of what he calls 'intellectual pilgrimage' so prevalent at the Colossos on Memnon, where there is almost an intellectual dialogue taking place between visitors through their graffiti. But the social status of visitors was different at Abydos, and they were arguably less interested in such dialogue (Rutherford 2003, 177).

The final example of a pilgrimage centre is the temple of Isis at Philae. The earliest evidence for the worship of Isis comes from the reign of Psammetichus II in the early 6th century BC, and the temple remained an important cult centre until the 6th century AD, surviving well into the Christian era. Again, the temple is rich in graffiti. But it was not just a focus of pilgrimage by Greek and Romans – indeed Philae must be placed within its geographic context in order to be fully understood. It lay in 'contested space' on the frontiers of the Roman Empire, and the region as a whole, the Dodekaschoenus, boasted temples like the Isis temple at Philae and the temple of Mandulis at Talmis or Kalabsha, which attracted regular pilgrimages from the Blemmyes in Nubia as well as Greeks, Egyptians and others. The latter seems to have been the focus of 'intellectual pilgrimage', judging by graffiti (Nock 1972).

At both Abydos and Philae, a pattern emerges in the inscriptions and graffiti left. There is very little sign of tourism. Rather, the inscriptions are votive in nature, and often either record a visit (as though that was the purpose of a journey), an act of adoration, but importantly also, acts of adoration on behalf of others (Rutherford 1998, 236–8 and generally Geraci 1971). Here we must remember the desire of Nearchos to inscribe *proskynemata* on behalf of his friends. So they are of definite religious nature, very different to the inscriptions found on what we might describe as tourist attraction – the colossi of Memnon, the tomb of Ramses, and the sphinx. Inscriptions on these record visits for the purpose of inquiry (often using a form of the word *historia*), and often record an individual's impression of what they have seen. Gods' names are invoked only rarely. So it is possible to determine a pattern of visits, and to achieve a rough impression of the importance of individual sites – whether religious or touristic.

Conclusion

First, it is clear that Graeco-Roman interest in the attractions of Egypt was driven by their fascination with natural wonders, odd habits and customs, and other spectacles. Many came to look at these from far-afield, others in the course of their professional duties, but there is almost a feeling of a 'been there-done that' mentality. These places are visited because they are well-known or odd, and are on the tourist itinerary, so a pattern of repetition gradually reinforces their cultural significance. Some certainly, as we have seen, were interested in inspecting or investigating, but most visitors seem to have been ticking a list. Secondly, there is the distinct impression, evident in our literary sources as well as the inscriptions and graffiti, that there was little interest in the Egyptian past or context of the sites, but rather a drive to place them within a Greek and especially Homeric context. It was Memnon with whom Hadrian conversed, not Amenophis III. The original context is forgotten, and the repeated visits of Greeks and Romans to these sites, and the setting down in literary works of a new Greek context for the monuments served – through repetition and appropriation – to further absolve the attractions of their Egyptian heritage. Monuments thus appropriated embodied a Greek past in Egypt and simultaneously, in the present, they confirmed Graeco-Roman domination of Egypt.

In some sense then, 'travel narrows the mind', in that it provoked reflection on the travellers' own culture, rather than a true and open approach to the other cultures. Greeks and Romans were not open to other cultures and histories, but sought only to place them within their own cultural context through re-interpretation. Their culture served as a binding link between travellers, which was re-enforced and perpetuated through the medium of graffiti. Greeks and Romans were separated from Egyptians, and the graffiti on the Colossus on Memnon further suggests a separation between the intellectual elite (the backbone of empire) and their subjects. This is clearly a facet of cultural imperialism, where the works of art and architecture of conquered foreign peoples are viewed as expressions of corruption and vanity until they can be appropriated by the dominant power.

Acknowledgments

This paper was delivered, in different forms, at the Universities of Calgary and Warwick. My thanks to Tom Harrison and Fiona Hobden for comments on an earlier draft.

Notes

1 The basic discussion of travel in the Roman world remains Friedländer 1908–13, i 268–428. For Greek travel, see Hartog 1996, English translation 2001, and generally Casson 1994. For a discussion of Greek and Latin terms for travel, see Hunt 1984, 394–6.

2 Germanicus – Tacitus, *Annals* 2.59.1, 'Germanicus Aegyptum proficiscitur cognoscendae antiquitatis', and generally 2.59–61; Severus – Dio 76.13.2 and HA, *Sev.* 17.

3 See Morgan in this volume, and on the strangeness of desert environments, Leigh 2000. On the image of Egypt, see Versluys 2002, 422–34.

4 This idea was well established in the Graeco-Roman world, see Herodotos 2.147, with Lloyd 1988, iii 118–9 and Hartog 2001, 216.

5 *P. Tebt.* I 33 = *Sel. Pap.* II 416 (112 BC) (trans. Hunt). Strabo describes the feeding of the crocodile at 17.1.38. The Labyrinth was a temple beside the pyramid of Amenemhet III at Hawara, near the entrance to the Fayum.

6 Lampela 1998, 216, who cites additional examples – Scipio Aemilianus (Diodorus 33.28B.2),

and Lucullus, who declined the opportunity (Plutarch, *Luc.* 2.6).

7 *I. Phil.* 63 (32BC) – Gaius Julius Papius. It is likely that Papius was attached to the army of Marcus Antonius, maybe as a praefectus fabrum. Two Latin inscriptions attest Roman presence at Philae in 116 BC, see Rutherford 1998, 236–7, citing *CIL* I2 4 2937a-b.

8 Rutherford points to the difficulty with the word 'pilgrimage', with its inherent Christian and Islamic connotations (2003, 171), but is happy with the definition 'travel to a sacred place for a sacred reason'.

9 For graffiti at shrines of Pan, see Bernand 1972, Cuvigny, et al 2000, and Adams, forthcoming. For passing trade at a local shrine, see *I. Herm.* 23 (second century BC), which records a visit of 7 slaves to the tomb of Petosiris at the necropolis of Touna el-Gebel at Hermopolis Magna. Graffiti left at the Hathor temple at Deir el-Medina, most of it Coptic, was probably left by pilgrims, but they may also have visited other sites, see Montserrat and Meskell 1997, 183.

10 On Egyptian religion, see Morenz 1973, esp. 88–90 of festivals, and David 1982, esp. 108–9 on pilgrims to Abydos, although it is not clear if 'pilgrim' is an appropriate description. Herodotos 2.58–59, with Lloyd 1976, ii 264–6. On pilgrimage in Ancient Egypt generally, see Yoyotte 1960, Bernand 1988, and Frankfurter 1998, *sv.* pilgrimage.

11 Abydos – Rutherford 2003; Deir el-Bahri – Lajtar 1991; Philae – Rutherford 1998.

12 Although, at 2.54–57 he mentions that he spoke to priests at Thebes, and compares the oracle at Thebes to that of Dodona.

13 Diodorus Siculus 1.45.6–7. We may here be dealing with a very garbled description, or perhaps a priestly guide's explanation, of the impressive reliefs of Ramses II's victory at the battle of Kadesh.

14 Herodotos 3.25–26; Diodorus Siculus 1.46.4–6. The accounts of Cambyses' destruction of the temples of Egypt can hardly be credible, see Lloyd 1983, 286, Arnold 1999, 91, and Mysliwiec 2000, 135–6.

15 Shelley no doubt borrowed from Diodorus' description at 1.47.4. – 'King of Kings am I, Ozymandias. If anyone would know how great I am and where I lie, let him surpass one of my works'. It has been suggested, however, that Ozymandias should be identified with Amenophis III, whose great mortuary temple was guarded by the colossi, see Bowerstock 1984, 21, citing Bataille 1952.

16 References to the colossi: Strabo 17.1.46; Tacitus, *Annals* 2 61; Pliny the Elder, *NH* 36.58; Juvenal, *Satires* 15; Lucian, *Tox.* 27 and *Philopseudes* 33; Philostratus, *Imagines* 1.7 and *VA* 6.4; Pausanias 1.42.3; HA, *Sev.* 17; Ptolemy 4.5.69; Dionysius Periegetes 250.

17 On the 'miracle of Memnon', see Bowerstock 1984, who discusses at length the different descriptions of the statue.

18 There is a question as to whether such professionally carved inscriptions can be classed as graffiti, but as the nature of their content is similar to other graffiti, is seems safe to treat them all together. The difficulty of classifying inscriptions is shown, for example, in *I. Memnon* 60 of Marcus Herennius, which records his visit to the statue but also has the attributes of a senatorial career inscription.

19 *I. Memnon* 60. Two other may date to the third century, *I. Memnon* 61 and 72, noted by Bowerstock 1984, 27.

20 References to the tombs of the Valley of the Kings: Diodorus 1.46; Strabo 17.1.46; Pausanias (the first to use the term *Syringes*) 1.42.3; Aelian, *NA* 6.43 and 16.15; Heliodorus, *Aeth.* 1.6 and 2.27; Ammianus Marcellinus 22.15.30.

21 Details of the inscriptions can be found in Letronne, but more reliable readings are to be found in Baillet 1926.

22 The temple of Kalabsha was itself of interest in terms of intellectual pilgrimage, see *I. Metr.* 166–8 with Nock 1972.

23 See Abdalla 1992. Perdrizet and Lefebvre no. 301 = *I. Metr.* 137 is dedicated by Polyaratos of Cyrene, who states that 'now the land of Egypt holds him'.
24 Seti's throne name was Menmaatre, and the name Memnon may reflect this. References to Abydos: Strabo 17.1.42; Pliny *NH* 5.60.
25 Noted by Rutherford, citing Perdrizet and Lefebvre no. 253.

Bibliography

Abdalla, A. (1992) *Graeco-Roman Funerary Stelae from Upper Egypt* (Liverpool).
Adams, C. E. P. (2001) 'There and Back Again. Getting around in Roman Egypt', in Adams and Laurence, 138–66.
Adams, C. E. P. and R. Laurence (2001) *Travel and Geography in the Roman Empire* (London and New York).
Arnold, D. (1999) *Temples of the Last Pharaohs* (Oxford).
Baillet, J. (1926) *Inscriptions grecques et latines des tombeaux des Rois ou syringes à Thèbes* (Cairo).
Bataille, A. (1939a) 'Sur un graffite de la Motagne Thébaine', *BIFAO* 38, 129–39.
Bataille, A. (1939b) 'Quelques graffites grecs de la Montagne Thébaine', *BIFAO* 38, 141–82.
Bataille, A. (1952) *Les Memnonia* (Cairo).
Bernand, A. (1969) *Les inscriptions greques de Philae* 2 vols (Paris).
Bernand, A. (1972) *Le Paneion d'el Kanais: les inscriptions greques* (Leiden).
Bernand, A. and E. Bernand (1960) *Les inscriptions grecques et latines du colosse de Memnon* (Cairo).
Bernand, E. (1983) 'Pèlerinage au grand Sphinx de Gizeh', *ZPE* 51, 185–9.
Bowerstock, G. (1984) 'The Miracle of Memnon', *BASP* 21, 21–32.
Casson, L. (1994) *Travel in the Ancient World* (Baltimore).
Cuvigny, H., A. Bülow-Jacobsen and N. Bosson (2000) 'Le paneion d'Al-Buwayb revisité', *BIFAO* 100, 243–66.
David, R. (1982) *The Ancient Egyptians: Religious Beliefs and Practices* (London).
Foertmeyer, V. A. (1989) *Tourism in Graeco-Roman Egypt* PhD thesis (Princeton).
Foti Talamanca, G. (1974) *Ricerche sul processo nell'Egitto greco-romano* i (Milan).
Frankfurter, D. (1998) *Religion in Roman Egypt: Assimilation and Resistance* (Princeton).
Frankfurter, D. (1998) (ed.) *Pilgrimage and Holy Space in Late Antique Egypt* (Leiden).
Friedländer, L. (1908–1913) *Roman Life and Manners under the Early Empire* 4 vols (London).
Geraci, G. (1971) 'Ricerche sul Proskynema', *Aegyptus* 51, 3–211.
Gikandi, S. (1996) *Maps of Englishness: Writing Identity in the Culture of Colonialism* (New York).
Hartog, F. (1986) *Mémoire d'Ulysse: Récits sur la frontière en Grèce ancienne* (Paris).
Hartog, F. (2001) *Memories of Odysseus: Frontier Tales from Ancient Greece* trans. J. Lloyd (Edinburgh).
Hartog, F. (1986a) ''Les Grecs égyptologues', *Annals* 41, 953–67, reprinted as 'The Greeks as Egyptologists', in T. Harrison (2002) (ed.) *Greeks and Barbarians*, 211–28 (Edinburgh).
Hunt, E. D. (1984) 'Travel, Tourism, and Piety in the Roman Empire: A Context for the Beginnings of Christian Pilgrimage', *Echos du monde classique/ Ancient Views* 28 (n.s. 3), 391–417.
Lajtar, A. (1991) 'Proskynema inscriptions of a corporation of iron-workers from Hermonthis in the Temple of Hatshepsut at Deir el-Bahri: New evidence for pagan cults in Egypt in the 4th cent. AD', *JJP* 21, 53–70.
Leigh, M. (2000) 'Lucan and the Libyan Tale', *JRS* 90, 95–109.
Lloyd, A. B. (1975) *Herodotus Book II: Introduction* (Leiden).
Lloyd, A. B. (1976) *Herodotus Book II: Commentary 1–98* (Leiden).
Lloyd, A. B. (1988) *Herodotus Book II: Commentary 99–182* (Leiden).

Lloyd, A. B. (1983) 'The Late Period', in Trigger, B. G., B. J. Kemp, D. O'Connor and A. B. Lloyd, *Ancient Egypt: A Social History*, 279–348 (Cambridge).
Matthews, R. and C. Römer (2003) *Ancient Perspectives on Egypt* (London).
Meyboom, P. G. P. (1995) *The Nile Mosaic of Palestrina: Early Evidence of Egyptian Religion in Italy* (Leiden).
Montserrat, D. and L. Meskell (1997) 'Mortuary Archaeology and Religious Landscape at Graeco-Roman Deir el-Medina', *JEA* 83, 179–97.
Morenz, S. (1973) *Egyptian Religion* (London).
Mysliwiec, K. (2000) *The Twilight of Ancient Egypt: The First Millennium B.C.E.* (Ithaca and New York).
Nock, A. D. (1972) 'A Vision of Mandulis Aeion', in Z. Stewart (ed.) *Essays on Religion and the Ancient World* i, 357–400 (London).
Perdrizet, P. and G. Lefebvre (1919) *Les graffites grecs du Memnonion d'Abydos: Inscriptiones Graecae Aegypti* III (Nancy).
Roullet, A. (1972) *The Egyptian and Egyptianizing Monuments of Imperial Rome* (Leiden).
Rutherford, I. (1998) 'Island of the extremity: space, language and power in the pilgrimage traditions of Philae', in Frankfurter (1998), 229–56 (Leiden).
Rutherford, I. (2003) 'Pilgrimage in Graeco-Roman Egypt: New Perspectives on Graffiti from the Memnonion at Abydos', in Matthews and Roemer, *Ancient Perspectives on Egypt*, 171–89.
Smelik, K. A. D. and E. A. Hemelrijk (1984) 'Who knows what monsters demented Egypt worships? Opinions on Egyptian animal worship in Antiquity as part of the ancient conception of Egypt', *ANRW* II 17.4, 1852–2000.
Schwartz, J. (1961) *Les Archives de Sarapion et de ses fils: une exploration agricole aux environs d'Hermoupolis Magna (de 90 à 133 p.C.)* (Cairo).
Versluys, M. J. (2002) *Aegyptiaca Romana: Nilotic Scenes and the Roman Views of Egypt* (Leiden).
Volokhine, Y., 'Les déplacements pieux en Égypte pharaonique: sites et pratiques cultuelles', in Frankfurter, *Pilgrimage and Holy Space*, 51–97.

Landscape and Local Identity in the Mosaics of Antioch

Zahra Newby

During the Roman period the eastern Mediterranean was a busy and bustling place, full of people travelling for the purposes of trade or warfare, as well as education, pilgrimage and tourism (Casson 1994, 128–37; Pretzler, this volume). My aim in this paper is to explore the impact that being part of such a cosmopolitan, much-travelled world had on the ways people represented their own city and culture, both to themselves and to visitors, and how they situated themselves within the wider landscape. The expression of local and civic identities can be explored in a number of ways, through consideration of public architecture, coins or inscriptions (e.g. Newby 2003; Harl 1987; Howgego, Heuchert and Burnett 2005; generally on identities in the Near East, see Millar 1993). Here, however, I will examine its expression in the domestic sphere, on the floor mosaics that decorated the houses of ancient Antioch and its surroundings (Levi 1947; see also Balty 1981; Campbell 1988; Cimok 2000 and Kondoleon 2000b. For another recent account which uses the Antioch mosaics to discuss identity, see Hales 2003b).

Antioch was a crucial meeting place within the Roman Empire. Initially founded by Seleucus Nicator, it had gradually become first the capital of the Seleucid empire and then the central city of Roman Syria (Downey 1961; Grainger 1990, 7–87). In the second century AD the traveller Pausanias likened it to Alexandria in Egypt in terms of size and prosperity (8.33.3, cf. Strabo 16.2.5). It was from Antioch that military campaigns against the east were prosecuted, with a number of emperors, including Trajan and Lucius Verus, basing themselves here. The impact on the city of the presence of the emperors can be seen clearly in a comment by Cassius Dio. When describing the earthquake which hit Antioch in AD 115, while Trajan himself was residing in the city, Dio asserts that so many traders, soldiers and embassies were present that 'not a province or community remained unharmed' (Dio 68.24.1–2). A further statement of the cosmopolitan nature of Antioch is given by the fourth-century Antiochene orator Libanius who asserted, 'If [a man] sits in our market-place he will make acquaintance with every city in the world, so numerous will be the people from all quarters with whom he will come into contact' (*Or.* 11.166).

The city was ideally positioned for its role as a centre of communications (Fig. 29). It lay on a major land route from Rome, which passed via the Balkans and Asia Minor and then down through Syria and Phoenicia towards Judaea and Egypt. It also

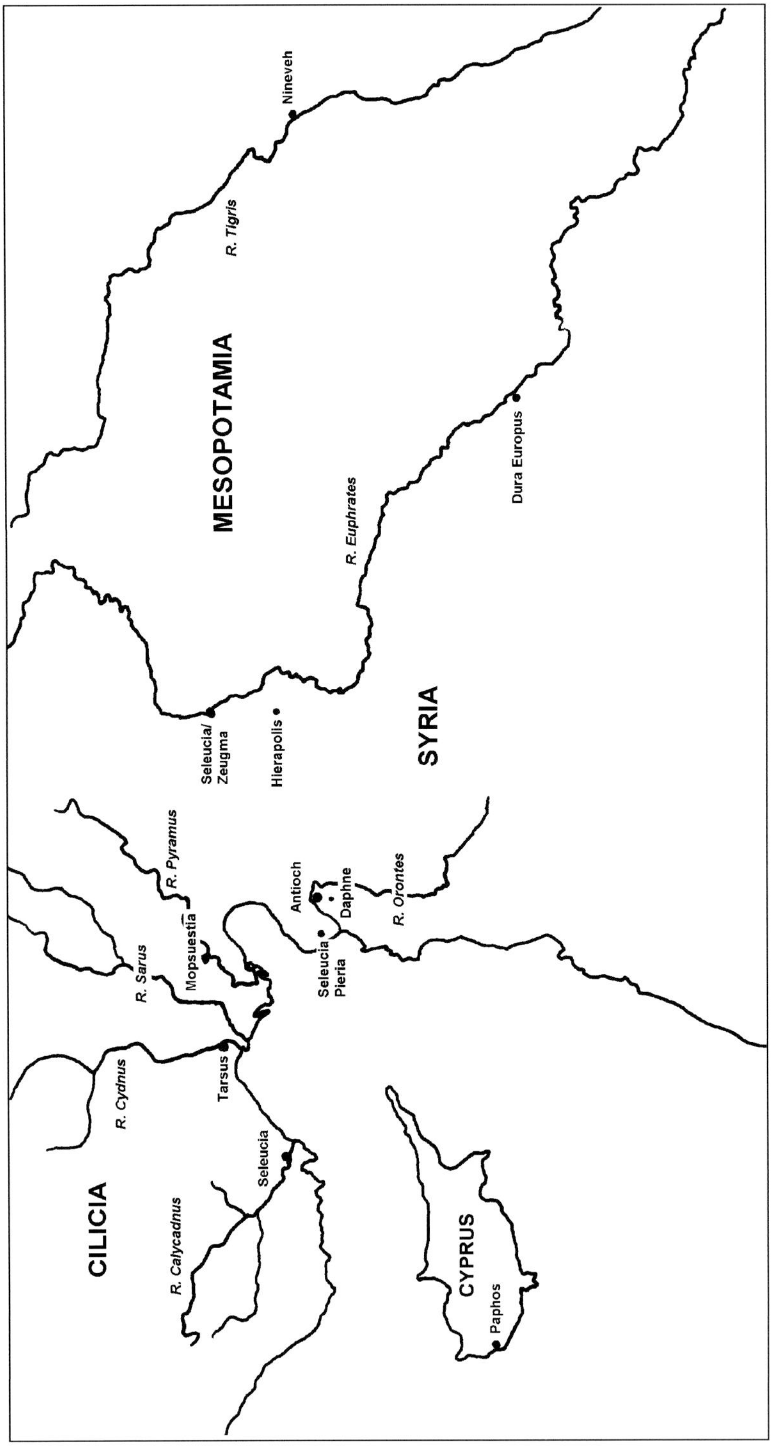

Fig. 29 Map of Antioch and its surrounding area.

controlled access to the east, towards Mesopotamia and Parthia. Antioch itself was connected to the sea via the river Orontes, and its port town of Seleucia seems to have played an increasingly important role as a naval base, particularly in the course of the second century AD (Millar 1993, 86–90, 103–5; Van Berchem 1985). While multitudes of people would have passed through both Seleucia and Antioch on their journeys elsewhere, the attractions of the city itself were also famed. In particular, the suburb of Daphne is widely represented in the literary sources as a haven of luxury, seducing the emperor Lucius Verus away from his military duties, and corrupting the morals of the Syrian legions (SHA, *Marcus Antoninus* 8.12; SHA, *Severus Alexander* 53.2). Antioch itself seems to have been called 'Antioch near Daphne' in the Roman period, an indication of Daphne's notoriety (Strabo 16.2.4; Pliny, *NH* 5.17).

Many of the visitors to the city would have stayed in the houses of the local elite. In Apuleius' novel, the *Metamorphoses*, the hero Lucius goes to an inn only to enquire the whereabouts of the house of a local notable for whom he has a letter of introduction from a friend (1.21–22). Another story in Philostratus' *Lives of the Sophists* tells of how the future emperor Antoninus Pius was rudely ejected from the house of the sophist Polemo in Smyrna (1.534). Antoninus is said to have chosen this particular residence as being the best in Smyrna and belonging to the most notable citizen. Polemo's rejection of him is clearly presented as unusual and a mark of the sophist's arrogance. In general, we presume, members of the local elite would have been glad to welcome important figures from Rome or elsewhere with the associated opportunity of developing personal contacts and showing off their hospitality, culture and status.

Recent studies of Roman housing have asserted the importance of domestic architecture and decoration in structuring social relationships and creating a particular self-image for the owner of the house (Clarke 1991; Wallace-Hadrill 1994; Hales 2003a). While many of these studies have focussed on the better-preserved houses of Campania and Ostia, similar motivations will have influenced the owners of houses elsewhere around the empire. The circumstances of excavation and preservation often make it difficult to reconstruct fully the houses of ancient Antioch, Seleucia and Daphne. However, the discovery of lavish mosaics that appear to have decorated reception and dining rooms suggests that here too decoration played a crucial role in presenting the correct image of the host to his friends and guests (Dobbins 2000). A number of the mosaics found around Antioch can be compared with other domestic mosaics around the empire, particularly in their representation of scenes of hospitality or images drawn from mythology. Such images present the host as a man of culture and generosity, and hold out the promise of an enjoyable evening ahead.

Apart from these more general messages, however, I will argue that some of the Antioch mosaics actually assert a stronger message about the delights and history of the local area. Civic identities were important throughout the Roman period, and we have plentiful references to civic rivalries particularly from the late first century onwards (e.g. Dio Chrysostom, *Or.* 34, 38; see C. P. Jones 1978, 71–94). Often these rivalries were expressed through legends and images on coins or architecture, proclaiming both the contemporary significance of a city and its remote mythological or historical origins (Ziegler 1985; Harl 1987; Lindner 1994). Yet there is no reason why similar statements of local identity should not have been asserted also through the medium of domestic imagery. Indeed, Maria Pretzler argues that one source of information used by the travel-writer Pausanias would have been precisely his conversations with members of the local elites in the various places he visited (Pretzler, 2005). The plentiful discussions over the origins of various customs, which we find in texts like Plutarch's *Tabletalk* and Athenaeus' *Deipnosophistae,* also suggest that the dinner table could provide a locus for educated conversation on a number of different matters. The images decorating domestic floors could act as prompts to such discussions, as well as being a means by which the host could promote his own identity as a citizen of a prestigious and important city.

In my discussion of this phenomenon I will confine myself to mosaics which have been assigned dates within the second and third centuries AD, though often we cannot ascertain their precise dating due to a lack of archaeological evidence (on dating see Levi 1947, with revisions by Balty 1981 and Campbell 1988). These mosaics come from a period when Antioch was a major centre of military and administrative activity, and would have experienced a host of visitors from around the empire. This is also the period of the so-called 'Second Sophistic', distinguished by the interest shown in the ancient Greek past, and the desire of cities and individuals to assert their own forms of Hellenic identity (Bowie 1974; Cameron and Walker 1989; Swain 1996; Goldhill 2001. On Antioch in later periods see Sandwell and Huskinson, 2004). The ways in which a Hellenic identity could be claimed and expressed by Antioch will be one strand of the discussion below.

An insight into the history, myths and local characteristics of the city of Antioch is provided by the speech in honour of the city composed by the orator Libanius. This was delivered at the Olympic games in Antioch in AD 356 (Norman 2000, 3–7). It lies in a tradition of laudatory oratory which goes back to Pericles' funerary speech in Thucydides (2.35–46), and to the Panathenaic orations by Isocrates and later, in the second century AD, by the sophist Aelius Aristides. Although we do not have a parallel speech in honour of Antioch from the second or third centuries, it seems reasonable to assume that the features which Libanius singles out for attention would also be those in which the city could take pride one or two centuries previously. Libanius' speech clearly works to a formula, outlining the benefits of the local landscape before moving onto the origins of the city, all themes that are common to laudatory speeches. However, the orator's skill lies in applying these common themes to the particular occasion, and the precise details that Libanius draws out would have to have been convincing to his audience. It seems certain, then, that his description of the local landscape, for example, would have adhered closely to the scenes the audience could see around them, even if it was embellished to some extent. Similarly Libanius' description of Antioch's myths and origins presumably reflects the versions current in his own day. Many of these may also have been current previously and indeed the second and third centuries were a period of intense interest in civic genealogies and civic assertions of ancient origins (Bowie 1974, 184–8). One such history of Antioch was certainly produced, since the sixth-century writer John Malalas refers to a work by one Pausanias entitled *Antiocheias ktisis*, 'The foundation of Antioch', though we are ignorant of its date (Downey 1961, 36–7 suggests a date in the second or fourth century AD). While Libanius' oration postdates the mosaics examined here, it can serve as a literary parallel to the sorts of civic self-promotion I perceive in the visual imagery.

The natural wonders of Antioch

A key feature of Libanius' oration is the natural benefits of Antioch and its surrounding area, prominently placed at the start of the speech. Antioch is praised for the fertility of its land and for its temperate climate. It produces abundant vines, olives, and corn, showing the favour of the gods Dionysus, Athena and Demeter (*Or.* 11.19–21). Moreover, it is especially favoured by rivers and streams, a claim that reappears elsewhere too in Libanius' speech. So, in chapter 27 he exclaims 'who could enumerate the streams which irrigate the land?' and declares that it is in these that the Antiochenes find their hallmark. Water reappears later in the speech too, when Libanius describes the luxurious resort town of Daphne which lies to the southwest of Antioch and was famous for its sanctuary of Apollo. It was also the site for the final events of the Olympic festival, where Libanius' speech was delivered. So in chapter 240 he declares 'The chief of the glories of Daphne, indeed of the whole world, are the springs of Daphne', springs which also adorn the city of Antioch itself, whose abundant supply of private fountains is praised (*Or.* 11.244–8). These references to Antioch's natural advantages, particularly her prolific water supply, thus frame the speech.

As others have noted, this very feature is also common in many of the mosaics decorating Antioch and its suburb, Daphne (Kondoleon 2000b, 71). Libanius' statement about the prevalence of private fountains has been proved correct by the archaeological findings which show that most houses had a private fountain, usually situated off a corridor and in view of the main reception room (Dobbins 2000, 57–8). Many nymphaea were decorated with mosaic floors showing marine scenes. So the nymphaeum from the House of the Boat of Psyches at Daphne was decorated with a fish mosaic, alluding to the natural abundance of the streams around the villa (Fig. 30). More marine themes occur elsewhere in this house (Levi 1947, 167–91; Kondoleon 2000b, 71–4). One of the rooms is decorated with a mosaic showing the bust of the marine goddess Tethys, surrounded by fish. She appears again, now accompanied by Oceanus, in the central triclinium, beneath a scene of Europa being carried off by Zeus in the form of a bull. The water theme was continued in the room next door in

Fig. 30 Detail of mosaic from the Nymphaeum of the House of the Boat of Psyches, Daphne.

Fig. 31 Mosaic showing Opora, Agros and Oinos, from the House of the Boat of Psyches, Daphne.

the central panel showing the eponymous Boat of Psyches. All these images reinforce the sense of an abundance of water in the surrounding area, the trait for which Daphne is so highly praised by Libanius.

Antioch's fertility is also represented in the house of the Boat of Psyches in the mosaic from room 8 (Fig. 31). A seated couple are shown dining, attended by a Silenus-like figure who serves them wine. All three are labelled above as the personifications *Opora* (Harvest/Vintage), *Agros* (Field) and *Oinos* (Wine). This scene of dining and relaxation, which parallels the real intimate feasts which could have been held in the room, is thus directly enabled by the fertility of the region. The natural advantages of Antioch help to ensure the luxury for which Daphne was so famous. The mosaics in this house probably date to the middle of the third century AD, by which time Daphne was already well established as a centre of luxury. Later, Libanius could boast that the suburb possessed 'gardens like those of Alcinous, fare of Sicilian profusion, the horn of plenty, sumptuous banquets and the luxury of Sybaris' (*Or*. 11.236).

The sensuous delights which awaited the visitor to this house did not lie in wine and water alone, however. Erotic pleasures also seem to be on offer here. So the semi-naked figures of *Opora* and *Agros* in this mosaic have iconographical parallels with the representation of pairs of lovers in Roman wall-paintings (Clarke 1998, 93–107). Erotic scenes crop up elsewhere around the house too, in the groupings of a satyr and hermaphrodite shown in the corridor panels (Levi 1947, 183–5). On one level these mosaics can be interpreted loosely as simply indicating the hospitality and luxury which a guest can expect to enjoy in this house. Yet the stress which Libanius puts upon Daphne's fertility and streams suggests that the mosaics also make a direct reference to the advantages of the local landscape in which the villa is set. This sort of interplay between art and nature could also have been reinforced in some houses by views out across the neighbouring hills, giving glimpses of the luxurious vegetation which Antioch's springs and soils nourished.

Local Myths

Apart from Daphne's luxurious vegetation, the suburb was also renowned for its Temple of Apollo which seems to have attracted people from across the empire. Among others, the author of the *Lives of the Sophists*, Philostratus, recalls in the preface to his work that it was in the Temple of Apollo at Daphne that he had first discussed the sophists with Gordian, the recipient of his book. In the *Life of Apollonius of Tyana*, Philostratus describes the myth attached to the sanctuary:

> *'[to this temple] the Assyrians attach the legend of Arcadia. For they say that Daphne, the daughter of Ladon, there underwent her metamorphosis, and they have a river flowing there, the Ladon, and a laurel tree is worshipped by them which they say is the one substituted for the maiden' (1.16)*
>
> (trans. Conybeare, Loeb).

The coexistence of two versions of the myth, one situating it in Arcadia in Greece, while the other locates the events in Syria, is also indicated by Pausanias. During his account of Arkadia he turns to the river Ladon, famous for its legend of Daphne. 'I pass over the story about Daphne current among the Syrians on the Orontes and will tell instead the account given by the Arcadians and Eleans' (8.20.2). Libanius strongly asserts the Antiochene version of the myth in his description of the foundation of Daphne by Seleucus Nicator (*Or.* 11.94–9). According to Libanius events ran thus: while Seleucus was out hunting, he found a golden arrowhead embedded into the ground at the foot of a tree. This was engraved with the name Phoebus, a sign that it had belonged to the god Apollo and that this tree was therefore the metamorphosed Daphne. Seleucus thus decided that he should honour the god by building a temple to him here.

This Syrian version of the myth thus strongly asserted the right of Daphne near Antioch to be seen as the location of Daphne's pursuit and metamorphosis. However, the literary sources may suggest a certain ambivalence amongst other Greeks concerning the Antiochenes' claim to the myth. In particular, the sage Apollonius of Tyana is scathing about the sanctuary, and rebukes the river Ladon for having become 'barbarian instead of Greek and Arcadian' (Philostratus, *VA* 1.16). It is notable that the texts refer to the Antiochenes either as Syrians (Pausanias) or Assyrians (Philostratus). As well as accusing the river of becoming a barbarian, Apollonius also insults those who attend the temple as 'half-barbarian and uncultivated' (Philostratus, *VA* 1.16). These authors thus suggest a certain reluctance on the part of others to see Antioch as fully part of the Greek world.

Yet Antioch was a Greek city. As a foundation by Seleucus its population probably included a great number of Macedonian veterans, as well as immigrants from Greece and it used Greek on its coins and inscriptions (Inhabitants: Grainger 1990, 60; coins: Metcalf 2000). Libanius is also very keen to paint his city as Greek, especially in its education and culture, and provides it with a mythological past going back to the settlement in this area of Argives who had come in search of Io (*Or.* 11.44–51; 270). Despite Apollonius of Tyana's scathing remarks about the lack of culture in Antioch, it does seem to have acted as a cultural centre in earlier centuries too. The empress Julia Domna, herself from the Syrian city of Emesa, based herself in the city for a time and is known to have enjoyed the company of some prominent Greek intellectuals, Philostratus amongst them (Philostratus, *VA* 1.3; Bowersock 1969, 101–9). The city also possessed prestigious Greek–style festivals, including the *Olympeia*, founded in the first century AD (Moretti 1953, 176–7).

The appropriation by Antioch of the well-known Greek myths concerning Daphne and Io was one of the ways in which the city's inhabitants could assert their identity as part of the Greek world. By localising traditional Greek myths in their own territory they were establishing their claims to Greek identity, even if, in reality, that identity only went back to the Hellenistic period (compare Newby 2003, on Asia Minor). We find the myth of Daphne represented in the suburb itself on a mosaic in the House of Menander (Fig. 32). The mosaic paved a corridor and

Fig. 32 Mosaic showing Daphne and Apollo, from the House of Menander, Daphne.

shows Daphne turning into the laurel tree while Apollo chases her (Levi 1947, 198–216, esp. 211–4).

Other mosaics in this house evoke other qualities for which Daphne was famed. Her springs and fertility are alluded to in the marine scenes decorating two separate courtyards, placed in front of nymphaea. A corridor mosaic in front of a triclinium elsewhere in the house also has a panel showing the reclining figures of two river gods, labelled Ladon and Psalis (Fig. 33). Ladon clearly represents the local river, the father of Daphne. Psalis is otherwise unknown but probably, as Levi suggested, represents another local water source, perhaps one of the many springs for which Daphne was so famed (Levi 1947, 205; Kondoleon 1995, 170–5). The same corridor mosaic also actively celebrates the resort's reputation for luxury. A panel to the right of the mosaic shows the bust of a female figure, holding up a cup and labelled Tryphe (luxury) (Fig. 34). Between the two end panels is a scene of olive harvesting. Together, all three images assert the fertility and abundance of Daphne – its rivers and springs, agricultural prosperity and the luxurious lifestyle which these support. Like the House of the Boat of Psyches, the mosaics of this house advertise a myriad of delights, alluding to the prosperity of the region, its local myths and landscape, and the entertainment which guests can expect, including

Fig. 33 Mosaic showing Ladon and Psalis, from the House of Menander, Daphne.

Fig. 34 Mosaic with a personification of Tryphe, from the House of Menander, Daphne.

the theatrical performances suggested by the eponymous Menander mosaic in room 11 (Levi 1947, 201–3; Kondoleon 2000, 74–6, 156, cat. 40; Huskinson 2002–3, 151–5). As well as presenting the owner of the house as a figure of culture, wealth and hospitality, these mosaics also act as a permanent eulogy of the benefits of the luxurious resort of Daphne.

Seleucia in its wider context

Thus far I have concentred on the mosaics from two houses in Daphne which extoll the benefits of that particular town and its mythological traditions. Elsewhere, however, we also find allusions to the wider landscape and the geographical situation of these cities. The House of Cilicia was discovered in the port town of Seleucia Pieria, to the west of Antioch. It is named after the mosaic decorating the central reception room (Levi 1947, 57–9). The central panel originally showed two figures, though only the one on the right remains (Fig. 35). In composition she is similar to the famous statue of the Tyche of Antioch by Eutychidas. She is labelled above as the personification of the province of Cilicia. The other figure is lost but was originally reclining and holding a cornucopia. In the corners of the mosaic are

Fig. 35 Mosaic showing landscape personifications, from the House of Cilicia, Seleucia.

roundels containing male heads. The one in the bottom right corner is bearded and labelled Tigris. Another in the top right corner shows a youthful beardless figure labelled Pyramus. Both are rivers. Two other busts of rivers would presumably have completed the mosaic on the left side, along with the figure of a second personification in the central panel. We can only speculate as to their identities but the surviving labels suggest an allusion to the wider geographical area within which the city of Seleucia was positioned (Fig. 29).

In Antiquity Antioch and Seleucia were within the province of Syria. Cilicia lay on Syria's northwestern border, the Pyramus being one of its three main rivers. The Tigris, however, was famous as the river which formed the eastern border of Mesopotamia, the area to the east of Syria. Levi was probably right to suggest that the left hand figure in this mosaic would have been a personification of Mesopotamia, and one of the two missing rivers the Euphrates, its western border. We would then expect a second river in Cilicia to balance the picture, perhaps the Cydnus or the Sarus, or alternatively perhaps a river which marked the eastern part of the region, such as the Calycadnus.

The mosaic thus alludes to the geographical situation of Seleucia, and northern Syria in general, between Cilicia to the north-west and Mesopotamia to the east, a position clearly described by Strabo: 'Syria is bounded to the north by Cilicia and Mt. Amanus…to the east by the Euphrates' (16.2.1). In practical terms, travellers are likely to have approached this area from the west either by land along the coast of Cilicia, or by sea, arriving at Seleucia itself. Yet it also served as an important staging post for military activities further east, particularly during the Parthian campaigns of the 160s. Indeed, an allusion to Mesopotamia may well have had political connotations, depending on the precise date at which the mosaic was laid (for a Hadrianic or Antonine date, see Levi 1947, 58; for late second century, see Kondoleon 2000b, 152). First annexed by Trajan, Mesopotamia had later been relinquished by Hadrian, before being reconquered by Lucius Verus (Birley 1987, 140–8). If the mosaic was laid after Verus' annexation of the new province, it may be a sign of pride in the extension to Rome's empire, and perhaps also the important role which the port of Seleucia had played in supporting military activity (Van Berchem 1985). Such statements of pride in the military successes of the Roman empire can be attested elsewhere in long-standing Roman provinces, most notably in the reliefs decorating the Sebasteion at Aphrodisias (Smith 1987, 1988).

Yet as well as its geographical and, possibly, contemporary relevance, the mosaic may also have suggested the many important mythical and historical links which both Cilicia and Mesopotamia shared with northern Syria. All three areas had formed part of the Assyrian and then Persian empires until the conquests of Alexander the Great in the fourth century BC. They then became part of the Seleucid empire, although the Ptolemies had also pressed their claims to Cilicia (A. H. M. Jones 1937, 192–226). The cities of the three regions had a number of connections. Many of the cities of Cilicia claimed, like Antioch itself, to have been founded by the Argives who had followed Triptolemus in search of Io (Strabo 14.5.12; 16.2.5; Libanius *Or.* 11.44–52). Many of the cities of Mesopotamia, on the other hand, were Hellenistic foundations, like Antioch and Seleucia Pieria itself. Indeed, Seleucus I Nicator is attributed with having founded a number of cities here (Appian, *Roman History* 11.57) and the area formed an important link between Syria to the west and the eastern part of the Seleucid empire with its capital at Seleucia on the Tigris (A. H. M. Jones 1937, 216–221; though note the caution expressed by Grainger 1990, 46).

Another Seleucia, the city on the Euphrates which later became known simply as Zeugma or 'Bridge' was also one of Seleucus I's foundations. Indeed, it is likely that an educated antiquarian, seeing the mosaic in the House of Cilicia, might be prompted to think of Seleucia Pieria's synonymous cities in the neighbouring regions. In addition to Seleucia on the Tigris and Seleucia on the Euphrates, the city of Seleucia on the Calycadnus lay at the western end of the Cilician plain and is also said to have been a foundation of Seleucus I (Strabo 14.5.4, Ammianus Marcellinus 14.8.2). On the Pyramus river itself, featured in our mosaic, the existing Greek city of Mopsuestia seems to have been given the dynastic title of Seleucia on the Pyramus during the Hellenistic period, though it had reverted to its traditional name by the Roman period (A. H. M. Jones 1937, 201).

As the literary works by Plutarch and Athenaeus attest, antiquarian research and conversations could form a key part of evening entertainment, and numerous coins and inscriptions suggest that cities were keen to explore their mythical or historical links with other cities during this period, a good example being Aegeae in Cilicia, which claimed kinship with Argos (Robert 1977, 120–9). An awareness of the area's Seleucid past is certainly suggested by Libanius, who describes this period of Antioch's history in some detail (*Or.* 11.72–128). While we cannot be sure precisely which other rivers were represented on the mosaic, and thus which cities might have sprung to mind, the mosaic asserts Seleucia-Pieria's place within its wider geographical context and its own importance. The precise message may have changed over time, from a statement about the importance which the city had in the Seleucid empire to more contemporary resonances. If those looking at it after AD 165 were prompted to think of the destruction of another Seleucia, Seleucia on the Tigris, by Avidius Cassius (Birley 1987, 140), they may also have contemplated the vagaries of fate (cf Pausanias 8.33.3), musing on the fact that of Seleucus' two great capitals, only that to the west, Seleucia Pieria, now remained.

Greek and Eastern Identities

We have already seen how the town of Daphne appropriated a Greek and specificially Arcadian myth and located it in her own territory. In the House of Cilicia at Seleucia, the mosaic helps to situate the house and its surroundings in a regional setting, while also alluding to its Seleucid history. Elsewhere, other mosaics replicate this shifting allegiance to both 'Greek' and local or regional origins and

Fig. 36 Mosaic showing river busts, from the House of the Porticoes, Seleucia.

identities. Another house in Seleucia, the House of the Porticoes, suggests a desire to link the wider area around Antioch with the Greek mainland and its myths. One of the porticoes of this house is decorated with a series of labelled river busts similar to those in the House of Cilicia (Fig. 36). Here, however, not all the rivers are local. Instead, we find the rivers Alpheius and Arethusa paired with Pyramus and Thisbe. The story of Alpheius' love for Arethusa, and her transformation into a Syracusan spring or stream was well known in the ancient world. The Peloponnesian Alpheius was said to have wandered through the ocean as a river to go in search of his beloved (Ovid, *Met.* 5.601f; Pausanias, 5.7.1–3). For Ovid, Pyramus and Thisbe were human lovers, living in Babylon (*Met.* 4.55–8). Their representation here as rivers, however, suggests instead an identification with the river Pyramus which flowed through Cilicia. The love story between the couple and its tragic end was also represented on a mosaic in the House of Dionysus at Paphos in Cyprus where Pyramus is also represented as a river. In the fifth century, Nonnus' *Dionysiaca* shows the River Alpheius calling out to Pyramus as a fellow river chasing an elusive lover (6.346). By representing the two couples together here, the mosaic draws a connection between a mythical couple from the east, in the region close to Seleucia, and a more famous pair from mainland Greece. The regional significance of this myth is also indicated by its appearance in the House of Dionysus at Paphos in a collection of erotic scenes including Poseidon and Amymone and Apollo and Daphne (Kondoleon 1995, 147–74). Like the mosaics from Seleucia, those in the House of Dionysus also help to situate the house they decorate in its regional setting by alluding to myths associated with Cilicia and Antioch.

While the rivers mosaic helps to equate an eastern love story with one from mainland Greece, elsewhere in Antioch there may also be allusions to the region's Assyrian past. The so-called House of the Man of Letters in Daphne yielded two mosaics which both feature figures known from the ancient novels (Hanfmann 1939, 242–6; Levi 1944; Quet 1992). One shows an interior scene with two couches set out (Fig. 37). On the left of these a young man is reclining, holding in his hand a small portrait of a woman, at which he looks longingly. From the right another young woman approaches him, offering something. Another mosaic found at nearby Alexandretta showed a similar young man holding a portrait and labelled him as Ninus, the king of Nineveh (Levi 1944: 422–3, fig. 3). It has thus been assumed that this mosaic too represents Ninus, who was the focus of a romantic novel, only known from papyrus fragments, in which the Assyrian king appears to be in love with his cousin. Through approaching their respective aunts the two endeavour to be allowed to marry before Ninus leaves for war. The rest of the novel appears to have involved shipwreck and separation, typical features of the Greek novels (Stephens and Winkler 1995, 23–71). As with other novels there is a clear historical setting. The historical figures of Ninus and Semiramis, already linked in earlier literature, are recast as a youth and modest young girl to suit the genre of the Greek novel. It is possible that in the Antioch mosaic we have some crucial scene of the novel represented, perhaps Ninus being tempted by another woman, as Theagenes is by Arsace in Heliodorus' novel, or even Semiramis' return to him in disguise, a feature which occurs in some of the other novels (Heliodorus, *Ethiopica* 7.7, 9–10).

There may also have been a local relevance of the story of Ninus and Semiramis which made it particularly appropriate for Antioch. As already noted, Ninus was an Assyrian king and Syria and Assyria were commonly conflated in literature, with the inhabitants of Antioch sometimes being referred to as Assyrians. In addition,

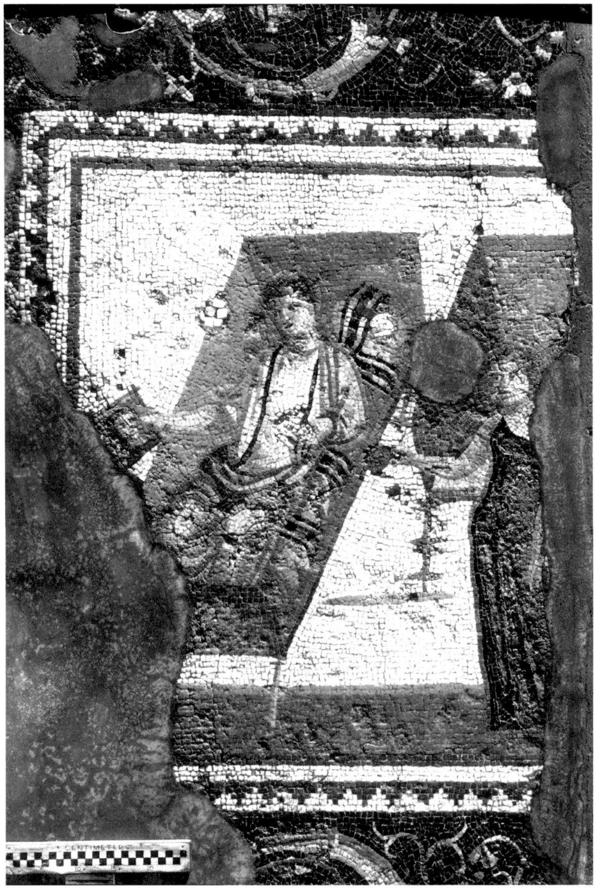

Fig. 37 Mosaic showing Ninus, from the House of the Man of Letters, Daphne.

there was already a connection between Antioch and Semiramis, as Libanius shows when he recalls a temple built by Semiramis to Artemis (*Or*. 11.59). The influence of Semiramis in Syria as a whole can be seen in Lucian's *On the Syrian Goddess* where he records, among the many legends about the foundation of the sanctuary at Hierapolis, one suggesting that it was founded by the Babylonian queen Semiramis in honour of her mother Derketo (14). In his description of the statues inside the temple he mentions one of Semiramis as well as others both of gods and key Greek mythical figures (33). One 'Xenophon of Antioch' is also said to have written a *Babyloniaca*. The title likens the work to some of the Greek novels, such as Heliodorus' *Ethiopica*, and may well have been a novel. If so, with such a title, it may have dealt with the story of Semiramis, particularly since she had links to the area (Stephens and Winkler 1995, 27).

Fig. 38 Mosaic showing Parthenope and Metiochus, from the House of the Man of Letters, Seleucia.

The other mosaic from this house shows two figures labelled as Metiochus and Parthenope (Fig. 38. They also appear on a mosaic from Zeugma, Önal 2002, 54–5). Here, too, a source in a Greek novel has been suggested. The couple appear in two Greek papyrus fragments as well as in an eleventh-century Persian verse version of the story which changes their names to Wamiq and Adhra – 'the lover and the virgin'. The fragments suggest that Metiochus is an aristocratic young man who scorns love. In a debate on the nature of Eros at the house of Polycrates, the historically attested sixth-century tyrant of Samos, Metiochus' expression of his views is countered by the passionate speech of the tyrant's daughter, Parthenope. Although the papyri tail off at this point, the evidence of the Persian version and of a coptic version which turns Parthenope into a martyr have been combined to suggest that in fact this young couple were at the centre of a Greek romantic novel telling of their love, travels and separation (Stephens and Winkler 1995, 72–81).

Hanfmann argued that the representation of the figures here as if standing on a stage, along with the theatrical gesture of Parthenope's hand, suggests that the mosaic might allude to a version of the story known through mime or pantomime (Hanfmann 1939, 244–6; Levi 1944: 425, n. 13 and Levi 1947, 119 n. 2 where Levi prefers to see a connection with the novel). Antioch was particularly famed for its performances of pantomimes (Lucian, *On the Dance,* 76). Indeed, it has been suggested that Lucian's speech in defence of this art, *On the Dance,* might have been delivered at Antioch during the AD 160s in honour of Lucius Verus, who is portrayed in his biography as a devotee of the theatre (SHA, *Lucius Verus,* 8.7; Robertson, 1913). Within the repertoire of the dancer, Lucian mentions the fate of Polycrates and 'his daughter's wanderings, extending to Persia' (54). It is possible that there may be a reference here to the story of Parthenope and her wanderings when separated from Metiochus. If *On the Dance* was composed for delivery in Antioch then its opening lines may be important. Here Crato attacks Lycinus, Lucian's mouthpiece, for attending the dance and forgetting his education in favour of watching erotic scenes of Phaedra, Parthenope and Rhodope (1). Elsewhere too Lucian alludes to performances in the theatre involving the characters of Ninus, Metiochus and Achilles (*False Critic,* 25). This suggests that the stories of Ninus and Semiramis and Metiochus and Parthenope represented in the mosaics from this house might also have been familiar to the people of Antioch through their performance in mime or pantomime (Quet 1992, 137–40 discusses the possible links between novels and performances). The decision to represent scenes from these myths in this particular house might not only have been a statement of the host's love of literature, or perhaps, alternatively, theatre, but also an assertion of his regional history. The appearance of Ninus, in particular, suggests an awareness of the area's Assyrian past, as well as its links with Greek myth and culture (Quet 1992, 147).

The complex issue of shifting cultural identities in the Near East has received masterly treatment by Fergus Millar. Throughout his book, Millar stresses the slipperiness of 'identity' and the difficulties inherent in pinning down how a certain population thought of itself (Millar 1993, 1–23, 225–35, and 489–532). With reference to the cities of northern Syria, he concludes, however, that the majority of the evidence tends in favour of the deep penetration of Greek culture into this area, with little evidence for a strong Syrian or semitic identity. While the religious cults of the area often presented themselves as 'ancestral', their architectural expression was firmly Graeco-Roman (Millar 1993, 236–63, esp. 253–5). This might suggest that when the inhabitants of the area stressed their allegiance to the ancestral gods, or, as in Lucian's *On the Syrian Goddess,* drew attention to the strangeness of their own customs, it was not intended as an assertion of their separateness from the Graeco-Roman world. Indeed, Millar points out that the cults which Lucian gives as parallels to that of the Syrian goddess are all located in Phoenicia and were well known to the Greek world (Millar 1993: 246). Lucian himself, while asserting an Assyrian identity in this text, also uses the Ionic dialect so strongly associated with Herodotus. He thus poses as both insider and outsider, explaining the exoticism of his native religion but also representing himself in part as an external observer (Elsner 2001, esp. 123–8 on the question of authorship; on Lucian's complex identity, see Swain 1996, 298–308).

In Pausanias' *Guide to Greece*, regional peculiarities of cult or ritual are part of what makes individual communities important, while they remain part of the wider Greek whole. The assertion of local cults and customs in the east too could have served as a marker of what made a city or region unique and important, rather than as a means of asserting its separateness from the all-pervasive Greek culture. The mosaics of Antioch seem to express both this allusion to the local region's own myths and advantages, as well as to its membership in a wider cultural whole. While Ninus was an important historical figure from the Assyrian past, and could be seen as asserting a specifically Assyrian identity in contrast to that of Greece or Rome, the way in which he is presented in this mosaic in fact argues against any strong assertion of separateness. Instead, the great king of Assyria is turned into a lovelorn Greek youth, just as the fearsome Semiramis of myth becomes a shy and bashful maiden in the fragments of the novel. Foreign figures and histories are thus represented through the medium of Greek culture, using Greek frames of reference. A similar attitude to non-Greek figures can be seen in Philostratus' description of the Persian queen Rhodogune, in the *Imagines*. While gazing at the beauty of this painted figure, the orator imagines her speaking out to him, in Greek (*Imagines*, 2.5.5). In Philostratus' pictorial fantasy world, even a barbarian queen addresses the viewer in Greek.

In contrast to the Ninus mosaic, a number of the mosaics discovered at Antioch and its surroundings depict scenes from well-known Greek myths. Many of these probably acted to assert the host's knowledge of Greek literary and theatrical culture, such as the scenes shown in the Red Pavement Mosaic (Levi 1947: 68–85; Huskinson 2002–3, 134–7). Others, however, are likely to have had a particular relevance for the local area in addition to their status as well-known Greek myths. So the scene of the Judgement of Paris which decorated the Atrium House at Antioch might have helped to assert a local tradition locating this episode at Daphne instead of Mount Ida, a claim which we find in Libanius' eulogy of the area (*Or*. 11.240; Levi 1947, 16–21).

While we cannot always be sure whether a local connection lay behind the choice of a particular scene, the mosaics examined here do strongly suggest that domestic imagery could be used to assert the individual claims of the local area. These claims to importance range from the area's natural advantages, to her reputation for luxury and entertainment and her mythical and historical past. While some mosaics seem to allude to the area's Seleucid and Assyrian past, this stress on her regional identity in no way undermines Antioch's claims to be part of the Graeco-Roman world. Rather, the claims of local and regional importance seem to be asserted either through the appropriation of Greek myths to the immediate locality, or through the presentation of Assyrian history and myth through the visual and narrative media typical of Greek culture. Such modes of representation formed the *lingua franca* of the Mediterranean world and were part of the educational background in which both hosts and guests would have been immersed. It was through such means, particularly the lavish floor mosaics decorating their houses and villas, that the inhabitants of ancient Antioch found a way of asserting to the wider world their pride in their city and her unique importance within the Mediterranean world.

Bibliography

Balty, J. (1981) 'La mosaique au Proche-Oriente I. Des origines à la Tétrarchie', *Aufstieg und Niedergang des Römischen Welt* II.12.2, 347–429.
Birley, A. (1987) *Marcus Aurelius: A biography* (revised edition, London).
Bowersock, G. (1969) *Greek Sophists in the Roman Empire* (Oxford).
Bowie, E. L. (1974) 'The Greeks and their Past in the Second Sophistic' in M. I. Finley (ed.) *Studies in Ancient Society*, 166–209 (London).
Cameron, A. and S. Walker (eds.) (1989) *The Greek Renaissance in the Roman Empire* (London).
Campbell, S. (1988) *The Mosaics of Antioch* (Toronto).
Casson, L. (1994) *Travel in the Ancient World* (second edition, Baltimore and London).
Cimok, F. (ed.) (2000), *Antioch Mosaics: A Corpus* (Istanbul).
Clarke, J. R. (1991) *The Houses of Roman Italy* (Berkeley, Los Angeles and London).
Clarke, J. R. (1998) *Looking at Lovemaking: Constructions of Sexuality in Roman Art 100 B.C.-A.D. 250* (Berkeley, Los Angeles and London).
Dobbins, J. J. (2000) 'The Houses at Antioch' in Kondoleon (2000a), 51–61.
Downey, G. (1961) *A History of Antioch in Syria from Seleucus to the Arab Conquest* (Princeton).
Elsner, J. (2001) 'Describing Self in the language of Other: Pseudo (?) Lucian at the temple of Hierapolis' in Goldhill (2001), 123–53.
Goldhill, S. (ed.) (2001) *Being Greek under Rome: Cultural Identity, the Second Sophistic and the Development of Empire* (Cambridge).
Grainger, J. D. (1990) *The Cities of Seleukid Syria* (Oxford).
Hales, S. (2003a) *The Roman House and Social Identity* (Cambridge).
Hales, S. (2003b), 'The Houses of Antioch: a Study of the Domestic Sphere in the Imperial Near East' in S. Scott and J. Webster (eds.), *Roman Imperialism and Provincial Art*, 171–91 (Cambridge).
Hanfmann, G. M. A. (1939) 'Notes on the mosaics from Antioch', *AJA* 53, 229–46.
Harl, K. (1987) *Civic Coins and Civic Politics in the Roman East AD 180–275* (Berkeley, Los Angeles and London).
Howgego, C., V. Heuchert and A. Burnett (eds.) (2005) *Coinage and Identity in the Roman Provinces* (Oxford and New York).
Huskinson, J. (2002–3) 'Theatre, Performance and Theatricality in some mosaic pavements from Antioch', *BICS* 46, 131–65.
Jones, A. H. M. (1937) *Cities of the Eastern Roman Provinces* (Oxford).
Jones, C. P. (1978) *The Roman World of Dio Chrysostom* (Cambridge, MA).
Kondoleon, C. (1995) *Domestic and Divine: Roman mosaics in the House of Dionysos* (Ithaca and London).

Kondoleon, C. (ed.) (2000a), *Antioch: The lost ancient city* (Princeton).
Kondoleon, C. (2000b) 'Mosaics of Antioch' in Kondoleon (2000a), 63–77.
Levi, D. (1944) 'The Novel of Ninus and Semiramis', *Proceedings of the American Philosophical Society* 87, 420–28.
Levi, D. (1947) *Antioch Mosaic Pavements* (Princeton).
Lindner, R. (1994) *Mythos und Identität: Studien zur Selbstdarstellung kleinasiatischer Städte in der römischer Kaiserzeit* (Stuttgart).
Metcalf, W. E. (2000) 'The mint of Antioch' in Kondoleon (2000a), 105–11.
Millar, F. (1993) *The Roman Near East 31 BC – AD 337* (Cambridge, MA and London).
Moretti, L. (1953) *Iscrizioni agonistiche greche* (Rome).
Newby, Z. (2003) 'Art and Identity in Asia Minor' in S. Scott and J. Webster (eds.) *Roman Imperialism and Provincial Art*, 192–213 (Cambridge).
Norman, A. F. (2000) *Antioch as a centre of Hellenic culture as observed by Libanius* (Liverpool).
Önal, M. (2002) *Mosaics of Zeugma* (Istanbul).
Pretzler, M. (2004) 'Turning Travel into Text: Pausanias at Work', *Greece and Rome* 51, 199–216.
Quet, M.-H. (1992) 'Romans grecs, mosaïques romaines' in M.-F. Baslez and M. Trédé (eds.) *Le monde du roman grec*, 125–60 (Paris).
Robert, L. (1977) 'Deux inscriptions de Tarse et d'Argos', *Bulletin de Correspondence Hellenique* 101, 80–132.
Robertson, D. S. (1913) 'The Authenticity and Date of Lucian *De Saltatione*' in E.C. Quiggan (ed.) *Essays and Studies Presented to William Ridgeway*, 180–85 (Cambridge).
Sandwell, I. and J. Huskinson (eds.) (2004) *Culture and Society in Later Roman Antioch* (Oxford).
Smith, R. R. R. (1987) 'The Imperial reliefs from the Sebasteion at Aphrodisias', *Journal of Roman Studies* 77, 88–138
Smith, R. R. R. (1988) '*Simulacra Gentium*: The *Ethne* from the Sebasteion at Aphrodisias', *Journal of Roman Studies* 78, 50–77.
Stephens, S. and J. Winkler (1995) *Ancient Greek Novels: The Fragments* (Princeton)
Swain, S. (1996) *Hellenism and Empire: Language, Classicism, and Power in the Greek World AD 50 – 250* (Oxford).
Van Berchem, D. (1985) 'Le port de Séleucie de Piérie et l'infrastructure logistique des guerres parthiques', *Bonner Jahrbücher* 185, 47–87.
Wallace-Hadrill, A. (1994) *Houses and Society in Pompeii and Herculaneum* (Princeton).
Ziegler, R. (1985) *Städtisches Prestige und kaiserliche Politik: Studien zum Festwesen in Ostkilikien im 2. und 3. Jahrhundert n. Chr.* (Düsseldorf).

Index